D1202537

"... important, path-breaking study in comparative colonial history, Professor Wiener engagingly and persuasively demonstrates the complex and conflicting pulls on the criminal justice systems of a range of multi-racial British colonies. Confidently steering between reductionist and complacent renderings of imperialism, he shows the extent to which British politicians, the Colonial Office, colonial officials, the judiciary, and, not least, the colonized pushed for genuine equality before the law for all residents of these possessions, typically in the face of visceral opposition by European minorities with their own limited and self-interested vision of the rule of law and its protections."

–John McLaren, Emeritus Professor of Law,
University of Victoria, British Columbia

AN EMPIRE ON TRIAL

An Empire on Trial is the first book to explore the issue of interracial homicide in the British Empire during its height – examining these incidents and the prosecution of such cases in each of seven colonies scattered throughout the world. It uncovers and analyzes the tensions of empire that underlay British rule and delves into how the problem of maintaining a liberal empire manifested itself in the late nineteenth and early twentieth centuries. The work demonstrates the importance of the processes of criminal justice to the history of the Empire and the advantage of a trans-territorial approach to understanding the complexities and nuances of its workings. *An Empire on Trial* is of interest to those concerned with race, empire, or criminal justice and to historians of modern Britain or of colonial Australia, India, Kenya, or the Caribbean. Political and postcolonial theorists writing on liberalism and empire, or race and empire, will also find this book invaluable.

Martin J. Wiener is Mary Gibbs Jones Professor of History at Rice University. He is the author of numerous works, including *English Culture and the Decline of the Industrial Spirit, 1850–1980*; *Reconstructing the Criminal*; and *Men of Blood*. Dr. Wiener is a Past President of the North American Conference on British Studies and a Fellow of the Royal Historical Society.

An Empire on Trial

Race, Murder, and Justice under
British Rule, 1870–1935

MARTIN J. WIENER

Rice University

CAMBRIDGE
UNIVERSITY PRESS

CAMBRIDGE UNIVERSITY PRESS
Cambridge, New York, Melbourne, Madrid, Cape Town, Singapore, São Paulo, Delhi

Cambridge University Press
32 Avenue of the Americas, New York, NY 10013-2473, USA

www.cambridge.org
Information on this title: www.cambridge.org/9780521735070

First published 2009

Printed in the United States of America

A catalog record for this publication is available from the British Library.

Library of Congress Cataloging in Publication Data
Wiener, Martin J.
An empire on trial : race, murder, and justice under British rule,
1870–1935 / Martin J. Wiener.
p. cm.
Includes bibliographical references and index.
ISBN 978-0-521-51365-4 (hardback) – ISBN 978-0-521-73507-0 (pbk.)
1. Great Britain – Colonies – Race relations.   2. Great Britain – Colonies – History – 19th
century.   3. Great Britain – Colonies – History – 20th century.   4. Criminal justice,
Administration of – Great Britain – Colonies – History.   5. Racism – Great Britain –
Colonies.   I. Title.
DA125.A1W487 2008
364.152'30917124109034–dc22   2008018061

ISBN 978-0-521-51365-4 hardback
ISBN 978-0-521-73507-0 paperback

Contents

Preface

In recent years many historians have become dissatisfied with the limitations of national history and have sought to move toward a broader perspective. Historians of the British Empire have been feeling a similar confinement. Consequently, interest has grown in studying the relationships between imperial "center" and "periphery" or, even better, between center and multiple locales, and between one locale and another, in the Empire. Such history, interactionist and comparative, might best be called "trans-territorial." Important recent works following one particular theme through different parts of the Empire, like Douglas Hay and Paul Craven's *Masters, Servants, and Magistrates in Britain and the Empire* and Philippa Levine's *Prostitution, Race and Politics: Policing Venereal Disease in the British Empire*, have shown how much about the workings and meaning of Empire becomes clear only when a wider and interrelated view is taken.

This book similarly takes one issue – interpersonal interracial homicide – and seeks to follow, through a broad range of imperial contexts, how it was dealt with and what that "dealing with" reveals about the nature of the British Empire at the height of its power. At first glance this problem may appear to be a rather small and limited one, but it involved portentous questions of how nonwhite races were to be governed, particularly where they came into regular interaction with whites, and of how the liberalism so strong in modern Britain was to be reconciled with the imperial rule of non-Britons. Large, indeed global, questions were worked through in small, specific contexts. Only through, in Clifford Geertz's words, "a continuous dialectical tacking between the most local of local detail and the most global of global structures" can the student of the British Empire come to a deeper understanding of its workings, past or present.[1]

I also aim here to move beyond the increasingly sterile debate between "celebratory" and "accusatory" histories of the Empire. If for many years the dominant note of imperial historiography, from the vigorous assertions of J. R. Seeley in 1883 through the more measured language of the *Cambridge History of the British Empire* (1925–1959), was close to a eulogizing of the Empire's contributions to the advance of "civilization" and "modernity," this was succeeded by an equally pervasive tone of indictment of "colonialism" as violent, racist, and exploitative. This accusatory historiography was at first strongly Marxist, but as Marxism lost its intellectual sway it became predominantly culturalist, taking its new lead from Edward Said's *Orientalism* (1978). It has matched the earlier historiography's self-satisfaction with a new self-satisfaction of the formerly colonized and their self-appointed Western spokespersons. As the distinguished historian of Africa and of British colonialism there, Frederick Cooper, has recently argued, it is past time to put away tendentious and abstract claims for and against colonialism, and to look more closely, and dispassionately, at the complexities of the historical phenomenon that was the British Empire.[2]

One of these knotted complexities was the endemic tension between everyday racial inequality evident throughout the Empire and the deep-rooted liberal premises of the criminal law that extended everywhere in that Empire. In exploring this complication, I have tried to also give due attention to the elements – of individual personality, of the contingency of events – that undermine the simple generalizations toward which both celebratory and accusatory history have inclined. As the great historian Marc Bloch (who never shied from generalizing when that was appropriate) warned, "the ABC of our profession is to avoid these large abstract terms" and instead "to try to discover behind them the only concrete realities, which are human beings."[3]

This study draws upon my previous exploration of the workings of the criminal law in England and of the relationships formed over time

---

[1] "From the Native's Point of View: On the Nature of Anthropological Understanding," in *Interpretive Social Science: A Reader*, ed. Paul Rabinow and William M. Sullivan (Berkeley, 1979), p. 239.
[2] See *Colonialism in Question: Theory, Knowledge, History* (Berkeley and Los Angeles, 2005), particularly the introductory essay.
[3] *L'Etrange Defaite: Temoignage Ecrit en 1940* (Paris, [1946] 1990), p. 57 (my translation).

between the law and the people making use of – or being used by – that law. The experience of writing my earlier books *Reconstructing the Criminal* and *Men of Blood* has convinced me that the criminal law was a crucial part of British society, and its export throughout the world was a significant if underexamined part of imperial history. It has also shown me how small a part of the criminal law can be understood through the doorway of legal history alone; only by integrating the operation of the law with social, economic, political, and cultural history, as this book attempts to do, can we come to an adequate appreciation of its place in the history of Britain and the British Empire.

Acknowledgments

The research for this book was made possible by a grant from the John Simon Guggenheim Memorial Foundation and by support from Rice University and its Dean of Humanities, Gary Wihl. I was greatly helped by everyone in Fondren Library's Inter-Library Loan office and by Anna Shparberg, a wonderful locater and acquirer of research material. Librarians and staff at the British Library, the National Archives, and the Bodleian Library (especially the watchman at Rhodes House who let me in after hours to retrieve a briefcase in time to catch a train) and the staff of the Queensland State Archives were all of invaluable assistance.

I am indebted to Michael Miller and Mary Lindemann of the University of Miami and to the organizers of various conferences at which parts of this work were first presented: the workshop "New Histories of Criminal Justice" at the Baldy Center for Law and Social Policy of the University at Buffalo Law School; the conference on the Cultural History of Violence at the University of York; the annual meeting of the North American Victorian Studies Association at Purdue University; the conference "Crime, Violence and the Modern State – Historical Perspectives" at the University of Crete; the Fourth British Worlds Conference, at Bristol University; the Fifteenth British Legal History Conference at Oxford University; and the First British Scholars Conference at the Center for British Studies of the University of Texas at Austin. Parts of this book were previously published in *The Cultural History of Violence*, ed. Stuart Carroll (London: Palgrave Macmillan, 2007); and in *Modern Histories of Crime and Punishment*, ed. Markus D. Dubber and Lindsay Farmer (Stanford: Stanford University Press, 2007), © 2007 by the Board of Trustees of the Leland Stanford Jr. University, all rights reserved, by permission of the publisher.

I would also like to thank James Epstein, Dane Kennedy, Elizabeth Kolsky, Philippa Levine, Roger Louis, John McLaren, David Philips, and

David Thomas for suggestions and criticism, and my students Martin Wauck, David Getman, and Chris Davis for assistance. Most of all (as always), I thank my wife, Meredith Skura, for stimulation, inspiration, support, and companionship, without which the writing of this book would have been not only much slower, but much less pleasant.

Introduction

How were men tried? There is no better touchstone for a social system than this question.

Marc Bloch, 1939[1]

I. LIBERALISM VERSUS EMPIRE?

The British Empire was built upon a contradiction: justified as a benevolent liberating mission to many millions of Asians, Africans, and other non-Europeans enslaved by ignorance, oppressive traditions, and misrule,[2] it depended at the same time upon the subordination of these millions to the authority of the small ruling British elite. This contradiction was highlighted by the workings of the legal systems the British established in their possessions. The single most important exemplar of the claimed beneficence of the Empire was its system of laws, and by the nineteenth century there was great pride in spreading the benefits of English law around the world. Perhaps the best-known principle of that law was the equality of individuals – that all were equally subject to its strictures, and that all could equally claim its protection. This had been established for the Empire as early as 1774, when in the case of *Campbell v. Hall* Lord Mansfield declared that "an Englishman in Ireland, Minorca or the Plantations has no privilege distinct from the natives." A century

---

[1] *Feudal Society* (Chicago, 1961), p. 359.

[2] An example of this pride in "British justice" can be seen in Elspeth Huxley, *The Flame Trees of Thika: Memories of an African Childhood* (Harmondsworth, 1959), p. 132. An official version from the same time was given by Sir Kenneth Roberts-Wray, legal adviser at the Colonial Office: "British administration in overseas countries," he wrote in 1960, "has conferred no greater benefit than English law and justice" ["The Adaptation of Imported Law in Africa," *Journal of African Law* 4, 2 (Summer 1960), 66].

later the noted political thinker and legal adviser to the Government of
India Henry Maine observed that the Government "is bound, by the
moral conditions of its existence, to apply the modern principle of
equality, in all its various forms, to the people of India – equality between
religions, equality between races, equality between individuals, in the eye
of the law."[3] Yet the most basic working principle of empire, as Maine
well knew, was *inequality* – a necessary inequality of power between the
British ruling class and the subject populations, a distinction that (as colonies of white settlement gained self-government) increasingly merged with
that between white and colored races. To put this contradiction another
way: in the course of the nineteenth century British society became ever
more based on "liberal" ideas. Yet the Empire this society constructed and
extended was deeply authoritarian. Could a liberal society run an authoritarian empire, without one or the other being corrupted? As Ranajit Guha,
founder of the "subaltern studies" school, observed, the British colonial
state in South Asia was "an historical paradox, an autocracy set up and
sustained by the foremost democracy in the Western world."[4]

How meaningful was the British commitment to "the rule of law"?
Many "postcolonial" scholars have argued that it meant little except as a
veil to cover the unpalatable realities of exploitation.[5] Guha influentially
claimed that colonial law was simply the "state's emissary," whose
function was to transform "a matrix of real historical experience" into a
"matrix of *abstract legality* so that . . . the will of the state could be made
to penetrate, reorganize part by part and eventually control the will of a
subject population in much the same way as Providence is brought to
impose itself upon mere human destiny."[6] Borrowing from Marx and
Gramsci, Guha described the notion of the "rule of law" as "mystifying"
the true relations of power in the Raj, and encouraging Indians to develop
a false consciousness, thus diverting the flow of discontents into harmless

---

[3] Quoted in Sir M. E. Grant Duff, *Sir Henry Maine: A Brief Memoir of His Life* (London, 1892), p. 40.
[4] *Dominance Without Hegemony: History and Power in Colonial India* (Cambridge, Mass., 1997), p. xii. Guha's terms – "autocracy" and "democracy" – render the paradox rather too starkly. Before 1918 Britain was still some distance from a democracy, while examination of the workings of colonial law reveals this "autocracy" to have been more complex than Guha portrays; see Peter Fitzpatrick, "Tears of the Law: Colonial Resistance and Legal Determination," in *Human Rights and Legal Theory*, ed. Katherine O'Donovan and G. R. Rubin (Oxford and New York, 2000).
[5] For the most recent such argument, see the forthcoming book by Karuna Mantena, *Alibis of Empire: Social Theory and the Ideologies of Late Imperialism* (Princeton).
[6] "Chandra's Death," *Subaltern Studies* 5 (1986), 141.

channels of legal appeals: "While the colonial regime first took it upon itself to inculcate the notion of rights and liberties upon its subjects and then deny these in full or in part in the principles and practice of governance, the disenfranchised subjects went on pressing the rulers to match their administration to their own ideals. Ironically, therefore, a large part of the politics of protest under the Raj, especially when initiated by the educated middle-class leaderships, turned on a certain concern about the 'un-British' character of British rule."[7]

Even the radical historian E. P. Thompson, Guha declared, had been a victim of English self-satisfaction when he had argued in his important work on eighteenth-century England, *Whigs and Hunters*, for seeing the development in England of the notion of the rule of law as "a cultural achievement of universal significance."[8] This critique of Thompson was elaborated by Robert Gregg, who noted Thompson's own colonial roots: his father, a liberal missionary in India, had been a noted critic of empire, but a critic from within empire's larger assumptions that Britain had brought valuable "gifts" to India. "The equity of the law," Thompson had declared, in a context of class inequality

must always be in some part sham. Transplanted as it was to even more inequitable contexts, this law could become an instrument of imperialism.... But even here the rules and the rhetoric have imposed some inhibitions upon imperial power. If the rhetoric was a mask, it was a mask which Gandhi and Nehru were to borrow, at the head of a million masked supporters.

"Here," Gregg insisted,

Thompson tried to have his cake and eat it too. First of all he pronounced the rule of law to be a cultural achievement. He then recognized that it might be an 'instrument of imperialism'.... But then we are told that its presence led to 'inhibitions upon imperial power' – perhaps because the imperialism was in this case British.... To imply, as this surely does, that there is some absolute benefit to be gained when nationalists learn the language of imperialism in order to overthrow it seems at the very least ironic when that imperialism has only been made effective by that same language.[9]

This critique of British "imperial liberalism" has become extremely influential among scholars of empire and of liberalism.[10] Yet at heart it

---

[7] *Dominance Without Hegemony*, p. 57.

[8] Ibid., p. 67.

[9] Robert Gregg, *Inside Out, Outside In: Essays in Comparative History* (London, 2000), p. 78.

[10] See for example, Uday Mehta, *Liberalism and Empire: A Study in Nineteenth-Century British Liberal Thought* (Chicago, 1999); Jennifer Pitts, *A Turn to Empire: The Rise of*

ignores the complexities and paradoxes of history that Thompson pointed
to. "Imperialism," for Guha and those who take their lead from him, is
close to being a single "project" with at root one nature, one aim, one
effective actor. The nearer one looks, however, the more this supposed
monolith dissolves into a multitude of often incompatible projects and
actors. Guha's critique of colonialism has by now been overtaken by more
subtle work. As Sally Engel Merry has noted, at the same time that the law
served as an instrument of control, it not only "provided a way for [colo-
nized groups] to mobilize the ideology of the colonizers . . . to resist some
of the more excessive demands of settlers for land and labor . . . [but also]
provided a way for the colonial state to restrain the more brutal aspects of
settlers' exploitation of land and labor." In practice, then "the legal arena
became a place of contest among the diverse interest groups in colonial
society," even if the contest was certainly an unequal one.[11]

Were British colonial governments, then, racist autocracies adorned
with a thin and self-serving veneer of legal liberalism? Or did the principle
of the "rule of law" ever provide a real check to arbitrary rule, and its
corollary, the equality of legal subjects, afford a mitigation of racism? Did
"home" Britain and its Empire constitute two separate worlds, as Guha
posited, one of liberty and expanding democracy, the other of autocracy,
or did these worlds interpenetrate and influence each other? This was
an issue that deeply concerned many Britons throughout the history of
empire, not simply something that was raised by postcolonial critics.

Imperial Liberalism in Britain and France (Princeton, 2005); Mantena, op. cit.; Allen
Beattie and Patrick Dunleavy, "New Perspectives on the British Imperial State,"
unpublished paper 2004; Gita Subrahmanyam, "Schizophrenic Governance and Fostering Global Inequalities in the British Empire: The UK Domestic State vs. the Indian
and African Colonies, 1890–1960," paper presented at the 2004 annual meeting of the
American Political Science Association, Chicago. Online <.PDF> Retrieved 2006–10–05
from http://www.allacademic.com/meta/p61046_index.html.

[11] "Law and Colonialism," *Law and Society Review* 25 (1991), 889–922. One can accept
this and still be strongly critical of imperialism. "Of course," John Comaroff has
insisted, "the historical fact that there were these 'tensions of empire' did not make
imperialism any the less exploitative. Or coercive. Nor did it soften the inequalities that
saturated colonial societies everywhere; if anything, it sharpened them. But, for the
colonized, conflict among colonizers sometimes opened up fissures through which the
contradictions inherent in colonialism became visible. In so doing, they gave the consciousness of 'natives' material to work on, material from which to fashion their own
understandings of European overrule, their insights into its ways and means, their
reactions to the challenge that it posed to vernacular cultural practices, even, at times,
their strategies of resistance" ["Colonialism, Culture and the Law: A Foreword," *Law
and Social Inquiry* 26 (2001), 313]. However, I would suggest that such tensions and
fissures did in fact diminish the "coerciveness" of British imperialism.

How was the inevitable tension between liberal ideals and myths on the one hand, and the pressures and inducements of authoritarian rule on the other, to be worked through?

II. INTERRACIAL HOMICIDE TRIALS

What in fact happened when the contrasting "principles" – of equality and liberalism on the one hand, and inequality and authoritarianism on the other – came into practical conflict? Or when, indeed, liberals' acceptance of the need for a period of tutelage for "backward" peoples slid, as it could easily do, into a prospect of indefinite authoritarian "tutelage"? This book addresses this question by exploring significant moments when the rule of law and its promise of equal treatment were put to the test. It examines revealing episodes in the ordinary operation of the criminal law across the Empire, cases in which this underlying conflict could not simply be argued in the abstract but had to be resolved by a courtroom decision over the fate of an actual defendant.[12] These cases disrupted the smooth everyday operation of the legal machinery, leading to moments of unusual illumination into the Empire's fundamental nature.

Law lay at the heart of the British imperial enterprise. And criminal justice was at the core of law. "The administration of criminal justice," the eminent jurist James Fitzjames Stephen argued, "is the indispensable condition of all government, and the means by which it is in the last resort carried on."[13] A modern historian has observed that "the legal colonisation of large parts of the non-European world as a result of the expansion of Europe has been one of the most thorough, and most durable, of the effects of imperialism."[14] Such legal colonization was particularly central to the efforts of the British. Indeed, one must ask, why did British colonial regimes put in place judicial institutions that have been characterized as "expensive, expansive, and far in excess of functional requirements" for maintaining their rule?[15] The

---

[12] Historians have recently become aware of the importance of "ordinary" civil and criminal law, and not just constitutional law, in empire building. See, for example, Radhika Singha, *A Despotism of Law: Crime and Justice in Early Colonial India* (Delhi, 1998); Peter Karsten, *Between Law and Custom: "High" and "Low" Legal Cultures in the Lands of the British Diaspora* (Cambridge, 2002).

[13] "Minute on the Administration of Justice in British India," selection from the Records of the Goverment of India, Home Department, no. 89 (Calcutta, 1872).

[14] Martin Chanock, "The Law Market: The Legal Encounter in British East and Central Africa," in *European Expansion and Law*, ed. W. J. Mommsen and J. A. De Moor (New York, 1992), p. 279.

[15] Comaroff, op. cit., p. 308.

answer, I would suggest, lies in British, more than imperial, needs. Such needs are suggested in Stephen's assertion; like Maine, Stephen served for a time as legal adviser to the Government of India. "Our law," he declared while serving in that post, "is in fact the sum and substance of what we have to teach them. It is, so to speak, the gospel of the English, and it is a compulsory gospel which admits of no dissent and no disobedience."[16]

This "gospel" was preached through the courts and the trials they conducted. As with religion, the law as it was practiced in the courts fell far short of its ideal. Yet, also as with religion, the ideal never ceased to exert its pressure on practice. The courtroom thus became an arena in which social, political, and ideological contests played themselves out, in which not only particular litigants and defendants struggled, but the contradictions of British law were exposed and the Empire itself put on trial.[17] Even more than other parts of law, the criminal law, with its sanctions of corporal punishment, imprisonment, and death, was deeply political, as Marc Bloch long ago recognized.[18] In criminal trials of Europeans for killing natives, and vice versa, implicit political visions clashed: for most non-official Europeans, colonial law's primary mission was to protect them in a threatening environment, while for those involved in government, it was to maintain the authority of the state by providing consistent, available, and equal justice. When European employers whipped disobedient native employees, they saw themselves as part of the apparatus of colonial authority, and not private individuals trespassing on the state's preserve. Such dissonant understandings of empire were bound to clash, quite apart from the expectations brought by natives themselves.[19]

---

[16] "Legislation under Lord Mayo," in W. W. Hunter, *Life of the Earl of Mayo* (London, 1875), vol. 2, 143–226. Even when the British intended to leave as much of the law of the colonized as unchanged as possible, the repugnancy principle (that nothing truly "repugnant" to the fundamental principles of English law could be left in operation) worked to expand the sphere of British law, especially in criminal law. Today the law – and particularly the criminal law – of nearly all the states that once were part of the British Empire remains based on colonial law.

[17] On the usefulness of criminal trials in understanding both British and imperial history, see Martin J. Wiener, "Murder and the Modern British Historian," *Albion* 36, 1 (Spring, 2004), 1–12.

[18] For an excellent argument for the inevitably political character of criminal law, see Victoria F. Nourse, "Reconceptualizing Criminal Law Defenses," *University of Pennsylvania Law Review* 151 (2003), 1691–1746.

[19] This study follows a call made by Foucault about power (even if he rarely followed it up himself): that historical analysis should be concerned not primarily with who possessed power but how power was *exercised* in day-to-day situations – the "*micro-physics*" of power.

Some of the most crucial tests for colonial law were thus posed by instances of homicide when one of the parties was "European" and the other was "native." Despite Lord Mansfield's dictum, often repeated by jurists thereafter, power differentials ensured that when natives and Britons assaulted one another, the law in practice was rarely the same for both. Yet a growing part of the legitimacy of British rule, in the eyes of subject peoples as well as of those back home, depended on such equality. As a result, such cases put the administrators of law in the colonies and back in Whitehall under great pressure, dividing the white ruling class while affording an opportunity for spokesmen for subject peoples to deploy British colonial ideology in criticism of British rule.

Homicide is perhaps the most attention-getting of crimes, and when it was perpetrated across the lines of race it was potentially inflammatory. Not that interpersonal violence was rare in the Empire; if anything, white-on-"colored" violence was ingrained in the everyday life of Empire. While state violence, particularly dramatic episodes like Governor Eyre's suppression of a rebellion in Jamaica in 1865, or the 1919 Amritsar massacre in India, has been much studied, everyday private violence, although far greater in total than that perpetrated by the state, has received far less attention. Recently, Jock McCulloch, on East Africa, and Elizabeth Collingham, on India, have shown how close violence was to the surface of imperial life. "Prestige," Collingham has observed, "manufactured at the level of face-to-face interaction, relied heavily on a deferential response on the part of Indians.... British sensitivity to the slightest hint of a challenge to their dignity or authority meant that they frequently met any act which suggested insolence with physical violence."[20] Beating of servants and employees, in particular, was frequent and unremarkable, usually only reaching the courts (and not always even then) if a victim died. This book will examine what happened when such cases did reach the courts.

The cases we will explore took place between the 1870s and the mid-1930s, an era in which the Empire was at its height, preoccupied neither with establishing itself nor with preparing for its end. It was a period in

---

[20] *Imperial Bodies: The Physical Experience of the Raj, c. 1800–1947* (Oxford, 2001), p. 142; see also McCulloch, "Empire and Violence, 1900–1939," in *Gender and Empire*, ed. Philippa Levine (Oxford, 2004). Even symbolic physical threats to European domination were worrisome; thus Lord Minto was pressed in 1910 to prohibit interracial showings of the "cinematographs" of a prize fight in which a Negro contender defeated his white opponent [Lawley (Governor of Madras) to Minto, 13 July 1910, cited in Stephen E. Koss, *John Morley at the India Office, 1905–1910* (New Haven, 1969), p. 126n].

which it was least shaped by external forces and most "itself," so to speak. Moreover, it was a time in which the ideal of "the rule of law" and its closeness to notions of "Englishness" and "Britishness" was strongest; A. V. Dicey's influential book on the constitution, published in 1885, made the term "the rule of law" into a byword, and identified it with the English way of life.[21] One of its essential characteristics, he declared, was equality before the law. "We mean," he wrote, "when we speak of the 'rule of law' as a characteristic of our country, not only that with us no man is above the law, but (what is a different thing) that here every man, whatever be his rank or condition, is subject to the ordinary law of the realm and amenable to the jurisdiction of the ordinary tribunals. In England the idea of legal equality, or of the universal subjection of all classes to one law administered by the ordinary Courts, has been pushed to its utmost limit."[22] Pushed indeed, as we will see, to a limit that was to press against the structures of imperial rule.

In this study we will move between five regions and, within them, seven colonies, ranging across the Empire and the world. The Empire, as we will see, was an extremely diverse and complicated entity, embracing a vast range of physical locales and inhabitants; even its forms of government varied greatly. Yet it had crucial common elements. All its parts were subject, if in different degrees, to the same British Government, acting through the Colonial Office and India Office, and the officials appointed by that Government – officials who were frequently moved from colony to colony (or in India from province to province) not only to give them varied experience but to prevent them from developing too-strong local loyalties and perspectives. Another element of commonality within diversity was the way the racial divide between "white" and "colored" subjects recurred everywhere. Further, nearly everywhere this racial divide was reinforced by the economic divide between laborers or servants and employers. Nearly all parts of the Empire followed essentially the same criminal law, based on England's. The Indian Penal Code of 1861, which became the basis for the criminal law not only of the Raj but of Burma, Singapore, Mauritius, and most African colonies, was a systematization and adaptation to Indian conditions of English criminal law,

---

[21] As he had put it in 1875: "English law is the most original creation of the English genius" [A. V. Dicey, "Digby on the History of English Law," *Nation*, 21 (9 Dec. 1875), 373–374].

[22] Dicey, *Lectures Introductory to the Study of the Law of the Constitution* (London, 1885), pp. 177–178.

and criminal law in other British colonies differed little from it. The administrators of the legal system tried as far as possible to maintain its uniformity across the Empire. In the 1879 case of *Trimble v. Hill*, the Judicial Committee of the Privy Council, the highest court of appeal, declared it to be "of the utmost importance that in all parts of the empire where English law prevails, the interpretation of that law by the Courts should be as nearly as possible the same."[23] Thus, in criminal trials throughout the Empire we can see common issues played out, with similar rules and procedures, under varying conditions of place and time.

III. THE COURTROOM AS ARENA

The actors that first spring to our minds are the nonwhite, usually indigenous, population of the Empire. Yet for our story they are for the most part secondary players. Occasionally, one or more of them were in the dock; more often, they were remembered victims, or else entered the courtroom as witnesses, "assessors" (advising Judges in place of jurors), spectators, and press reporters. Their spheres of action were more limited than that of whites, their voices usually less audible. Nonetheless, they too often had decided views and pursued their own strategies. Their presence, real or in the minds of the white actors, was always a factor.

The leading set of actors in interracial homicide trials were the usual offenders, non-official Europeans. Whites who were not part of Government – settlers, businessmen, clerks, and ordinary soldiers and sailors – varied by class but felt a common bond racially, against all nonwhites as subject peoples. Left to themselves, they would have placed racial distinctions in the formal law. However, wherever they retained final authority, officials, bound at least in principle to look out for the rights and welfare of all the subjects of the Crown, prevented this. As Lord Kimberley, Secretary of State for the Colonies in Gladstone's second ministry, remarked to Lord Ripon, Gladstone's Viceroy for India, the "dislike of anything which tends to the treatment of natives on an equal footing with European British subjects," which Ripon had complained of in Anglo-Indians, was true of "colonists generally throughout the British Empire." "The chief difficulty of a Colonial Minister," he reflected, "is to avoid a collision between the Liberal policy towards colored races which is now on the whole firmly established at home as the only just policy, and

[23] Cited in Janet McLean, "From Empire to Globalization: The New Zealand Experience," *Indiana Journal of Global Legal Studies* 11, 1 (Winter 2004), 164.

the narrow-minded views of most of the colonial communities."²⁴ Such
collisions were not easy to avoid. Non-officials were almost everywhere
strong believers in the notion of the "rights of freeborn Englishmen,"
carried as a personal entitlement throughout the world, including the
right to trial by a jury of one's peers – that is, other white men.²⁵ Officials,
in the Empire and particularly in the Home Government, were aware that
this was not in fact the law. However similar to England's the laws of the
Empire were, they ultimately rested first on royal prerogative and then
on parliamentary sovereignty, and such unwritten rights as trial by jury
applied only where and to the degree that they were embodied in sta-
tute.²⁶ Often settlers from Britain gained such an embodiment; sometimes
not. Thus, criminal trials, especially between Britons and nonwhite others, evoked deep clashes of ideology about "Britishness" and the rights of
Britons.²⁷ Even more, however, this fundamental ideological difference

²⁴ Quoted in *Liberal by Principle: The Politics of John Wodehouse, First Earl of Kimberley*, ed. John Powell (London, 1996), p. 164.
²⁵ The *locus classicus* of this settler claim in formal law was a famous opinion given in 1720 by Richard West, recently appointed counsel to the Board of Trade and Planta- tions in London. West advised that the common law of England was also the common law of the plantations. "Let an Englishman go where he will," he declared, "he carries as much of law and liberty with him as the nature of things will bear" [Anonymous (1722) 2 P Wms 75; 24 ER 646]. Two years later, in an appeal from Barbados, the Privy Council officially endorsed the principle that English people who went to settle in the overseas dominions of the Crown took their laws with them.
²⁶ "Mid-nineteenth-century constitutional writers," Miles Taylor has noted, "poured cold water on the idea that emigrating Britons took their freedoms with them. . . . George Cornewall Lewis and Alpheus Todd, amongst others, pointed out that English case law, as long ago as the 1780s, had settled that Englishmen only enjoyed those rights which existed at the time of their departure, and were they to settle in conquered territories, such as parts of the formerly French, Spanish and Dutch Caribbean, or the Cape, then they were subject to local laws, until if and when the British parliament chose to amend them" ["Colonial Representation at Westminster, c. 1800–1865," in *Parlia- ments, Nations and Identities in Britain and Ireland, 1660–1850*, ed. Julian Hoppit (Manchester, 2003), p. 208].
²⁷ Alan Lester has observed that British settlers in different colonies "co-constructed a particular, trans-imperial discourse of colonialism. This discourse was immediately informed by the imperatives of rationalizing projects of capitalist expansion and defending personal security (itself threatened precisely because of commercial expansion on to indigenous lands). But settler discourse was also built around the need to defend settler colonial practices from a critique elaborated by British humanitarians" – a cri- tique, I would add, often accepted by governing officials. In response to this critique, Lester continued, settlers were "forced to define the ways in which they, as respectable Britons, were distinguished from colonized others, and to specify the forms of behavior that such Britons could legitimately adopt in relation to those others." Thus, the struggles between settlers and humanitarians were in part "struggles over the nature of Britishness itself" ["British Settler Discourse and the Circuits of Empire," *History*

between officials and non-officials was sharpened and often embittered by a social gap. Officials were recruited from the professions, the gentry, and aristocracy, and felt socially, as well as intellectually and morally, superior to other Britons (and of course foreigners) in the Empire. Indeed, officials in Whitehall usually regarded even officials out in the colonies, both military and civilian, as a cut below them. Such condescension did not of course sit well with non-officials (or, more subtly, with officials on the spot vis-à-vis their Whitehall masters), and social resentment of the pretensions of officials was a lively force in the approach of Europeans in the Empire to these trials, particularly when they did serve on juries, and also to the larger issues surrounding them.

The other crucial group of participants, in some ways the decisive one, was that of officials, first of all those running the trial – prosecutors, magistrates, and Judges – and secondly, those who were called upon to alter its outcome in one direction or another – Judges of Appeal, Governors, and Colonial Office and India Office bureaucrats and ultimately the Secretary of State for the Colonies or for India. Judicial posts in the Empire were not easy to fill, and the imperial Government depended on the ambitions of British barristers, in excess supply during most of the nineteenth century, coupled with the very small number of judgeships at home.[28] There was no formal examination to take, as existed after 1860 for the Indian Civil Service, and appointment depended upon patronage. Lawyers in the colonies themselves were more eager for judgeships, but the Colonial Office much preferred Britons, to prevent the growth of localism, favoritism, and corruption. Sometimes, however, it was forced to accept local candidates – relatives or protégés of powerful persons there – but it tried throughout our period to limit their number. Colonial judgeships were more "political" than home ones, and not only in being less based upon professional ability. Unlike English and Scottish High Court Judges, appointed essentially for life (removable only by parliamentary impeachment), colonial Judges were appointed at the pleasure of the Crown, and could be removed by their colony's Governor, if the Colonial Office approved. In practice, this was rarely done, but the sword of removal always hung over their heads, and sometimes (as we will see)

Workshop Journal, issue 54 (Autumn 2002), 25. See also Alan Lester, *Imperial Networks: Creating Identities in Nineteenth Century South Africa and Britain* (London and New York, 2001)].

[28] See Henry L. Hall, *The Colonial Office* (London, 1937). We very much need a general study of the colonial judiciary.

indeed fell.[29] Executive officials, at home and in the colonies, saw this lack of complete security for Judges as appropriate to the more Baconian role they were supposed to fill, as arms of a more authoritative, if not authoritarian, Government of distant dependencies. What was wanted were men who could cooperate, and not contend, with colonial Governors. Yet this was not always what was gotten.

Despite holding their positions as other colonial officials did, colonial Judges, as part of a separate arm of Government with a long tradition of independence at home, had the potential to clash with the executive arm – if Governors looked for Bacons, sometimes they were to get Cokes, starting with Robert Thorpe in Upper Canada in the 1800s and Chief Justice Forbes in New South Wales in the 1820s and 1830s.[30] Nor were they as easily removable in practice as they were in principle. As Lord Kimberley, who headed at various times the Colonial Office and the India Office, privately noted in 1884, "no class of man is more difficult to deal with than a wrong-headed Indian or colonial Judge. The public always thinks that any rebuke of a Judge means interference with his judicial independence although his proceedings may be anything but judicial."[31] Tensions with Judges are a thread running through the papers of many colonial officials. To take just one: Sir Frederick Lugard, when Governor of Hong Kong in 1907, wrote a friend that "the Chief Justice [Sir Francis Piggott] is like all Chief Justices, I [hadn't] been here a week before I got letters about 'ignoring the position and dignity of the Bench' and so on, and since then he has shot me in a series of letters raking up every conceivable grievance."[32]

Their relations with local officials and others below the level of Governor were not necessarily easier; like Governors, Judges were centripedal actors in the Empire, moving frequently from colony to colony, their loyalty fixed on the Empire as a whole and the more-or-less uniform imperial criminal law. As John Lonsdale has pointed out, "they circled the world on promotion within one legal service; their precedents were

---

[29] See Chapter 4.

[30] See John McLaren, " 'The Judicial Office . . . Bowing to No Power but the Supremacy of the Law': Judges and the Rule of Law in Colonial Australia and Canada, 1788–1840," *Australian Journal of Legal History* 7 (2003), 177–192.

[31] Letter to Lord Ripon, Viceroy of India, 24 Oct. 1884, quoted in *Liberal by Principle*, op. cit., p. 173.

[32] From the Lugard MSS, quoted in Peter Wesley-Smith, entry on Piggott in the *Oxford Dictionary of National Biography* [henceforth *ODNB*]. Piggott may not have been popular with the governor, but he seems to have been well liked by the Hong Kong bar.

imperial. Unfamiliarity with local ruling culture was deemed to be a strength, a shield of impartial judgment that relied not on 'some one who knew the people and their ways' but on evidence proven in court." Not that Judges were always oppositional; Lonsdale went on to note that "a desire to fit in with local culture could also create . . . a nervous complaisance with local prejudice."[33] Judges could irritate Governors or locals by being confrontational, or they could annoy Whitehall by falling in with local interests, and on occasion they could manage to do both over the period of an appointment. The official historian of the Colonial Office reflected in 1937 that a Judge "may be at loggerheads with the governor and his council, or may be so oppressed with a sense of the ill-treatment of one class that he becomes too biased the other way, does something wrong and thus has to be removed, or he may try to curry favour with the planter class, or he may simply prove unfit for the post."[34] All these kinds of judicial behavior will be on display in the chapters ahead. Perhaps most important for our concerns, however, were the significant number of Judges who sought to follow British norms of equal justice in situations of colonial inequality, and by so doing provoked serious confrontations with local whites.

The most important other colonial officials – Governors and Colonial Secretaries – were also appointed by the Secretaries of State at home, as advised by their civil servants, but, like Judges, were not necessarily at one with their appointers. Some of the same tensions that existed between these officials and the local white population also operated between them and their superiors in Britain. The top permanent Whitehall officials, both before and after the introduction of competitive examinations in the 1860s, usually came from a higher social class, and were increasingly better educated than the men holding most colonial posts, who continued to be recruited more informally. As one historian of the Colonial Office in the second half of the century put it, "a candidate's politics and friends remained frequently more important than his ability or experience. Defeated members of Parliament . . . or politicians out of favor were often given administrative posts in the colonies."[35] Whitehall men sharing an Oxbridge background carried an underlying sense of intellectual superiority over the officials out in the Empire with whom they daily

[33] John Lonsdale, "Kenyatta's Trials: Breaking and Making an African Nationalist," in *The Moral World of the Law*, ed. Peter Coss (Oxford, 2000), p. 200.
[34] Hall, op. cit., p. 136.
[35] Brian Blakeley, *The Colonial Office, 1868–1892* (Durham, N.C., 1972), p. 119.

corresponded. When Secretary for the Colonies in the 1890s, Joseph Chamberlain, as Robert Kubicek noted, "found it necessary on several occasions to modify the language of drafts to governors which were 'too peremptory in their terms.'"[36] Reinforcing the sense of intellectual superiority was the social distance existing for most of the century between high Whitehall officials and typical officials in the colonies. Until open competition had been in operation for some time, the top permanent officials in the Colonial Office had close aristocratic connections, while Governors and Colonial Secretaries were drawn for the most part from more middle-class levels. From the standpoint of Robert Herbert, youngest son of the Earl of Carnarvon, or Robert Meade, second son of the earl of Clanwilliam, both prize-winning Oxford graduates and successively Permanent Undersecretaries at the Colonial Office, Governors were usually both socially and intellectually "very inferior persons" (as Meade put it in 1892).[37] By then, if the social distance was lessening, the intellectual one was only widening, and the tone of condescension from the more middle-class meritocrats under Herbert and Meade, and after them, continued to be noticeable in Office minutes in the twentieth century. Sydney Olivier, the Fabian Socialist who was one of the many Oxford "firsts" in the Office by the end of the century, did not take long to decide that "most Governors were exceedingly stupid."[38]

The social background of colonial Governors changed during the later nineteenth century, from military ranks to the professional middle class; the proportion who were military officers halved between 1860 and 1900, from 40 percent to 20 percent. This was not by chance; the Colonial Office, moving from an era of conquest to one of administration, consciously aimed to diminish the military character of the position and at the same time make it more of a professional career. Few of the new generation of high officials, however, were from business families, and very few indeed had not been to a "proper" public school. By the end of the nineteenth century the most common paternal occupation of high officials

---

[36] Robert V. Kubicek, *The Administration of Imperialism: Joseph Chamberlain at the Colonial Office* (Durham, N.C., 1969), p. 46.

[37] Blakeley, op. cit., p. 117.

[38] Cited in Ronald Hyam, "The Colonial Office Mind, 1900–1914," in *The First British Commonwealth: Essays in Honour of Nicholas Mansergh*, ed. Norman Hillmer and Philip Wigley (Cambridge, 1979), p. 39. Blakeley has observed that "there was a general feeling at the Colonial Office that many men entered the colonial service because they had failed in other endeavors" (op. cit., p. 117).

in the colonies was that of Anglican clergyman.[39] These changes may have done something to narrow the intellectual and social distance between them and Whitehall; they also tended to widen the gap between them and the non-official white community in their colony. Like Judges, Governors were moved around a good deal. The average length of a governorship in our period was less than five years, and one rarely lasted more than seven years. Governors thus had a commitment to the Empire as a whole much more than to the particular colony they were administering. Like Judges, Governors (and Colonial Secretaries, who often were promoted to governorships) tended to enforce a common pattern of rule based on instructions received from Whitehall.[40] Further, as not only men of Government but professional gentlemen, they often held low opinions of the scantily educated commercial men seeking to make their fortune in the colonies by farming or by trade.

Here imperial policy created an additional tension: it was Treasury doctrine, in an age when the Treasury dominated British Government, that colonies were to pay for themselves. This imperative pressed officials to support economic development, which largely meant the activities of white farmers, traders, and entrepreneurs, even if they were doubtful of the moral character of these men, whose drive for enrichment often sacrificed the welfare of indigenous inhabitants and imported nonwhite laborers. Governors, unlike Judges with their more limited role, were thus often pulled in opposite directions, to support and yet also to control economic development in the interests of all the Crown's subjects. Whatever they did, Whitehall usually backed them up. Although it guarded its ultimate authority, and required Governors to use the telegraph to check with it whenever possible before making decisions, the Colonial Office was prepared to go along with Governors. Even if it had doubts about a Governor's course, "once a decision was made," one historian has noted, "the Colonial Office usually made every effort to support the actions of their 'man on the spot.'" The top officials in Whitehall "regarded any governor or administrator working in the tropics or dealing directly with colonists as worthy of their sympathy and understanding."[41]

---

[39] See Anthony Kirk-Greene, *Britain's Imperial Administrators, 1858–1966* (Oxford, 2000).

[40] See Mark Francis, "Colonial Political Culture and the Mentality of British Governors, 1825–1860," *Political Science* [Wellington, New Zealand] 38 (1986), 133–146.

[41] Blakeley, op. cit., p. 117.

Much of the political dynamics of a colony was thus shaped by individuals – sometimes by chief justices but, most of all, by Governors. At times Governors were so anxious to encourage development (or so desirous of praise from those they lived among and socialized with) that they became co-opted into the world of the local "Europeans," and became virtual lobbyists for "their" settlers to Whitehall; but at many other times they clashed with them. Most often, they sought to tread a middle way between conflict and co-option, and Whitehall had to accept a more accommodating man on the spot than it would have liked.[42] All of these situations will come up in the following chapters.

Whitehall itself was changing throughout our period. After a remarkable if short-lived era of activism in the 1830s and 1840s, the Colonial Office's propensity to intervene and direct affairs overseas gradually diminished, even as the Empire itself expanded.[43] With this expansion, and the growth of its white population, it became increasingly difficult to think of controlling it all from London. The sheer volume of paper coming in grew alarmingly, and the Office became more and more a reactive body, simply trying to respond to this mountain of paper. Permanent Undersecretary Herman Merivale was much less ambitious than his predecessor, James Stephen, and Frederick Rogers, who succeeded him, less ambitious still. As early as the 1860s, it was being described as "a sleepy and humdrum office" in which nothing of substance was initiated.[44] Yet through the term of Rogers, a deeply religious man, missionaries and humanitarian critics retained a receptive ear at the highest level. When he retired and was succeeded by the more worldly and skeptical Robert

[42] Revisionists have sometimes overreacted against self-indulgent "old colonial hand history" and reduced imperial officials to nothing more than mere agents of an impersonal "colonial project" or, if looked at as individuals, to self-interested hypocrites, busily advancing their careers while congratulating themselves for their disinterested concern for their backward charges [see, for example, Bradford Spangenberg, *British Bureaucracy in India: Status, Policy and the I.C.S. in the Late Nineteenth Century* (Delhi, 1976); Douglas M. Haynes, "Victorian Imperialism in the Making of the British Medical Profession: An Argument," in *Decentering Empire: Britain, India, and the Transcolonial World*, ed. Dane Kennedy and Durba Ghosh (London, 2006)]. See the useful critique of such indictments of British Indian officials in David Gilmour, *The Ruling Caste: Imperial Lives in the Victorian Raj* (London, 2006).

[43] For "official" accounts, see Hall, op. cit.; Sir Lawrence Guillemard, *Trivial Fond Records* (London, 1937); Sir Charles Jeffries, *The Colonial Office* (London, 1956). Also, see Arnold P. Kaminsky, *The India Office, 1880–1910* (New York, 1986).

[44] R. C. Snelling and T. J. Barron, "The Colonial Office and Its Permanent Officials 1801–1914," in *Studies in the Growth of Nineteenth Century Government 1801–1914*, ed. Gillian Sutherland (Cambridge, 1972), p. 153.

Herbert in 1871, they lost that ear. From this point through the rest of the century, the Colonial Office's dominating concern (which was generally shared or accepted by the politicians nominally in charge of it) was to maintain orderly and effective government throughout the vast holdings of the Crown, without having to go to the Treasury, and without having to face embarrassing questions in Parliament. Mistreatment of indigenous peoples or indentured laborers, and miscarriages of justice between the races, were concerns when they threatened to bring the authority of the Crown into disrepute or become political embarrassments, but not very much otherwise. This was the case also at the India Office, whose long-sitting Permanent Undersecretary, Arthur Godley, shared Herbert's outlook; indeed, even more than the latter he saw his role as that of protecting the Government of India from criticism at home. Both men had served in their youth as private secretaries to Gladstone, and had thought of themselves as Liberals, but both had moved in their careers in the opposite direction from their mentor, becoming increasingly attached to the opinions of "men of practical experience" in imperial matters. "No opinion about Indian administration," Godley declared in his memoirs, "is worth the paper on which it is written, except in so far as it is... founded and supported by the opinions of those Englishmen who have spent the best years of their life in actual contact with the people of that country."[45] By 1904, Arthur Gordon, the extremely active first Governor of Fiji in the 1870s, could lament in the House of Lords that "the whole action, tone, and spirit of the Colonial Department of the present day show a grave and growing departure from the maxims which prevailed there some thirty or forty years ago."[46] Behind this bureaucratic shift was the larger shift in national politics, from an era of Liberalism to one of often-"jingoist" Conservatism.

[45] Lord Kilbracken [Sir Arthur Godley], *Reminiscences*, (London, 1931), p. 185. This was a common pattern among colonial administrators; even the authoritarian Lieutenant Governor of Bengal, Sir Charles Elliott, regretting the Liberal electoral victory in 1892 because of the party's commitment to Irish Home Rule, described himself as "a Gladstonian all my life." Elliott to Lord Lansdowne, 18 July 1892, British Library Oriental and India Office Collection [henceforth BL OIOC] Mss Eur. D 558/23 (Lansdowne Papers).

[46] 11 Aug. 1904, quoted in J. K. Chapman, *The Career of Arthur Hamilton Gordon, First Lord Stanmore 1829–1912* (Toronto, 1964), p. 368. By this time, the Permanent Undersecretary was Charles Ommanney, whose support for business interests and whose ideological conservatism made his cautious predecessor, Robert Herbert, look positively radical in retrospect.

This situation began to change for India in the 1890s and for the rest of the Empire after the Liberal election victory of 1906, when new men and reformist ideas came into government. As central government became more activist, so, gradually, did government of the Empire, and both Colonial and India Offices in the twentieth century came to intervene more and more in the affairs of their dependencies, showing a greater concern to see justice done between the races.[47] Holding together a multiracial Empire, in an age of emerging mass political consciousness, was, as the Colonial Office official H. W. Just put it in 1906, "a daily miracle," only accomplished against the grain of the inclinations of its white inhabitants.[48] While the newly titled Dominions, self-governed by white settlers, could only be dealt with very gingerly, the rest of the Empire, under the common heading of Crown Colonies, was still subject to central control, and the Colonial Office certainly intended to maintain that control. These colonies, one official summarized the policy at this time, were to be administered "first of all and chiefly in the interests of the inhabitants of the Territories; and secondly, in accordance with the views of the people in this country (and not a small and interested section of them [the merchants]) as represented in Parliament."[49] Indeed, after the World War the Colonial Office regained something of the activist spirit of the early Victorians.[50] By 1937, Henry Hall, in his quasi-official history of the Colonial Office, could contrast the virtual independence of nineteenth-century colonial governors with the situation in his day, when the general "complaint is of too minute an inspection of laws and ordinances" by Whitehall.[51]

[47] Churchill, speaking for his fellow Liberals, criticized Joseph Chamberlain's power-oriented imperial vision in 1904: if the British Empire held together, he argued, it would not be because of its size or soldiers, but because "it is animated by respect for right and justice" [Ronald Hyam, *Elgin and Churchill at the Colonial Office* (London, 1968), p. 50]. On the post-1906 shift in colonial policy, see Ronald Hyam, "Bureaucracy and 'Trusteeship' in the Colonial Empire," in *The Oxford History of the British Empire*, vol. 4: *The Twentieth Century*, ed. Judith M. Brown and William Roger Louis (Oxford, 1999).

[48] Cited in Hyam, "The Colonial Office Mind, 1900–1914," op. cit., p. 43.

[49] R. L. Antrobus, cited in Hyam, ibid., p. 46.

[50] Describing the prevailing decentralism of later Victorian and Edwardian colonial Government, M. K. Banton has noted that "only from the 1920s and 1930s did the office seek to play a role in standardizing legislation" throughout the empire ["The Colonial Office, 1820–1955: Constantly the Subject of Small Struggles," in *Masters, Servants, and Magistrates in Britain and the Empire, 1562–1955*, ed. Douglas Hay and Paul Craven (Chapel Hill, N.C., 2004)].

[51] Hall, op. cit., p. 150.

It is the argument of this book that a close look at interracial homicide trials, and their variation over time and place, will display British colonialism as more complex and divided than some have made it out to be. It will be shown to have been not a single "project," but an enterprise at any given moment fractured into a number of incompatible and competing projects, all of which were subject to change over time. Law in the Empire took on many faces. It was both a tool to further British rule and a resource with which the colonized could tellingly criticize that rule. It was a means of empowerment for the unofficial white minority, helping them resist British officials and dominate the nonwhite majority, but also the means by which politicians in Westminster and officials in Whitehall maintained ultimate control over these white minorities and restrained their power over nonwhites. Most directly, these trials expose dissonances within the ranks of colonizers that made British colonialism, even at its later nineteenth-century peak and all the more thereafter, a deeply contested enterprise. As Dipesh Chakrabarty asked Amitav Ghosh in an illuminating correspondence a few years ago, "how seriously do we take the ambiguity that lies at the heart of [imperial] liberalism, the ambiguity caused by the tension between the universal applicability that it claims for itself and the unacknowledged racism that runs through it?"[52] We should, I suggest, take it quite seriously indeed, for otherwise the history of the British Empire is not comprehensible.

[52] Amitav Ghosh and Dipesh Chakrabarty, "A Correspondence on Provincializing Europe," *Radical History Review*, issue 83 (Spring 2002), 146–172.

On the High Seas

I perceived that the pennant was up for punishment. . . . I took it for granted that some aggravated offence, such as theft or mutiny, had been committed. . . . [Boatswain's mates took turns with the "cat."] . . . The tails of this terrific weapon were three feet long, nine in number, and each of them about the size of that line which covers the springs of a traveling-carriage. . . . The last dozen being finished, the sum total was reported by the master-at-arms, "five-dozen!"

"Five dozen!" repeated Captain G – ; "that will do – cast him off. And now sir," said he to the fainting wretch, "I hope this will be a warning to you, that the next time you wish to empty your beastly mouth, you will not spit on my quarter-deck."

Captain Marryatt, *Frank Mildmay: The Naval Officer* (1829)

All Britons love the British sailor.

Lord Shaftesbury, in Parliament, 1873

The shocking scene imagined by Marryatt was set on a naval ship, during the Napoleonic wars, but captures the cruel possibilities of all life at sea before the Victorian era, where there was little check short of mutiny on the authority of merchant captains as well. An early testing ground of the "rule of law" beyond the United Kingdom was in the rapidly growing merchant fleet. Private ships flying the Union Jack constituted a liminal zone between Britain and her Empire. Until the nineteenth century this zone formed in practice largely a world of its own, and the "law of the sea" was understood as something rather distinct from the law of mainland Britain. In the course of that century, this distinction was erased.

When a merchant shipmaster, Francis Temple, who had regularly ordered a sick seaman flogged with the cat until the man died from his wounds, was charged with murder by a coroner's inquest in 1805, a grand jury threw out all charges. In the assize files the phrase "on the High Seas" was doubly underlined: a different standard was understood to apply at sea than on land, and such cases appeared in those days very rarely indeed at the assizes. As late as 1841, a Kent grand jury no-billed a murder charge brought by a coroner's inquest against two merchant marine officers who had a sick young sailor towed astern of a ship for forty days. William Sago, the unfortunate youth, had been picked up in Constantinople and then found to have sores on his legs and "relaxed bowels." He was forced to, in the words of the inquest, "inhabit a certain boat attached to the said vessel . . . without any proper bedding, proper accommodation or proper covering for the protection of the body." Sago was not given any medical attention, but was periodically beaten with ropes and doused with freezing water. Not surprisingly, he died before the end of the voyage. Still, this was not enough for the gentlemen of the grand jury, and the men were never tried.[1] It took a great deal of mistreatment to bring ships' officers before the bar of criminal judgment.

Early nineteenth century Judges spoke of masters of ships as stern fathers, or analogized a ship at sea to a small kingdom, the master being sovereign.[2] His legal powers were far more extensive than that of any employer on land. Baron Alderson, in an 1838 case, declared that "persons on board a ship are necessarily subjected to something like a despotic government, but when they are on land the laws of the country are to protect them in cases of improper treatment."[3] "Seamen," as N. A. M. Rodger has reminded us, "have always dwelt on the fringes of settled society."[4] If anything, the psychological distance between life on land and on the seas even increased in the last years of the age of sail, as industrialization and urbanization transformed land life, while comparatively little changed on sailing ships. To step, in the nineteenth century, from explosively growing Liverpool or London onto a merchant ship was almost to step back in time. On board, long-familiar patterns of hard physical labor and traditional skills continued, as did the corresponding patriarchal authority of the master, especially on long-distance voyages.[5]

[1] The National Archives [henceforth NA], ASSI 35/281/2, ASSI 36/4, Lent and Summer, Kent 1841 (Renum ASSI 94/2327–2328).

[2] Bruce Kercher, "Sovereigns at Sea," unpublished paper, 2005.

[3] *R v Leggett and Nesbitt* (1838): 8 *Carrington & Payne* 191, 173 *ER* 456. In *Murray v Moutrie* (1834): 6 *Carrington and Payne* 471, 172 *ER* 1324, for instance, Chief Justice Tindal said that a master had the same power of "moderate chastisement" as a parent or schoolmaster.

[4] *The Wooden World: An Anatomy of the Georgian Navy* (London, 1996), p. 1.

[5] See Daniel Vickers, *Young Men and the Sea: Yankee Seafarers in the Age of Sail* (New Haven, Conn., 2005). The expression "master" normally applied to those in charge of merchant ships, "captain" being the term used in the navy.

While life and law were being transformed on land, until the middle of the century, as Bruce Kercher has reminded us, "the basic law concerning discipline at sea remained the same across the English-speaking world, and remained little changed across the decades."[6]

In these years, British trade and power were rapidly growing and the ships plying the world's oceans were forming an increasingly significant part of "Greater Britain." Without the ships that traversed these oceans under the British flag, merchant as well as naval, there would have been no Empire. Between 1840 and 1900, the British merchant fleet increased from 2.7 to 9.3 million tons (rising, even as competition emerged from Europe and America, from 30 percent to 36 percent of the world total).[7] The number of merchant seamen on British ships rose from about 175,000 at mid-century to about a quarter million at century's end.[8] Even as steam power advanced, sail persisted: the tonnage of sailing ships in the British merchant fleet did not peak until around 1870.[9]

The British maritime world was also a multi-ethnic one; it had long been so,[10] and it became still more so in the nineteenth century, certainly far more than homeland Britain. Blacks from the West Indies and Africa, and Indians from the subcontinent, made up a growing part of the crews of British ships. Yet the nineteenth century also saw a sharper racism taking hold. The Merchant Shipping Act 1823 stipulated for the first time in legislation that Indian seamen were not British subjects and were not entitled to become so. Its successor Act of 1854 went further and required Asians hired for voyages henceforth to agree to return afterwards to their country of origin.[11] In 1858, the newly established India Office was given responsibility for the repatriation of Indian seamen.[12] Nonetheless, the numbers of Asian and West Indian seamen on British ships continued to

[6] Kercher, op. cit., n.p.
[7] H. J. Dyos and D. H. Aldcroft, *British Transport: An Economic Survey from the Seventeenth Century to the Twentieth* (Harmondsworth, 1974), p. 248.
[8] Henry Mayhew in 1850 gave the number of 200,000: *The Morning Chronicle Survey of Labour and the Poor: The Metropolitan Districts*, vol. 3 (Horsham, 1981), p. 251. G. Balachandran more recently gives the number of 175,000: "Recruitment and Control of Indian Seamen: Calcutta 1880–1935," *International Journal of Maritime History* 9 (1997), 1.
[9] Ben Marsden and Crosbie Smith, *Engineering Empires: A Cultural History of Technology in Nineteenth-Century Britain* (Basingstoke, 2005).
[10] Philip Morgan, "Encounters Between British and 'Indigenous' Peoples, c. 1500–c. 1800," in *Empire and Others*, ed. Martin Daunton and Rick Halpern (Philadelphia, 2000), p. 59.
[11] John Solomos, *Race and Racism in Britain* (London, 2003), p. 45.
[12] Rozina Visram, *Ayahs, Lascars and Princes: Indians in Britain 1700–1947* (London, 1986).

increase; indeed, as British wages rose and better opportunities for workingmen opened up at home and abroad, the population of merchant seamen on British ships became steadily less British. By 1891, non-Britons, from many nations, accounted for more than 22 percent of seamen employed on British vessels. This proportion peaked at close to a third by the turn of the century, before diminishing a bit when public concern about the implications of these figures for national security led the authorities to make serious efforts to increase the attractiveness of seafaring to Britons.[13] During the second half of the nineteenth century a clear racial hierarchy existed on board merchant ships, with the job of cook or steward being given to blacks, usually from the West Indies, and both blacks and Indians working as common seamen. The coming of steam increased the number of unskilled positions, particularly in the boiler room. The better-paid and less onerous positions of "able-bodied [skilled] seamen" were usually reserved for whites, although a few Asians or blacks of long experience could attain those jobs. Rare indeed, however, was a nonwhite officer.[14]

Nonwhites, South Asians (known as "lascars") most of all, not only worked for much lower wages but were seen as more docile than "Jack Tar." Some masters preferred lascar crews. One wrote: "Taken altogether a much more efficient state of discipline prevails on lascar-manned steamers than can ever be hoped for on similar vessels manned by ordinary types of European crews."[15] As might be expected, they were often mistreated on board ship, and, as one historian has noted, "their only remedy then was to desert, giving up their wages and risking destitution in an alien land."[16] However, occasionally their submissiveness would be tested too far. In 1883, two crews of 120 Indian seamen were reported to be in revolt at the news of British suppression of a rebellion in Egypt. A London newspaper announced that "fanatical Moslems have been on a mission to the docks, proclaiming as unholy the English crusade against

---

[13] Balachandran, op. cit.

[14] Shompa Lahiri, "Patterns of Resistance: Indian Seamen in Imperial Britain," in *Language, Labour and Migration*, ed. Anne J. Kershen (Aldershot, 2000); Alan Cobley, "Black West Indian Seamen in the British Merchant Marine in the Mid-Nineteenth Century," *History Workshop Journal*, issue 58 (Autumn 2004), 259–274; Vickers, op. cit.; Tony Lane, "The Political Imperatives of Bureaucracy and Empire: The Case of the Coloured Alien Seaman Order 1925," in *Ethnic Labour and British Imperial Trade: A History of Ethnic Seafarers in the U.K.*, ed. Diane Frost (London, 1995).

[15] W. H. Hood, *The Blight of Insubordination: The Lascar Question and the Rights and Wrongs of British Shipmasters* (London, 1903), p. 49

[16] Visram, op. cit., p. 35.

the faithful in Egypt, and forbidding Lascars, under penalty of future torture, to take any part in the expedition."[17] This scare quickly passed, but such events reminded the British public that docile Indians might yet turn savage at a moment's notice, as they had in 1857.

Over the same period as this shift in the seafaring population, however, went a second trend that provided some benefit for lascars and West Indians, along with their white fellow seamen. Two simultaneous changes in Britain – first, the emergence of trade unions and, with them, a degree of democracy in the workplace and, second, a rising intolerance for violence, whether from below or above – together promoted the extension of the rule of law to "Britain at sea," increasingly limiting the permitted brutality of seamen but also the despotic authority of shipmasters.[18] The very images of "Jack Tar" and of shipmasters became softer, more good-natured, more "civilized."[19] Such seamen should receive more caring treatment, and such masters would naturally provide it; any master failing in that would more and more be seen as an aberrant monster, deserving of severe punishment. What happened on merchant ships was thus of increasing concern to British authorities and the British public. What one labor organizer called in 1893 the traditional expectation for seamen – "blind, unreasoning, unqualified obedience" – was coming to be qualified by rising expectations of care and reasonableness in the behavior of their masters.[20] These growing expectations meant that excessive or unjustified violence by ships' masters and officers on the high seas was ever more likely to be denounced in the press and proceeded against in the courts.

Until the mid-nineteenth century, the reach of the criminal law to the high seas largely depended on whether a ship on which a crime had taken place returned to England. This limitation was ended by the Admiralty Offences (Colonial) Act 1849, which provided that crimes committed

---

[17] Lahiri, op. cit., p. 174.

[18] Markers of the first trend were measures reforming employment law in 1871 and 1875; for the second trend, see Wiener, *Men of Blood* (Cambridge, 2004).

[19] Marryatt's sea fiction exhibits this development. In his later and more famous novel, *Mr. Midshipman Easy* (1836), the harsh side of sea life was less visible, and the only figures to be flogged were obvious villains. For a discussion, see John Peck, *Maritime Fiction: Sailors and the Sea in British and American Novels, 1719–1917* (London, 2001). See also Anthea Trodd, "Collaborating in Open Boats: Dickens, Collins, Franklin, and Bligh," *Victorian Studies* 42 (1999), 201–225, and Mary Conley, "From Jack Tar to Union Jack: Images and Identities of British Naval Men, 1870–1918," Ph.D. dissertation, Boston College, 2000.

[20] Benjamin T. Hall, *Socialism and Sailors*, Fabian Society Tract 46 (London, 1893), p. 3.

within the jurisdiction of the Admiralty (in other words, on a ship flying the British flag) could be tried in any colony as if they had been committed within the waters of the colony. This was followed the next year by a measure that raised the bar for treatment of seamen, the Merchant Shipping Act 1850. This act, with amendments over the following few years, came to be called the "Seaman's Charter." Although it was primarily motivated by the desire to raise the standard of British seamanship, it also was meant to protect seamen from being exploited by the shipowners or tyrannized by their officers. It obliged all masters to keep official logs, which recorded illness, birth or death on board, misconduct, desertion, and punishment, and a description of conduct. It established local marine boards in all main ports and a shipping master appointed by each to take administrative responsibility for examinations for certificates of competency administered to all masters and mates of foreign-going ships. Such masters could withdraw the certificates if officers proved incompetent or unfit. Unfitness could arise not only from lack of capable seamanship but also from unacceptable treatment of the crew. The new shipping overseers were empowered to interfere with employment contracts and to inquire into disputes arising out of voyages, which meant that for the first time there existed paid officials with the responsibility to see that the laws were followed at sea, just as the new police being created at the same time were doing on shore.[21]

Such measures were responding to pressures from below that were brought to light in the reporting of Henry Mayhew. While this Merchant Shipping Bill was going through Parliament, Mayhew recorded London seamen's complaints at length in the *Morning Chronicle*: "We are not treated like men at all," one man told him. "We're worse than the black slaves; they are taken care of and we are not," said another. "On board ship," this man continued, "they can do anything with us they think proper. If in case you are a spirited man, and speaks a word against an officer that tyrannicalises [*sic*] over you, he will put you in irons and stop your money – six days for one: for every day you're in irons he stops six days' pay, and maybe forfeits your whole wages. There's as good men before the mast as abaft of it." Social notions were changing: "It ain't the same now as it used to be," this seaman remarked. "Our fathers and mothers, you see, gives us all a little education, and we're now able to see

---

[21] Charles Abbott and William Shee, *A Treatise of the Law Relative to Merchant Ships and Seamen* (London, 1854).

and feel the wrongs that are put upon us; and if in case people doesn't do better for us than they do now, why, they'll turn pirates."[22]

In these years the navy was forced to steadily curtail the violence of its disciplinary procedures.[23] Already by mid-century the incidence of flogging in the fleet was falling, although an officer could still later recall of a voyage in 1852 that "a week rarely passed without some man receiving his three or four dozen lashes at the gangway."[24] It took a wave of mutinies in the late 1850s to force official inquiries and bring about explicit reforms in discipline. Quarterly returns of all floggings were required to be submitted to Parliament, where they were available to the press, and under this prod the Admiralty was more thoroughly inquiring into complaints. The Gladstone Government's Admiralty issued in 1871 an instruction suspending all corporal punishment in peacetime. This was extended to wartime in 1879, and the last authenticated flogging on board a naval ship took place in 1880.[25] By then the issue of excessively violent naval discipline had faded, but any such instances on merchant ships, with their more racially and nationally heterogeneous crews, stood out all the more, and came to be the subject of some highly publicized trials.

Such proceedings were facilitated by the transfer of the criminal jurisdiction of Admiralty courts to the regular assize courts. An 1834 act empowered the Old Bailey and other assize courts to hear cases involving offenses committed within the jurisdiction of the Admiralty; ten years later another act removed criminal charges entirely from Admiralty courts. And, as we have seen, in 1849 this change was extended to the colonies, empowering all colonial courts to proceed against persons charged with crimes on the high seas; in case of conviction, offenders were to be punished as if their crime had been committed in England. From this point it would be up to regular juries and Judges to determine the limits of

---

[22] Henry Mayhew, op cit., vol. 3, p. 265. Another grievance was the frequent use of the Master and Servant laws: seamen who failed to join their ships were liable to be thrown in jail, and many were. After 1854, such sanctions were less and less resorted to [Captain A. G. Course, *The Merchant Navy: A Social History* (London, 1963), pp. 241 on].

[23] Change had come first to the army. A parliamentary campaign against army flogging had begun in the 1830s, leading to a Royal Commission and new restrictive regulations [J. R. Dinwiddy, "The Early Nineteenth Century Campaign Against Flogging in the Army," *English Historical Review* 97 (1982), 308–331]. A further act in 1868, provoked by the scandal of a flogging death, drastically reduced what was left of the practice, and it was finally abolished when the Liberals returned to office in 1881 [Edward M. Spiers, *The Late Victorian Army 1868–1902* (Manchester, 1992), p. 74].

[24] Peter Kemp, *The British Sailor: A Social History of the Lower Deck* (London, 1970), p. 190.

[25] Eugene Rasor, *Reform in the Royal Navy: A Social History of the Lower Deck 1850 to 1880* (London, 1976).

acceptable violence at sea. The Recorder of London stated the principle while charging a grand jury in 1853:

In order that the necessary discipline should be observed on board ship, it was permitted to persons in authority to make use of a description of violence that would not, under any circumstances, be tolerated on shore; but if that violence were carried to an improper excess the parties were still answerable for the consequences if death ensued. In the case that would be brought before them, it was suggested that the mate had beaten the deceased very violently with a thick stick, and if the grand jury should be of opinion that this was made out, and that the correction administered was altogether violent and in excess, and that it was the cause of the death of the man, it would be their duty to find the bill for manslaughter.[26]

Even when the victim was not an Englishman but African, West Indian, or Asian, and one would expect to find a sharp racial double standard, criminal prosecutions for excessive official violence were being taken up. As early as 1845, Captain George Hill, master of the *Challenge*, trading between Liverpool and the coast of Africa, found himself, to his great surprise, upon return to Liverpool charged with murder. The facts related in court were grim. After having a black ordinary seaman, Benjamin Johnson, who had several times fallen asleep on his watch, flogged, Hill had then exclaimed, "Damn that rope; it is too light," and personally laid into Johnson on the head and shoulders with a canoe paddle, with fatal results. The paddle was dramatically produced in court: it was broken, and there were bloodstains on it. Hill was apparently hated by his crew, some of whom gave evidence that he had subsequently had the ship's log altered to record the man falling and then receiving a short flogging, losing consciousness, and dying thereafter. He was found guilty of manslaughter. That his victim was black did not prevent his Judge, Baron Rolfe, from denouncing Hill as a brutal tyrant, calling his act a "crime only just short of murder" and awarding him the most severe sentence possible, transportation for life.[27] "You have numbers of

---

[26] *The Times*, 1 Mar. 1853, p, 7. The grand jury apparently "no-billed" this particular indictment, for it never came to trial.

[27] Isaac Land has argued by contrast that arguments by seamen and their sympathizers against brutal discipline built their case on a sharpened distinction between white Britons, who had the full rights of Englishmen against such treatment, and other races and nationalities, who did not, and thus that the eventual abolition of flogging was inseparable from intensified British racism ["Customs of the Sea: Flogging, Empire, and the 'True British Seaman' 1770 to 1870," *Interventions* 3 (2001), 169–185]. However, although his claims are for the nineteenth century in general, Land's evidence does not extend beyond the very early years of the century, and even then is highly

persons under your dominion," the Judge declared, "and to your violence they are all more or less obliged to submit."[28] Hill was shipped out to the penal colony of Van Diemen's Land.

In Exeter in March 1857 Captain Hugh Orr was brought up to the bar of justice for repeated beatings of his ship's cook, a black man from the United States, treatment that finally led to the man's death. "A case of such fearful cruelty and atrocity," *The Times* reporter began, "was, perhaps, scarcely ever heard." At the close of arguments Justice Williams went so far as to instruct the jury that a murder verdict would not be unreasonable, for while that usually required use of a dangerous weapon, lacking in this case, "the instruments of violence used [here] were used so often and so cruelly that the jury might come to the conclusion that they could not but infer that such a depraved and malignant spirit existed in him as would satisfy the imputation of malice." The Judge continued that "although it was true . . . that the master of a merchant vessel had authority over all persons in the ship, and might administer reasonable correction, yet his authority in that respect was that of a parent over a child. He must take care that there was sufficient cause for chastisement,

selective. Indeed, the single incident to which he devotes the most space, a London magistrate's 1814 indictment of a lascar supervisor for assault for the flogging of a lascar seaman while berthed in London, is on balance evidence *against* his claim. Moreover, racial distinctions, while no doubt often made colloquially and also no doubt affecting treatment of seamen, never entered legislation or case law. In practice, also, as the likelihood of criminal prosecution of excessively violent shipboard discipline rose, cases with "colored" victims rose more or less proportionately.

Indeed, when race did play a role in a maritime homicide trial at the Old Bailey, it was to mitigate responsibility for the man of color. In 1864, eight sailors were tried for mutiny and murder of their master, and seven convicted and sentenced to death. Five – an Englishman and four Spaniards – were hanged, while two lascars, their "Asiatic temperament, prone to sudden fits of resentment, quick to feel outrage or insult, and prompt to revenge it," cited in mitigation, were reprieved [*The Times*, 5 Feb. 1864, p. 11; Charles Hindley, *Curiosities of Street Literature* (London, 1871), p. 217 (broadside); Roger Chadwick, *Bureaucratic Mercy: The Home Office and the Treatment of Capital Cases in Victorian Britain* (New York, 1992), p. 344]. In the first complete study of the subject, Carolyn Conley has found that in the later nineteenth century, "only one of the 28 Africans and Asians tried for homicide in England and Wales was executed." Further, she noted, "English judges also gave lighter sentences to defendants from 'uncivilized' countries. Justice Cotton explained [in 1879] that he was reducing a sentence from 15 to 10 years as 'the prisoner was a man of colour and therefore the use of the knife under provocation he had received was somewhat more excusable than it would have been had he been a white man' " [*Certain Other Countries: Homicide, Gender, and National Identity in Late Nineteenth-Century England, Ireland, Scotland, and Wales* (Columbus, Ohio, 2007), pp. 58–59].

[28] *R v Hill: Liverpool Mercury*, 29 Aug. 1845, p. 2; see also NA, HO 18/158 /48.

and that the chastisement was reasonable, or he would be criminally responsible. There did not appear to him to be any evidence of any occasion for such chastisement." The jury did not go as far as invited, but they did find the captain guilty of manslaughter and withheld any mercy recommendation; Williams then, as Baron Rolfe had for Hill, pronounced the maximum possible sentence of transportation for life.[29] In neither trial was there any indication that the victim's race lessened the outrage of Judge or jury.

In 1874, Captain Charles Barnes of the *Locksley Hall* had the misfortune to return to London with a seaman in irons for being insubordinate and mutinous at the height of Samuel Plimsoll's agitation for seamen's safety, which relied on melodramatic portrayals of disasters at sea made possible by wicked shipowners who neglected the welfare of their workers in order to maximize their profits. Charging the man, as usual, at magistrate's court, he was amazed to find the magistrate "playing up to the sentiment of the time" by dismissing the charge and instead jailing him for a month. A delegation of shipowners to the Prime Minister won his release; two years later, however, after fresh incidents of magistrates and British Consuls "undermining" shipmasters' authority, the London Shipmasters' Society was established, to lobby in their defense.[30] Still, the trend continued, culminating in the Merchant Shipping Act 1894, which set out a detailed list of rules for shipowners and masters.

A series of well-publicized murder trials in the 1870s and 1880s firmly put merchant shipmasters on warning to rein in their resort to force, whether against British or foreign crewmen, including men of color. The first murder case at the Old Bailey with a lascar victim took place in the same year that Captain Barnes found himself imprisoned. Captain Horatio Walters, a 32-year-old American, was charged in 1874 with causing the death of three Indian seamen on a voyage from a Burmese port to London. He had had the men repeatedly beaten over a period of days with

---

[29] *R v Orr: The Times*, 23 Mar. 1857, p. 11. In Liverpool in 1858 another captain and mate were charged with murder for kicking a Spanish seaman to death; convicted of manslaughter, the captain was given penal servitude for life and the mate one year's imprisonment [*Liverpool Mercury*, 27 Mar. 1858, p. 3 (for their committal for trial, see *Liverpool Mercury*, 30 Nov. 1857, p. 6)].

[30] W. H. Hood, op. cit., p. 30. See also David Williams, "Mid-Victorian Attitudes to Seamen and Maritime Reform: The Society for Improving the Condition of Merchant Seamen, 1867," in *Merchants and Mariners: Selected Writings of David M. Williams*, ed. Lars U. Scholl (London, 2000), 229–252.

a belaying pin, and sometimes did the beating himself, adding powerful kicks. Justice Keating began by noting that "the law intrusted to the captain of a ship immense power, and anything approaching to mutiny he would be justified in putting down with the strongest hand." Still, he continued, "the power of a captain was to be used, not abused, and there could be no question, in point of law, that a subordinate officer was not bound to obey an order which would make him a contributing party to the death of another." The jury found the Captain guilty of manslaughter, but recommended him to mercy in consideration of "the very difficult and trying position of the captain with an inefficient crew of Lascars, and that many of the acts of violence were committed under great provocation." For his part, Walters declared that "no ship with a Lascar crew could sail the ocean without recourse being had to the 'serang' (boatswain) and the rope's end." But the Judge refused to accept this, noting that "the acts of violence to which the unfortunate men at length succumbed had been continuous, so far as he could see, and unjustifiable, at least to the extent to which they had been carried.... That Lascars were not able seamen and required management he could well understand; but he could imagine nothing so distressing as the state to which the deceased men were brought in this case." He told the prisoner that "if it had not been for the recommendation of the jury" he would have thought it his duty to give him the maximum sentence allowable. "He gave that recommendation all due effect, but he must say he could not surrender his opinions or feelings on the subject." Instead of life, he reluctantly sentenced the Captain to fifteen years' penal servitude.[31]

The death of a black cook aboard the *Cutty Sark*, bound from London to the Dutch East Indies, led to a widely followed murder trial at the Old Bailey in 1882. John Francis, who had signed on as an able seaman, had been found to have exaggerated his skills and was relegated to cooking; he apparently did not take that demotion well.[32] He quarreled with the first mate, John Anderson, and threats from the mate led to counterthreats from Francis. Finally, one night, while Francis was acting as lookout as the ship rounded the Cape of Good Hope, a fight broke out between Anderson and him. Francis was carried below deck with a wound on his head four inches long, deep blood flowing. The ship's master dressed his

---

[31] *The Times*, 26–28 Nov. 1874, pp. 11, 10, 12.

[32] At the inquest, the sailmaker testified that "Francis acted that night only as look out because he was incapable of anything else; he had been a cook and steward on a Yankee ship and signed onto this one without the proper skills of an Able-bodied seaman."

wound, but to no avail (all that was done for Francis, the second mate later claimed, was a sticking plaster and cutting his hair around the wound, nothing else). The following morning the chief mate said to the steward, "I have done for that son of a bitch. He will never lift no capstan bar to me again." Francis died that night and was buried at sea. The master, Anderson later claimed, exclaimed that "it served him damned well right." Along with Francis's body, the Captain dropped overboard the capstan bar with which he was struck. When they reached the East Indies, the Captain arranged for Anderson to leave the ship. Adding to the grimness of the story, two days after Anderson's departure the master fell into a depression and committed suicide by jumping overboard. The second mate got the ship to Singapore, where he went before the magistrates to give a statement about the killing of Francis. Eventually all got back to England, and Anderson was taken into custody. Unfortunately for Anderson, there were quite a few witnesses to the quarrel; when at his trial he claimed that "that nigger" had threatened him with a knife at one moment and a capstan bar at another, only one other seaman supported these claims, while numerous others explicitly denied them. The second mate testified that the master had forced him to sign an untrue statement in the log, to the effect that there were high seas and the ship was rolling. Anderson was at least able to produce a series of character witnesses, who seemed to impress his Judge, James Fitzjames Stephen. Stephen accepted that "he was a man of good character generally speaking and of humane disposition" and that "the deceased had certainly acted in a manner which was calculated to make the prisoner very angry." However, he directed a verdict of manslaughter, observing that "it must be clearly understood that the taking of human life by brutal violence, whether on sea or on land, whether the life be that of a black or a white man, was a dreadful crime, and deserving of exemplary punishment." Stephen sentenced Anderson to seven years' penal servitude.[33]

The death of another black cook, from a French colony, led to the trial of a ship's master, a Spaniard, at the Old Bailey in 1884. Enraged at what he saw as the cook's incompetence, the master had had the man tied to the rigging and beaten, and after he was let down beat him some more, finishing off with a kick to the head while he was lying out. A little while later, the dazed man fell overboard and drowned (although there were suggestions that he was pushed). The master was first tried for murder

[33] *R v Anderson, The Times*, 4 Aug. 1882, p. 4; his inquest is recorded in NA, CRIM 1/16/1.

and acquitted, but then convicted of causing "grievous bodily harm." In summing up in the second trial, Justice Day declared that

a captain was not justified in inflicting punishment, *qua* punishment, on any seaman. Captains were allowed to use any amount of violence to protect the ship, the lives of the crew, the cargo, and the other interests intrusted to their charge. But that was a very different thing from punishing a man simply as punishment.... A master of a ship was not at liberty, because a man had given him some offence, or because he was not a good cook, and not sufficiently economical of the provisions, to inflict punishment upon him.

After the jury returned a manslaughter conviction, strongly recommending mercy on the ground of previous good character, Day observed that "the law looked with jealousy upon any abuse of that great power [vested in ships' masters], and it was absolutely necessary in the interest of all seafaring men and in the interests of society that when that authority was abused, severe punishment should follow upon it." If it were not for the jury's recommendation, he announced, he would give the man the sentence he had given before to similar ship's masters – five years' penal servitude; in light of their recommendation, he pronounced a sentence of eighteen months' hard labor.[34]

In 1887 Justice Stephen presided over another Old Bailey murder trial of a ship's captain: James Cocks of the *Lady Douglas* and three of his crew stood charged with the deliberate shipboard killing of a Malay prisoner, being shipped from Western Australia back to Britain after a mutiny.[35] Malays, described as "naturally indolent" and "entirely destitute of moral capacity," with "habits which are so repugnant to all Englishmen's ideas of comfort," occupied possibly the lowest rung on the maritime ladder of esteem.[36] During the voyage in 1886, this Malay, named Hassim, had escaped custody, got hold of a knife, and run "amok." No one was seriously harmed, but he then retreated to a difficult-to-reach spot within the ship near the stores of coal for cooking, from which he threatened to come out at night and attack his fellow seamen. After days of failed efforts to dislodge him, the frightened crew (who were also facing a consequent lack of coal for cooking) urged the Captain to kill him if necessary. The Captain then organized a dislodgment party, one of whom shot the Malay. Dragged up on deck, the man, in great pain, appeared to be fatally injured. The Captain gave his pistol to a

---

[34] *The Times*, 21 Mar. 1884, p. 5.
[35] Quotations on this case are from NA, HO 144/199/A47104B; *The Times*, 30 June 1887.
[36] Visram, op. cit., p. 47.

mate who "put him out of his misery" with a shot to the head. After returning to England, he and the men who had shot were arrested. The defense took its stand, as we might expect, on the broad discretion allowed a Captain to maintain discipline and protect the safety of his crew and ship. Now, however, such discretion was seen to threaten the imperial civilizing mission itself, the fundamental moral justification for Britain's unprecedented world power. As Justice Stephen declared, "If they once broke through the principle that the law laid down – that except in certain excepted cases people were not to be put to death deliberately – how easy it would be to slide into the abominable doctrine that as soon as a man became a nuisance to his neighbours they were to put him to death, not that it was necessary to do so but because it was highly convenient."

Stephen's remarks echoed those of Baron Huddleston in the famous Dudley and Stephens trial also at the Old Bailey just three years before, in rejecting the claims of "the law of the sea" and convicting two shipwrecked sailors who killed and ate their cabin boy; if they could be found criminally liable for killing, as they saw it, for their survival, the case of Cocks and his men was all the weaker. To justify the actions of Cocks and his men on the ground of self-defense, Stephen argued, "it must be shown that they were in instant and immediate danger of death or some desperate injury." Instead, what they did were the actions of "timid men" in "cowardly terrors" (a judgment repeated within the Home Office).[37] Casting aside any pretense to neutrality, Stephen used his summation to urge the hesitant jurymen to return such a verdict: "It has been said," he told them, "that this was an important case, as it will tell captains and crews how to behave in future. It *is* an important case, and the jury must be careful that their verdict did not encourage timid men in circumstances of difficulty to get out of that difficulty by taking life." At the same time he signaled the jury that it would be safe to find murder, for he strongly implied that he would see to it that no one would actually hang. The jury was out for an hour. Pressed by the Judge, they finally returned not the manslaughter verdict of Hill's and Orr's trials a generation earlier but a symbolically important conviction on the full charge of murder. Cocks

---

[37] The Permanent Undersecretary remarked that "the conduct of these men seems to have been guilty of the most cowardly character and quite unnecessary." Stephen, whose book *Liberty, Equality, Fraternity* (1873) was a powerful and influential critique of John Stuart Mill's version of liberalism, was a believer in the necessity of upholding authority, but an authority that was lawful and self-disciplined.

and his men were, as Stephen had virtually promised, readily reprieved:
for his men a sentence of merely eighteen months' hard labor (for the
officer) and one year's (for the seaman) was substituted; for Cocks, five
years' penal servitude. It was less punishment than the usual murder
convict was dealt, but it delivered a public lesson – as the prosecutor had
told the jury, their verdict "would tell captains and crews how to behave
in future" – that there was no longer a law of the sea distinct from the
English common law, which applied in full on British ships anywhere in
the world.

Race, and indeed culture, did enter into the discourse of the case: the
Malay, a Moslem, was regarded by all on the ship, Cocks claimed in his
petition for mercy, "as a dangerous madman armed with a deadly
weapon, possessed with the idea that the death of a Christian at his hand
would ensure his entrance into paradise and consequently quite indif-
ferent to his own life as long as he could take that of another." This claim
was, however, ignored by the authorities. In addition, Malays' supposed
tendency to unpredictable violence – running "amok" (the English word
is borrowed from Malay) – was made much of during the trial by the
defense, which read out from news clippings describing such occur-
rences.[38] Yet it also cut no ice: Stephen dismissed the clippings as irrel-
evant, and later Thomas Gray, the head of the Merchant Marine
subdepartment of the Board of Trade, consulted by the Home Office in
deciding the terms of the reprieve, observed, lumping the Malay with
"coloured" men in general, that rather than being more dangerous, "as a
rule coloured men are more amenable to discipline than whites – and
severe but reasonable punishment in this case would I think tend in the
direction of making officers more instead of less careful in prescribing
discipline, and would not weaken their hands at all, while it would certainly be a salutary warning not to abuse their authority." Cocks's resort
to lethal violence, like Anderson's, was branded "cowardly" and
"unmanly." It is notable that, despite our assumptions about the prevalence of racism in nineteenth-century Britain, the victim's inferior racial
and colonial status did not help his killers' defense.

Two years later Liverpool assizes saw another maritime murder trial,
but this time the victim was a Captain and the man in the dock charged
with murder was a black crewman, Charles Arthur, a native of Barbados.

[38] Indeed, modern psychologists have verified and explored this cultural trait. See Joseph
Westermeyer, "On the Epidemicity of Amok Violence," *Archives of General Psychiatry*
28 (1973), 873–876.

While the sailing ship *Dovenby Hall* was returning to Liverpool from India via San Francisco, Arthur, a steward, disemboweled his Captain with a carving knife. Before dying, Captain Baillie swore that he had never struck Arthur, and being seized and put in irons Arthur admitted that he had had no immediate provocation – only, as his counsel was to describe, "a long period of bullying and extreme verbal provocation" – and that it had been "a cold-blooded murder."[39] Although at the trial Arthur retracted this admission and claimed that he had acted in immediate hot blood, his self-command cracking under fresh insults, he could offer no supporting evidence for this new claim. Most of the witnesses were officers, who described the gruesome scene, and confirmed Arthur's confession upon seizure. They did agree that Captain Baillie was known to be a bully, and that he had taken a particular aversion to Arthur, despite (or perhaps because of) the man's being "a favorite of the crew." However, not only had Captains traditionally been allowed wide scope to maintain authority at sea, but also blacks were almost always at the bottom of the maritime social hierarchy. The jury convicted on the full charge, as it could hardly help doing – before withdrawing, its members were informed by the judge, again Stephen, that "mere ill-usage is no provocation [that could reduce a charge of murder to manslaughter]." The "only thing which had this effect," he had continued, "was a serious actual assault or possibly such threatening gestures as if a man was to make such an assault."[40]

It is fair to say that in previous generations Arthur's path to the gallows would have been smooth. In this case, however, there was a great deal of sympathy for Arthur – the *Liverpool Evening Express* had headed its account of the trial "A Tragedy on the High Seas." The jury made a strong recommendation to mercy on account of provocation. And after the trial concluded additional seamen, a sailors' missionary, and even the Captain's former employers came forward with accounts of the Captain's history of abusing men under his command, particularly those of color, turning even Stephen – a man not easily swayed by others' views – to

---

[39] Quotations on this case are from HO 144/216/A59165.

[40] Indeed, he went on, resentment of previous ill-treatment could actually strengthen the case for a murder conviction: "If the Captain was a provoking and ill-conditioned person and had treated the prisoner improperly and violently on former occasions this not only was not provocation, but inasmuch as such treatment was calculated to produce resentment it was considered in law to give evidence of ill-will or malice on the part of the prisoner against the prosecutor. The law upon that point was very strict and clear" [*Liverpool Evening Express*, 3 Aug. 1888].

sympathize with the Barbadian. When asked by the Home Office to comment on the jury recommendation, Stephen replied that although insufficient evidence had been offered in court to justify it, he had since seen new evidence that "suggests a course of tyrannous conduct [by the victim] which would be sufficient" for reprieve, and indeed, for a lighter sentence than usual in reprieves. Stephen proposed a sentence of fifteen to twenty years, rather than the normal sentence of life imprisonment given to murder convicts reprieved from execution. The Home Office made further inquiries, and concluded that the Captain indeed was well known as an inveterate bully. Arthur was reprieved, although only to life imprisonment. However, his many friends – constituting most of the ship's crew as well as his previous Captain – continued to petition for his early release (a petition organized by a Liverpool seamen's missionary gained more than thirteen hundred signatures, many of them seamen's), and he was set free after eleven years. He had no trouble immediately finding employment as a ship's rigger. In effect Arthur was punished as if the jury had found him guilty only of manslaughter. This well-publicized case delivered a lesson to ship's masters: they mistreated even a lowly black steward at their peril. And a question was raised for later historians about the supposed hegemony of racism at sea, or in Liverpool.[41]

Three years later, in 1891, another colored sailor was in the Liverpool dock for murder. At Calcutta, on the merchant ship *Buckingham*'s voyage from Australia to Dundee, Bhagwan Jassiwarra, a Hindu, was recruited. He was apparently made to serve as cook unwillingly, and complained to the Dundee police about his treatment.[42] However, not surprisingly they took no action and he signed up again for the ship's next voyage, from Dundee to New York. On this voyage Jassiwara repeatedly quarreled with his Captain, who had him locked up for a time. After this he was seen sharpening his knife, and remarked to another sailor that if the Captain struck him again he would kill him. The following day the Captain was seen to strike him twice on the face, and shortly afterwards the Captain's body was found in the storeroom into which he had gone alone with Jassiwarra, stabbed in the head in several places. Although a few seamen testified for the prosecution that the Captain was "a kind man," the

---

[41] *Liverpool Evening Express*, 3 Aug. 1888; *The Times*, 29 June 1888, p. 5: "A Captain Murdered at Sea"; HO 144/216/A49165.
[42] The prosecutor claimed this was done "out of consideration for his nationality," and the Captain's subsequent displeasure was due to his bad performance of these duties [*Liverpool Evening Express*, 16 Mar. 1891].

accused's counsel was able to obtain a witness who had sailed with the Captain, and who agreed with the suggestion that he was "a man of brutal character," indeed one "likely to bring upon himself that which had happened."[43] The defense counsel in his closing "called attention," the *Liverpool Courier* reported, "to the fact that the captain was alone with the prisoner in the storeroom, and he might have done a thousand things to him there during the few minutes they were alone. To strike a man in the face was as great an insult as they could offer to a man, and if the contemptuous slap and kick would raise their [the jury's] blood, what effect would it have upon the warm-blooded races of the South? The blood of the European was but as ice to the hot blood of the Hindoo or negroes generally." Justice Day informed the jury that such provocation as had been shown would not be sufficient to reduce the crime to manslaughter, and the jury dutifully complied, returning a murder verdict. But it appended to the verdict a strong recommendation to mercy on the grounds of "great provocation." The secretary of the British and Foreign Sailors' Society, writing in support of a commutation, pointed out that the Captain had first broken the law by personally and repeatedly striking Jassiwara, treating him "like a dog."[44] The Home Office followed the jury's recommendation. Jassiwarra's death sentence was commuted to life imprisonment. Again, a Captain's "tyrannical" repute and allowance for the "hot blood" of non-European races worked together to save a killer from the gallows.[45] Jassiwarra was released in poor health after seven years and returned to India.[46]

In a very real sense, Britain's Empire began on the ships that left it under the Union Jack for worldwide voyages. The trials of interracial killings on board these ships point to three developments of great significance for this Empire. First, the lines of maritime authority, of the

---

[43] *Liverpool Courier*, 17 Mar. 1891.

[44] "Some captains," he continued, "do not know the art of governing, and treat hot-blooded Southerns and Easterns, who use the knife, as they might take the liberty of treating with comparative safety and impunity the more cold-blooded Northerns. . . . If a captain will take these foreign seamen in his ship, their nationality, antipathies, and the art of governing and managing these should be taken into consideration. But to treat them as dogs may be safely done for a voyage or two, but often ends in death" [*The Times*, 7 Apr. 1891, p. 12].

[45] On this case see HO 144/239/A52652: *Liverpool Courier*, 17 Mar. 1891; *Liverpool Evening Express*, 16 and 17 Mar. 1891; *The Times*, 7 Apr. 1891.

[46] BL OIOC L/P&J/6/484: 4 July 1898 (request from Home Office to India Office to make inquiries to two locations Jassiwarra has written to with no replies, to see whether, if he were released from Parkhurst prison, he would be properly looked after).

border between legitimate force and illegitimate "violence," were being redrawn. Masters and officers were increasingly restricted in their use of force to maintain discipline. Second, the world of maritime Britain was increasingly a multiethnic one. It was becoming more multicultural not only in numerical terms, as residents of different parts of the Empire were recruited to fill the ranks of "British" seamen, but also in conceptual terms, as the authorities were adapting to the position of a global power by learning how to deal with – and make allowances for – a population drawn from widely varying cultural backgrounds. And third, a contrast was sharpening between a Britain in which race did not appear to make much difference in the trial of serious offenses (except, if anything, to mitigate the punishment of nonwhite offenders) and a colonial Empire in which, as we will see, race weighed heavily upon criminal justice.

2

Queensland, 1869–1889

Great as the British race has been in the work of colonisation, it has not always been particularly happy in its treatment of inferior races.

Sydney Morning Herald, 11 July 1878

I

In early 1884, the merchant ship the *Hopeful* was cruising off New Guinea, a land then outside the claims of any "civilized" state, seeking men to work the sugar plantations of the young and rapidly developing Australian colony of Queensland. At Moresby Island, impatient at the slow methods of negotiation, the second mate and recruiting agent, Neil McNeill, had the crew begin their operations by ramming native canoes that had come out to see what they wanted, and dragging their occupants aboard. They moved from island to island, repeating this brutally effective technique. When they met resistance, they shot the resisters; when two captives escaped one night, in the morning McNeill set fire to the village opposite where they were anchored, again shooting several natives who rushed out of the burning village. "Look here steward," the shipmaster replied to a concerned seaman, "if you want to be in this trade you have got to be blind and see nothing." On another day, several men escaped into the water, where McNeill and Barney Williams, the boatswain, shot them dead. It was for these last murders that they were to be tried in Brisbane, the capital of the colony, later that year, along with the master and the Government Agent, placed there by law to protect native recruits, but in fact, as he was later described, "a hopeless drunkard."[1] Before it was over, this single

---

[1] E. W. Docker, *The Blackbirders: The Recruiting of South Seas Labour for Queensland, 1863–1907* (Sydney, 1971), p. 199; the judge's notes of the trial are in NA, CO 234/45.

voyage cost probably thirty-eight Pacific Islanders their lives – the fuller and more appalling toll was not known until after their trial had concluded. The Commissioners later appointed by the Queensland Government to inquire into the state of labor recruitment were moved to declare that "the history of this cruise . . . is one long record of deceit, cruel treachery, deliberate kidnapping and cold-blooded murder."[2]

Three years later, in the Union Camp, a small grouping of seventeen or eighteen Europeans outside the town of Thornborough in northern Queensland, not far from today's booming resort city of Cairns, a different kind of killing took place. On October 19, 1887, William Nichols, a twenty-six-year-old quartz miner, was observed beating a fourteen-year-old Aboriginal girl named Maggie, who worked in the small settlement as a servant. Two nearby housewives saw him beat Maggie around the head with a length of wood as thick as a shovel handle. The next day he was seen chopping down a sapling and taking it into his house. Screams and the sound of blows were then heard coming from inside the house. These incidents were reported to a local police constable, who visited Nichols's home three days later and found the girl lying unconscious in the chicken coop. Finding what he took to be "marks of violence" on her, he came back in half an hour with the senior constable and a doctor from the nearby hospital. The girl was moved to a hospital and Nichols was arrested. He admitted to the constable that he "had chastised the gin with a whip." She died that night without regaining consciousness. Post-mortem examination revealed a skull hemorrhage. Nichols was held for trial in Townsville on the charge of murder.[3]

II

Occupying the northeast quadrant of Australia, Queensland was carved off from New South Wales in 1859 and made a separate, internally self-governing colony. With a climate ranging from semitropical to tropical, and a rainy zone along the coast separated by a range of mountains from a vast arid interior, Queensland was less attractive to European settlement

---

[2] Hugh Hastings Romilly, *From My Veranda in New Guinea: Sketches and Traditions* (London, 1889), p 207; see materials in Queensland State Archives, Brisbane [henceforth QSA], CRS 146 (Crown Solicitor's Papers).

[3] This account is based on Gary Highland, "A Tangle of Paradoxes: Race, Justice and Criminal Law in North Queensland, 1882–1894," in *A Nation of Rogues? Crime, Law and Punishment in Colonial Australia*, ed. David Philips and Susanne Davies (Melbourne, 1994), pp. 123–124.

than the more temperate earlier colonies of New South Wales and Victoria. However, its southern coastal areas were well suited for agriculture and especially pasturing, and farther north for cotton and especially sugar plantations, all of which grew rapidly after the creation of the state, along with the mining of quartz and gold. The plantations needed cheap and disciplinable workers who would put up with the hot climate and heavy physical labor. Europeans, it was assumed, could not be attracted to such work (at least not at affordable wages); as Queensland's first Governor, George Bowen, told the Colonial Office the year after the constitution of the colony, "the climate is unfavourable to European fieldwork."[4] Aborigines, it was felt, could not be trained nor would they remain, as they could always desert into the bush. In the 1860s efforts to import indentured labor from India, as West Indian colonies had begun to do, were blocked by the combined opposition of the Colonial and India Offices, and so recruitment turned to nearby Pacific islands and was given legal recognition in 1868.

The combination of a not-quite-acknowledged frontier war with Aboriginal peoples and the increasing presence of Islander workers intensified the majority's concern with maintaining a color line in the colony. Against "savage blacks," gradually retreating, and newly arrived "Kanakas," drawn from islands where cannibalism was still known to be practiced – not to mention a growing number of Chinese immigrants – whites, particularly outside the capital city of Brisbane, felt powerful pressure to stick together. By the 1880s Queensland was an unusually racially mixed colony, holding a rapidly growing white majority with substantial Aboriginal, Pacific Islander, and Chinese minorities. The Aboriginal population, however, was in sharp decline; as Europeans poured in, Aborigines died in large numbers from diseases and violence, or were pushed further into the interior. This decade saw the end of the fiercest frontier fighting and the acceleration of white immigration.[5] Those Aborigines remaining in the "settled" areas increasingly lived on

---

[4] Quoted in Tracey Banivanua-Mar, *Violence and Colonial Dialogue: The Australia-Pacific Labor Trade* (Honolulu, 2007), p. 76. On the issue of the suitability of the tropics for European settlement, see Richard Eves, "Unsettling Settler Colonialism: Debates over Climate and Colonization in New Guinea, 1875–1914," *Ethnic and Racial Studies* 28 (2005), 304–330.

[5] In the course of the 1880s, stimulated by the Agricultural Depression in the U.K., the colony's official population almost doubled [Jennifer Harrison, "The People of Queensland, 1859–1900: Where Did the Immigrants Come From?" *Journal of the Royal Historical Society of Queensland* 13 (1988)].

the fringes of white settlement, mostly dependent on a combination of charity and work as occasional hired labor.

In contrast with Chapter 1, English courts no longer figure in this chapter or those following. Unlike the happenings on board British vessels traveling to or from Britain, what took place in Queensland was outside the authority of such courts. Even crimes committed on the high seas in such ships, by labor "recruiters" in the Pacific for instance, while under imperial legal authority and after the Colonial Courts Act of 1849 triable in Queensland's courts, were in practice very difficult to prosecute. The Empire, even while under the same sovereign authority as the United Kingdom itself and drawing on the same English common law, constituted a different legal world or, rather, collection of worlds. Queensland criminal law was essentially English law with some local modifications, but its chief distinction from the latter was that it was largely administered by Queenslanders. While their legal definitions might be the same, crimes were often understood differently in late-nineteenth-century Queensland and England; some, like sheep-stealing, were seen as more heinous in the former; others, like the killing of nonwhites, generally as less so. Moreover, Queensland, as a colony of settlement, enjoyed almost-complete internal autonomy. In contrast to either India or to directly ruled Crown colonies, the Home Government was extremely limited in its ability to influence Queensland justice. Here we will see British imperial authority at its weakest, just as Chapter 1 showed it in its full power. In regard to Queenslanders' treatment of Aborigines in the courts and outside them, the Colonial Office had only the frail tools of exhortation and persuasion. Since the Colonial Laws Validity Act of 1856, colonial legislation no longer required the prior approval of the Home Government; the Government, through the Colonial Office, did retain the power to disallow existing legislation, but this power was potentially inflammatory and very sparingly used.

While Aborigines were left in the hands of colonial authority, the imperial Government had more to do with Pacific Islanders. When Queenslanders left their state to recruit Island laborers, they came at least in principle within the sphere of direct imperial authority. The Pacific Islanders Protection Act of 1872, together with the creation of the Western Pacific High Commission in 1877, established a framework for imperial regulation of recruitment activities and, if necessary, prosecution of major crimes committed by recruiters. In practice, such prosecution outside of Queensland was very difficult, and by the 1880s the Government of Queensland (and those of other Australian states) had accepted responsibility to normally mount such prosecutions of its own citizens. Indeed, a series of trials for murder and kidnapping in 1884 and 1885 drew intense public interest, and led to the first abolition of the Pacific Islands labor trade. The 1880s were a watershed decade also for the treatment of Aborigines. With increasing security, the imperative of white solidarity eased, and the humanitarian, constitutional, and, one might say, reputational concerns of the great majority of Queenslanders who did not live on the frontier, particularly those living in and around Brisbane, began to predominate.[6] Even for those away from the capital, racial solidarity could now begin to be trumped by other values. In the wake of the establishment of "order," "law" could come into its own. A pair of murder trials in 1888 bore witness to this novel state of affairs.

The central actors in these legal dramas were the white settlers and traders, rapidly growing in number, overwhelmingly emigrants from either the United Kingdom or the earlier Australian colonies of New South Wales and Victoria. Like their counterparts in other parts of the Empire (or in the United States), they tended to share similar social backgrounds and a distinctive worldview. Coming by and large from unprivileged, sometimes desperately poor, circumstances, these men (and they were very disproportionately, in the earlier years, men) were there first of all to make money – if not wealth through mining finds, then at least solid prosperity through sheepherding, farming, planting, or trading. This fierce economic drive aimed to conquer nature and exploit its untapped economic potentialities, and could readily slip into simple greed, for which they were often taken to task by observers from more elevated backgrounds.

A second, even less attractive, facet of their view of the world was an unabashed racism. A major obstacle to their hopes to "make it" in their new country were the people who already inhabited it; these "natives," it appeared obvious to settlers, were essentially and probably irredeemably savage, indeed, hardly human. One popular novel of the time characteristically opened with a scene of a European shipwreck in the 1830s, in which all on board fall victim to "the blood-frenzy and love of slaughter common to all aboriginals of Australia."[7] An already-violent continent,

---

[6] In 1890, North Queensland held only 80,000 persons, and Central Queensland 50,000, compared with 280,000 in South Queensland (none of these figures included Aboriginal people).

[7] Simpson Newland, *Paving the Way: A Romance of the Australian Bush* (London, 1893), p. 17. Yet by the time he was writing, with the inevitable violence largely over, even

Australia, it seemed obvious, could not be settled without violence. As one English visitor sympathetic to settlers noted in 1884, "amongst the human family the Australian black occupies the lowest place; how much the lowest only ocular demonstration can make one understand." After a lengthy description, suffused with disgust, of the Aborigine's animal-like existence, he concluded that "the most striking characteristic of the 'black fellow' is the utter incapacity for anything like civilisation which he displays. . . . I never heard of more than one black man who had been civilised, and he was sent by a philanthropic Victorian to be educated in [England], with the melancholy result, that he was hanged in Queensland for an offense which is not to be mentioned in polite society."[8] Pacific Islanders were regarded similarly. Not that it was difficult to do so: practicing cannibalism, head-hunting, and frequent warfare, and lacking most of the habits of settled civilizations, they were feared or, occasionally, pitied exotics, and not perceived as people with a future. In particular, any violence used against them was seen in the context of their own violent societies and their presumed inherently violent natures.[9]

Australian settlers were for the most part certainly racists eager to exploit indigenous peoples; yet there was more to them than that. As a group they too could claim a degree of victimhood, often forced as they were from lack of opportunities to leave the motherland. Their romantic self-image as pioneers into the wilderness was not entirely divorced from reality; they indeed carried a new spirit of enterprise with them, and accepted hard conditions of life in order to create the conditions for a better future. Indeed, it was this spirit of enterprise that inevitably brought them into collision with native peoples. As a correspondent to the *Sydney Daily Telegraph* remarked in calling for naval action against

---

Newland could admit that "the darkest stain on Australia's fair fame is her treatment of the aboriginal race" [p. 64].

[8] A. W. Stirling, *The Never-Never Land* (London, 1884), pp. 80, 90.

[9] Even a writer critical of "slave-trading" labor recruiters described a horrifying instance among Melanesians of torturing captives: "the ceremony of torturing," he concluded, "was a form of entertainment, almost as popular as the cannibal feast that followed" [Gilbert Bishop, *The Beachcombers, or Slave-Trading under the Union Jack* (London, 1889), p. 45]. A popular memoir later recalled Melanesia at this time; it was a place where "cannibalism went on unchecked and tribal warfare was the order of the day" [John Cromar, *Jock of the Islands* (London, 1935), p. 112]. Recently, Banivanua-Mar [op. cit.] has emphasized the exaggerations of such writers, and interprets their characterizations as constructions meant to justify European violence against Melanesians. However, one can condemn European violence without refusing to acknowledge the undoubted existence of frequent warfare with public tortures and even cannibalism of captives in Melanesian societies.

Islanders who had massacred "recruiting" colonists, "the un-enterprising may say that if we leave the islands alone the natives will not seek us out to plunder and murder us; but as the spirit of enterprise is too deeply implanted in the heart of the Anglo-Saxon to ever allow his restless nature to remain in quiescence while there are new lands to conquer, or new sources of commerce to open up, we are afraid that the 'let well alone' policy of these pseudo philanthropists will hardly be acquiesced in by less heavenly-minded people."[10] Further, closely bound up with settlers' racism was an equally strong egalitarianism, and the society they created was also a democratic and rights-conscious one, hostile to much of the social privilege of old England and sensitive to hints of "oppression." Queensland politics thus early enshrined a hostility to any interference by the imperial Government that was to make the life of colonial Governors difficult. However, sometimes cutting across this resistance was the emergence of two parties, tending to represent the two chief interests of rural planters and squatters on the one hand and urban workingmen on the other – the National and the Liberal Parties, respectively. This party division was to open up space for changes in policies and practices toward peoples of other races. As it took form, the predominantly urban Liberal Party came to be the home of those who sought both internal law and order and better treatment for Aboriginal people and Pacific Islanders, while the competing National Party gave voice to the concerns of countrymen, seeking to protect their freedom of action to pursue their economic interests by "dispersal" of Aborigines and recruitment and indenture of Islanders. The desire to see the rule of law firmly established tended to spread from Brisbane in the south northward through the rural areas toward the northernmost frontier areas. As the danger from Aborigines faded, most settlers turned to taming their own wilder members and establishing a domestic and peaceable society.

Another influential group in the shaping of policy in regard to indigenous peoples were missionaries. Hoping to win converts among these peoples, missionaries were deeply worried by settlers' and traders' depredations, and working closely with humanitarian organizations like the Aborigines Protection Society, were instrumental in bringing abuses and crimes to light, influencing "respectable opinion" in Brisbane and back in Britain as well. Their outlook and self-image shaped by the long

---

[10] *Sydney Daily Telegraph*, Dec. 1880, in *Correspondence Respecting the Natives of the Western Pacific and the Labour Traffic*, PP 1883 (C. 3641), p. 21 [precise date not given (enclosed with letter from Governor of New South Wales to Kimberley)].

struggle against slavery, missionaries often described the Pacific labor trade simply as a revived slave trade. Where labor recruiters and planter employers saw violence in the trade as atypical, a result of the violence of Islander societies, missionaries viewed the trade as inherently violent, not only destructive of Islander life but demoralizing of its European practitioners as well.

Officials at the Colonial Office shared some of the missionaries' disapproval; after all, they too were comparatively disinterested gentlemen and not settlers seeking to rise in the world. Indeed, with their established gentry-professional upbringings, Whitehall bureaucrats were even more removed than missionaries were from the world of enterprising (or avaricious) settlers. The Permanent Secretary between 1848 and 1859, Herman Merivale, had remarked on the "perverse wickedness of those outcasts of society whom the first waves of our colonization [in the Antipodes] are sure to bring along with them." Merivale had warned that "if their violence and avarice cannot be restrained by the arm of power – and it must be confessed that there appears scarcely any feasible mode of accomplishing this – it is impossible but that our progress in the occupation of barbarous countries must be attended with the infliction of infinite suffering."[11] Merivale's successor, Frederick Rogers, was a devout Churchman and a friend of the missionary enterprise. With Rogers heading the Colonial Office and many supporters in the Liberal Party, the influence of missionary societies on British policymaking may have reached a peak during the early years of William Gladstone's first Ministry, which began in 1868. Yet it was a peak from which they were to fall quite rapidly thereafter. Officials charged with the maintenance of a continually expanding Empire were coming to look askance at the impracticality of missionary jeremiads about endangered natives. After Rogers was succeeded in 1871 by Robert Herbert, whose religiosity was purely conventional, and who had in fact served as the first (non-elected) Premier of Queensland, hard-nosed pragmatism soon characterized the Office. Herbert's experiences in Queensland in the 1860s had made him well aware of the unpleasant side of settlers (he had once been manhandled by unemployed protesters in the street near Parliament House in Brisbane), but also of missionaries' tendencies to embroider their accounts of settler evil, and even more crucially, had educated him in the economic needs of the colony (he retained economic interests there long after he had left it)

---

[11] *Genocide and Settler Society: Frontier Violence and Stolen Indigenous Children in Australian History*, ed. A. Dirk Moses (Sydney, 2004), p. 29.

and in the limits to the exercise of British power on the far side of the world. In any event, he seems to have shared the widely held colonial view that "troubles" between Aborigines and colonists "can never terminate except with the gradual disappearance of [this] . . . unimprovable race."[12] As head for the next two decades, he did much to set a new tone for the Colonial Office as a whole.

III

Labor recruitment in Melanesia had begun in 1863, with the arrival in Queensland of the first shipload of sixty-seven Islanders, and in 1864 the first arrival of Island laborers in the settlement at Fiji, as yet beyond British rule. By the late 1860s recruitment of Islanders for plantations in both Queensland and Fiji had become a large-scale enterprise; by the end of the century, over fifty thousand Islanders had been brought to Queensland.[13] It was a speculative trade, promising substantial profit to those ready to deceive and, if necessary, use force. It was also dangerous: the Islands were beyond the authority of any European state, outside "civilization," and anything could happen to intruders. Under these conditions, the trade tended to attract, as one historian has noted, "a shiftless, drunken set of seamen, who were kept under scant discipline."[14]

---

[12] Memorandum to Queensland Executive Council, 20 June 1866, CO 234/16 f. 300. His colonial education had been shared with his second-in-command at the Colonial Office after 1876, John Bramston, a friend from Oxford days who had gone to Queensland with him. Bramston served as Attorney General there after Herbert had returned to Britain. The missionary viewpoint evoked little sympathy in Herbert, Bramston, or their chief clerk, William R. Malcolm, all of them, in contrast to most of their predecessors, trained as lawyers. This new generation of officials were, as O. W. Parnaby has noted, "only too ready to dismiss [missionary] evidence as untrustworthy." "Unfortunately," Parnaby conceded, "this was often the case" [*Britain and the Labor Trade in the Southwest Pacific* (Durham, N.C., 1954), p. 78]. As Prime Minister of Queensland, Herbert had pushed for opening indentured immigration from India, but had been rebuffed by Rogers at the Colonial Office because of Queenslanders' bad treatment of Aborigines [Parnaby, p. 53]. Luke Trainor has observed, "Herbert was to provide the acceptable face of the Colonial Office to those in the white colonies who had criticized the office. One of his particular achievements was to cultivate good relations with some prominent people in those colonies. He was tactful and pleasant to such visitors and to their representatives in London." Trainor noted that "the intense racial prejudice which Herbert shared with his contemporaries . . . was sometimes modified by a scepticism of the motives of colonial inhabitants whose skin colour was similar to his own but whose social class was different" ["Sir Robert Herbert," *ODNB*].

[13] Rev. William Gray, *The Kanaka* (Adelaide, 1895).

[14] Deryck Scarr, *Fragments of Empire: A History of the Western Pacific High Commission* (Canberra, 1967), p. 139.

Between 1869 and 1872 a series of Australian trials first drew public
attention to the trade and its violence. These trials and the public discussion around them were shaped by two contending frameworks, one of
class and one of race, both of them inflected with geographical concerns.
Many of the more respectable parts of Australian society blamed the
violence on the "scum" of the mother country, the criminal classes drawn
to the lawlessness of the fringes of civilization. There, in the hot tropics,
the climate further "degenerated" them.[15] The outcome was "scenes of
wickedness...blood-shedding and drunkenness, and kidnapping and
treachery" that deeply shocked the respectable.[16] Such shock was shared
by many of the imperial officials on the spot, such as the naval officer
Captain George Palmer, formerly of the West African slave trade patrol,
who had in April 1869 seized a recruiting ship, the *Daphne*, when it
docked in Levuka, Fiji, with a hundred "recruits" and brought charges of
slaving against the ship's officers. "What is it," Palmer wondered, "that
causes a certain class of persons to throw off all restraint and decency
when they live under a tropical sun, and see other human beings with
skins darker than their own?"[17]

If these trials had been held in England, such a view would have been,
as we have seen, familiar and readily accepted. In Australia, however,
those like Palmer found themselves up against another way of understanding these events that excused or mitigated the defendants' behavior –
a mental framework of racial, and geographical, difference. These men, it
was said, in carrying on the drive to extend commerce that had made the
British great, had ventured into "dark" regions beyond the reach of law,
and there had to face on their own the unpredictable behavior of barbarous and uncivilized races. In such circumstances, violence on all sides
was almost inevitable, inherent in the remoteness of the world of the
frontier from civilization.[18] Reinforcing this understanding was the fear

[15] On the widespread and intense debates in this era over the relation of climate and
character, see Eves, op. cit., and David Arnold, *The Problem of Nature: Environment,
Culture and European Expansion* (Oxford, 1996).

[16] The Chief Justice of New South Wales, Sir Alfred Stephen, letter to the Governor, 10
July 1869; quoted in Capt. George Palmer, *Kidnapping in the South Seas* (London,
1871; reprinted 1971), p. 148.

[17] Palmer, p. 182. Palmer was the son of an Anglican clergyman (like so many of the new
generation of colonial officials), and later retired as Rear Admiral. One of his daughters
married the 17th Earl of Moray.

[18] As the Rev. George Brown asked in his memoirs, in defending his leading a retaliatory
expedition in 1878 into the interior of Fiji after four Fijian mission teachers were
murdered there, an expedition that killed between ten and fifty natives: "Does he

of Islanders that was already a rooted part of Australian culture. In the first children's book published in Australia, Charlotte Barton's *A Mother's Offering to Her Children* (1841), children are told long stories about shipwrecks and the gruesome sufferings of those on board who fell into the hands of Pacific Islanders.[19] Many Australians had since grown up with fearful images of wild cannibals. In responding to criticisms of the labor trade, Australians drew on three established but not necessarily harmonious cultural narratives. One told of the gradual settlement and cultivation of a new land, in which economic and moral progress went hand in hand. However, a second portrayed a conflict among Britons, between selfless humanitarians and selfish enterprisers, in which only the humanitarians could be trusted with the fate of the backward Islanders, backward in military capability as in economic and cultural pursuits. Both of these narratives were colored by a third that had been developing from the first days of contact – of the Islands as a dark zone outside civilization, which, if it failed to kill the civilized Britons who ventured into it, could easily ruin them, morally and even materially. If the enterprisers – or even the humanitarians – harmed the natives, it could be seen as not really their fault, but in a sense the inevitable degeneration awaiting those who ventured beyond the borders of civilization.[20]

The violent abuses of labor traffickers threatened the first narrative, and more broadly the moral standing of Australian colonials in the eyes of the "Home country." Thus they could be condemned not only by humanitarian missionaries, but also by urban Australians uninvolved in the trade but jealous of the respectability of their new country abroad. Yet the effort to prosecute such "recruitment" as simply a new form of slaving failed when Captain Palmer was humiliatingly rebuffed in the Sydney courts. Defense counsel denounced the high-handed and indeed "monstrous" actions of "this Wilberforce of the Pacific" against ordinary men of business, and a magistrate threw out the charge. The magistrate cited the lack of evidence that force had been employed on the *Daphne*, or that the contracts of indenture that Islanders had signed had placed them in the

[a critical Australian journalist] think that in becoming missionaries we cease to be men, and, above all, cease to feel and act as Christian Englishmen?" [George Brown, *George Brown, D.D., Pioneer-Missionary and Explorer: An Autobiography* (London, 1908), p. 276].

[19] See Alan Atkinson, *The Europeans in Australia. A History*, vol. 2: *Democracy* (Sydney, 2006), pp. 108–109: "Islanders and Aborigines are more prone that we are, so the mother says, to 'unrestrained passions'."

[20] See Banivanua-Mar, op. cit., ch. 1.

condition of slaves.[21] Palmer would not give up, and pressed the case before the Vice-Admiralty Court. Yet here also he failed: Chief Justice Sir Alfred Stephen clearly sympathized with him and with the Islanders, but found there was no legal ground on which to convict; the recruits may not have been dealt with fairly or honorably, but they had not been enslaved, nor had any act of violence against them been proved.[22]

If a charge of slaving could not stand, perhaps one of kidnapping could. A new attempt two years later to proceed against the trade tested that possibility. Since the *Daphne* trial, the Queensland Government had issued new regulations requiring the presence of a Government Agent on every recruiting voyage from the colony. It was one of the first such voyages that led to a prosecution in Brisbane Supreme Court in the fall of 1871. When the shocking news of the clubbing to death by relatives of kidnapped islanders of Bishop John Patteson, who had been a fierce critic of labor recruiters, reached Queensland in September, a reluctant colonial Government decided to act against the men who had provoked the Islanders. Attorney General John Bramston charged Captain John Coath of the *Jason* and some members of his crew with kidnapping nine Islanders. The Government Agent, who upon protesting their forcible capture of these Islanders, had been handcuffed and chained for the duration of the voyage, was a key witness, and while the crew were acquitted, Coath was convicted and sentenced to five years' penal servitude.

Coath immediately appealed to Queensland's Supreme Court, and obtained for his counsel a figure to match Bramston – Charles Lilley, a leading urban radical, former Attorney General, and at that moment Leader of the Opposition in the Legislature. Lilley drew on the narrative of "dangerous alien races beyond the pale of civilization" to move past the particulars to the broad argument that taking nine Islanders into captivity against their will was not a crime under British law. The crime of kidnapping, he claimed, could not be committed "on a savage or barbarous people captured and brought within the protection of British law and landed free" in Queensland. He maintained that it was no offense

---

[21] "Seizing a vessel in these circumstances," remarked E. W. Docker, reconstructing the popular state of mind in Sydney, "might have been all right had one been dealing with a crew of shifty Arabs off the coast of Zanzibar. But it was quite another thing to do so in face of a community of freeborn British subjects" [op. cit., p. 64].

[22] "The morality of the proceeding," he had noted, "cannot be taken into consideration"; the case was more strictly one of slaving or not. This and the "shocking" case of the *Young Australian* showed, he wrote to the Governor, that "some legislative action is urgently required on the part of the Imperial Government" to remedy the gap in the law.

to "bring these people within the protection of the English law," and just as before "the Slave Acts, inferior races could be enslaved" legally, this case of capturing savages in places outside the protection of English law was, as long as they were not then enslaved, not yet illegal. He even conceded that what was done might "be morally wrong," but yet was not unlawful.[23] He did not say, but his listeners could be assumed to understand, that such behavior was almost to be expected in the strange world of the Islands, where violence was ubiquitous, inherent, and almost unavoidable.

In response, the Attorney General took an even more general line, arguing that wherever British law reached it protected all men: "the savage has as much right to protection [of his personal liberty] under this law as the most highly educated." Acts that the recruiters, flying the British flag, would have been prohibited from performing against their own were also prohibited against those who lived outside civilization. Bramston also made a more pragmatic argument about the prestige of British law and the "public peace" of Queensland, as well the individuals kidnapped, that had been struck at: if such deeds were unpunishable, terrible consequences might follow. The pragmatic argument won the day. Justices Cockle and Lutwyche could find no fault in the logic and legal correctness of the defense; nonetheless, in the interests of the safety and credibility of the law, and the Empire as a whole, they felt unable to overturn Coath's conviction.[24] Yet in upholding the conviction without affirming its solid legal basis, they underlined the uncertain state of the law. It was clear after this trial, and Bishop Patteson's murder, that fresh legislation (blocked for the previous decade by Treasury opposition) was now unavoidable in order to directly address the problem of kidnapping.

The passage of new legislation in Parliament, and its acceptance in Australia, was aided by the worst scandal by far, that of the voyage of the *Carl*, which emerged in the spring of 1872. It was then that Dr. James Murray walked into the office of the British Consul in Fiji and described the massacre on board of as many as seventy helpless Islanders. Murray himself was actually the organizer of the voyage, and a participant in the

---

[23] At least not *yet*; Lilley implied that it could certainly be made so, as it indeed was to be. *R v Coath, Reports of Cases Argued and Determined in the Supreme Court of Queensland*, vol. 2 (Brisbane, 1900), p. 179. See the accounts of this trial in Docker, op. cit., and Banivanua-Mar, op. cit., pp. 140–141. Lilley personally was probably in sympathy with the prosecution; he was later to be a judge who gave severe sentences to the defendants in the even more notorious *Hopeful* trial in 1884.

[24] Coath was released after serving three years of his five-year sentence.

massacre, but his quick action in turning Crown witness saved his skin. The tale as it was recounted first in the press, and later in 1872 in courtrooms in Sydney and Melbourne by several members of the crew, was shocking: the *Carl* had set out from Melbourne the previous year, frankly aiming to kidnap as many Islanders as possible. When masquerading as missionaries failed to work (that was an old ruse by then), the investors and their crew set to work ramming native canoes, seizing their occupants, and locking them below deck. One night fighting started in the hold, it appeared that the prisoners were trying to break out, and the Captain ordered men to fire into the hold. Firing went on for eight hours, until dawn. About fifty dead bodies were thrown overboard, as well as sixteen men badly wounded but still alive. Here was the worst single outrage produced by "recruiters," one that made it impossible to ignore the evil.

The Captain and first mate were tried in Sydney and convicted of murder, their death sentences later being commuted to life imprisonment; five seamen were found guilty of assault on the high seas and each sentenced to two years' imprisonment. Two other participants in the shootings were apprehended in Victoria and tried a month later in Melbourne; recipients of some public sympathy since the chief villain, Murray, had escaped any punishment, they were found guilty of manslaughter only and sentenced to fifteen years (and, indeed, they were freed a year later on a technicality). Attitudes toward these men varied by class and degree of respectability: the release of the two in Melbourne was sharply regretted by most newspapers, but, as one reported, "as soon as this judgment [releasing them] was announced, the crowd in the court began to cheer, but were soon stopped, and they then made a rush to gain the outside of the building so as to obtain another view of the prisoners as they left the court."[25]

By the time of these trials, the Pacific Islanders Protection Act, popularly known as the "Kidnapping Act," had become law.[26] It made it a crime to "decoy away" or "enlist against his will" any native of the Pacific. It also empowered the Supreme Courts of any of the Australasian colonies to try any British subjects for offenses committed in any area of

[25] *The Australasian Sketcher*, quoted in Hector Holthouse, *Cannibal Cargoes* (Sydney, 1969), p. 111. For fuller accounts of the Carl case, see Holthouse, pp. 106–111, and E. W. Docker, op. cit., pp. 79–85, 93–94.
[26] A draft had been drawn up in 1861 at Rogers's order, but had been unable to win the agreement of the Treasury, concerned about the addition to expenditure it might entail, until now [Parnaby, op. cit., pp. 3–27].

the Pacific not under the jurisdiction of a civilized (meaning European) power, and further gave these courts the authority to compel the attendance of witnesses from outside British territory, and to hear native evidence, even if unsworn. Also, a license from the Governor of one of the Australasian colonies or from a British consular officer would henceforth be required of all vessels engaged in the labor traffic, and colonial Governments were required to appoint Recruiting Agents to accompany voyages. However, the Act only empowered but did not require colonial courts to act; doubting colonial governments' interest in pursuing such cases, imperial officials in the region pressed the Colonial Office for additional legal powers. In 1875 they won a victory: Parliament amended the 1872 Act to allow the creation by Order in Council of a High Commissioner having jurisdiction over all British subjects throughout the Western Pacific, empowered in HM's name to make regulations for their government, to issue the licenses required by the 1872 Act, and to "constitute a Court having cognizance of all offenses committed in those regions." Two years later the Order in Council was issued, and Arthur Gordon, the activist Governor of Fiji, was made High Commissioner. At last, it would seem, law and order had reached even this distant region, and a labor traffic purged of abuses could go forward. After he used his new powers to prosecute several recruiters, the *Sydney Morning Herald* praised Gordon for fixing "a system of labour traffic that was threatening to degenerate into a disguised form of slavery" while at the same time producing a prosperous colony (Fiji) that has revenue equal to its expenditure, placing no "burden on the British purse."[27]

The newspapers' satisfaction was echoed in Whitehall; an annoying problem, it seemed, had been solved. Although missionary complaints continued, the Colonial Office no longer paid them much heed; as one clerk minuted on such a complaint written to a Melbourne newspaper by a Rev. Morrison and forwarded to them, "we should get a report

---

[27] 11 July 1878 [NA, CO 83/17, file 91: clipping]. "For Polynesia to be prosperous under British superintendence," it continued high-mindedly, "there must be an equitable adjustment of the relations between the two races. The actual work of agriculture cannot in tropical islands be undertaken by persons of European descent, and either native islanders or imported Asiatics must do the toil. At the same time there must be neither slavery nor any institution which could drift into slavery; and while the planter is entitled to the fruits of his capital, his skill, and his enterprise, the workman must be assured of his liberty and his earnings." Polynesians, it assured its readers, were civilizable, if not quickly, and it was our duty to assist. "It is as wrong to wish that Polynesians should remain in barbarism, as it is foolish to expect them to emerge from it at a spring."

from Queensland, even though Mr. Morrison's forecastle *yarns* may be *distrusted* I think altogether." Another clerk observed that other sources showed that "whatever was true formerly, there is little to find fault with [in the Pacific labor trade] now."[28] Yet such contentment was premature. From the start of the High Commission, Herbert cautioned Gordon to use his new powers with "judgment" and discretion.[29] After early protests by traders and colonists, the Commission's powers and funding were gradually constricted. At the same time, with colonial opinion distrustful of imperial interference, the new regulations were easily evaded. The Government inspectors now mandatory on voyages could do little, and soon ceased to try. To an official inquiry in 1876, Immigration Agent Richard Sheridan cited the prevalence of the mistreatment of recruited laborers but when asked why he didn't take action, replied, "I could not procure a conviction . . . and I was not going to appear in a Police court and fail."[30] Despite evidence such as his, the inquiry found claims of widespread abuse unfounded; Sheridan subsequently resigned his post. A few years later the *Brisbane Telegraph* was moved to complain that "any person in the public service of the colony who dares to report any gross breach of the Pacific Islander Labourers' Act, either on the part of the captains and crews engaged in the recruiting of islanders, the agents who send out the these vessels and conduct the traffic, or the planters who take the men from the Agents, does so at the imminent risk of dismissal in disgrace, because the chances are twenty to one against him."[31]

At the same time, colonists involved in the labor trade deeply resented the criticism they received in the press, both in Australia and even more back in Britain. As one Queensland planter visiting London remarked to the Royal Colonial Institute in 1882, "I represent the interests of probably the best-abused and most ill-used Colonists in Her Majesty's dominions."[32] Such men strenuously objected to what they saw as a double

---

[28] CO 234/43, File 13890, "Slavery and the Slave Trade in Australia," June–Sept. 1883.
[29] Quoted in Scarr, *Fragments*, pp. 31–32. When in 1870 Gordon had been made Governor of Mauritius, Herbert, then Assistant Undersecretary, wished that his "judgment and discretion were at all times equal to his energy and ability" [quoted in Chapman, op. cit., p. 101].
[30] Quoted in Banivanua-Mar, op. cit., p. 130.
[31] Editorial, 17 July 1883 [quoted in Scarr, *Fragments*, p. 152].
[32] He went on to justify his role: "I am myself one of these much-talked-about and sat-upon 'slaveholders' – and I am proud of it; not only because I may derive some benefit from it, but I flatter myself that we also confer some benefit on those we employ. . . . [T]hey come to us half-naked semi-savages. . . . [W]e teach them the value of industry, fair dealing, and economy, and last but not least, the benefits of the use of soap"

standard in British public opinion, stirred up by missionaries and some officials – a sentimental solicitude for savage Islanders combined with a reluctance to protect British subjects who were often attacked by these savages in the course of their lawful trade. There was often obvious class resentment evident in this complaint: Hugh Hastings Romilly, an official deputed by Gordon in 1883 to investigate recruiting practices in New Guinea, and whose subsequent reports denouncing abuses were published in the press the following year, was pilloried by the pro-trade *Cooktown Independent* as "a pitiful scion of baronetcy, a relation of a red-tape Downing Street functionary."[33]

New economic developments were also undermining the law. A switch to disease-resistant cane varieties in the 1870s had ended "rust" disease outbreaks in Queensland and prompted the Crown in 1878 to open new lands for cultivation in the North. This was immediately followed by an unprecedented surge of capital investment. Under the assumption that white workers would not work in tropical conditions, a renewed search for laborers in the nearby Melanesian Islands was set off, a more intense search than ever before.[34] By the early 1880s, then, just as the reach of the Western Pacific High Commission had been restrained, the number of indentured recruits was rising to record heights, and the ensuing discord – violence perpetrated in obtaining them and counterviolence perpetrated by Islanders against recruiting ships – was being publicized in the Australian and British press as never before. The Western Pacific appeared to be returning to the greed-fueled violence that was supposed to have been banished by the 1872 Act. In 1883, *The Times*, although generally Conservative in its politics, could yet describe Queenslanders as "a nation of slaveholders" and "a blot on the Empire."[35]

The situation was increasingly ripe for explosion, which came in 1884. Elections in Queensland in November 1883 had put in a new Liberal Government. Drawing the bulk of their support from urban and working-class voters, the Liberals were not beholden as previous Governments had been to planter and merchant interests. Many of their supporters feared competition from "cheap coloured labor" and saw the recruitment of

[Thomas Archer, comments appended to John Gorrie, "Fiji As It Is," *Proceedings of the Royal Colonial Institute*, vol. 14 (1882–1883), 191–192].

[33] 2 Oct. 1884; quoted in Ronald K. Huch, "Hugh Hastings Romilly," *ODNB*.

[34] Peter Griggs, "Sugar Plantations in Queensland, 1864–1912: Origins, Characteristics, Distribution and Decline," *Agricultural History* 74 (2000), 609–647.

[35] Quoted in Docker, op. cit. p. 203.

Islanders on indenture contracts as a threat to free (white) labor in the colony. Queensland Liberalism thus married genuine humanitarian feeling to class and racial interests to pose a mortal challenge to the profitable recruitment of Islander laborers. The new Prime Minister, Samuel Griffith, son of a Congregational minister, feared that the growth of a plantation society worked by unfree labor in Queensland would ultimately undermine the free institutions so recently established. In the election campaign Griffith had promised to clean up or end the labor traffic, and as a first step indicated his readiness to try criminal cases against Queensland recruiters that the previous Government had left for the High Commission to tackle, if it could. Such cases soon emerged.

In the autumn of 1883, on the *Alfred Vittery*, searching for laborers in the Solomon Islands, two natives who caused a disturbance on board were shot dead. When the ship returned to Queensland, several officers and crewmen were taken into custody, charged with murder, and tried in April 1884 at the Supreme Court in Brisbane. The trial heard damning evidence from a procession of seamen that the Islanders causing the disturbance in the hold were no serious threat, and that the captain ignored their reports scotching rumors that the Islanders had tried to set fire to the ship and had firearms. As one able seaman testified: "I intended to follow into the hold but I was told not to go down. . . . The Government Agent said 'we are going to fire.' When the shooting started I saw the Government Agent and the Captain and [the first mate] standing close together. The captain and [first mate] had revolvers, I don't know if the G.A. did." Firing into the hold continued for about twenty minutes. One Islander was killed and another seriously wounded; the latter was shot in the head, and both were thrown overboard.[36] Despite such testimony, the defendants (unlike Captain Cocks at the Old Bailey) were all acquitted but the one who had fired the shot into the wounded man's head; he was found guilty only of manslaughter. The Colonial Office was dismayed and the Griffith Government embarrassed. The verdict, the *Brisbane Courier* lamented, "must fill every thinking man with despair." If, it observed, "the two unhappy men who were slaughtered had been white, it would not have entered the head of a single man on the *Alfred Vittery* to shoot them." Of course, it went on, the "institution of Government Agents is altogether discredited." This "shameful story . . . will not be forgotten. It will be held to justify every accusation brought against us concerning our

[36] QSA, CRS/146: Crown Solicitor. Briefs and Papers in Cases Involving Pacific Islanders.

dealings in the South Seas."[37] This embarrassment was intensified a few weeks later by the acquittal of the master and boatswain of the *Jessie Kelly* of charges of kidnapping.

Prime Minister Griffith, urged on by Governor Musgrave, appointed a Royal Commission to inquire into the labor traffic as a whole. Musgrave forwarded a full report on both trials with his critical remarks to the Colonial Office, urging the imperial Government to act. Even Griffith's Government, he argued, was politically constrained, and would not be able on its own to fully address the abuses inherent in the trade. As he was to put it most plainly a few years later, Musgrave believed it "to be absolutely futile to expect effective action to put a stop to these horrors . . . from any government resting upon popular suffrage in a community such as this."[38] Whitehall officials agreed that the cases represented gross miscarriage of justice; Colonial Secretary Lord Derby even observing that "it will become a question whether the traffic is to go on at all at this rate." Still, officials worried about Musgrave's lack of "discretion" among a people always prepared to resent imperial interference; moreover, some still felt he was "too ready to believe the worst" of planters and traders.[39]

As the Royal Commission held its meetings, the facts surrounding the most terrible of these cases, that involving the voyage of the *Hopeful* with which this chapter opened, were circulating in the Queensland press. Seven men from that vessel were put on trial in November for murder, aiding and abetting murder, and kidnapping. Hearing the cases was the man who had defended Captain Coath in 1871, Charles Lilley, who was now Chief Justice of the Supreme Court. Freed from the duty of representing a client, he summed up strongly against the defendants, emphasizing the weight of incriminating evidence and pointing out that "the question for the jury to consider was a very narrow one indeed." Such

---

[37] *Brisbane Courier*, 2 Apr. 1884, p. 4 (editorial). In earlier years, this newspaper's attitude had been quite different: in 1847, after a series of violent clashes between Aborigines and settlers in the vicinity of Brisbane, it declared: "Let it not be said that British subjects may be struck down like deer. . . . The Hydra must be crushed now . . . a treacherous, ignorant, grovelling yet bloodthirsty race." "For self-protection," it urged settlers, "rise *en masse* and take the law into our own hands" [quoted in *Radical Brisbane*, ed. Raymond Evans and Carole Ferrier (Melbourne, 2004), pp. 37–38].

[38] CO 234/49, Gov. Musgrave to Secretary of State, 15 Sept. 1888 (marked "Secret").

[39] CO 234/44, Musgrave to Secretary of State, 18 Mar. 1884, and n.d. (probably May 1884), with officials' comments. Derby was following the lead of Herbert, who made similar observations before forwarding the file to him. In a late letter to the Colonial Office, Musgrave exasperatedly called even the "reformed" labor traffic "a system which is only a bitter travesty of anything like free contract" [CO 234/49, 15 Dec. 1888].

pressure helped convict all the men.[40] The recruiter and boatswain were found guilty of murder while kidnapping, the master and Government Agent guilty of abetting the murders and given life sentences, and three other members of the crew were given sentences of ten and seven years. In pronouncing sentences, Chief Justice Lilley made his feelings clear:

Not much more than a year ago we were strenuously assured that [recent legislation] was sufficient, that crimes such as have been testified to in this court if they had ever been had now ceased to be perpetrated by persons sailing under the authority of this country. Here now the veil is drawn aside and we see only too distinctly the dark figure of the murderer, the pirate and the slavehunter – where he believes himself to be, with kindred or corruptible spirits, beyond the reach of human authority.

Lilley privately told Griffith and Musgrave that he had no doubt that "a deliberate and cruel murder in furtherance of the commission of the felony of kidnapping was committed," and saw no grounds for commutation.[41] Griffith felt just as strongly, telling a deputation of petitioners seeking commutation of the two death sentences that he had never heard of a voyage of such murderous atrocity and that he would have preferred to have seen every one of the men in the dock "hanged from their own yard-arm."[42]

Yet if earlier acquittals had shocked some, these convictions outraged many more. Public meetings of protest, focusing on the two death sentences, were held all over Queensland, giving voice to widespread racial and class enmities. "Hanging two white men on the evidence of cannibals" was denounced at one, and at another a speaker inveighed against the "smooth-tongued, oily wretches that those high in power in Queensland wanted to sacrifice two of our white men for." The condemned men were widely seen as scapegoats for inevitably violent confrontations with savages, and offerings up by their presumed "betters" on the altar of hypocrisy. A Government that had sanctioned many years of open killing of Aboriginal "blacks" now had turned around and presumed to hang white men for some particularly understandable killings of other blacks at sea. Even the *Brisbane Courier*, which had attacked the *Alfred Vittery* acquittals and had called for ending the labor traffic, urged clemency, arguing that it would be unjust to hang these men when many

---

[40] One speaker at a public protest afterwards declared that "if His Honour the Chief Justice had summed up as favourably to the prisoners as he had against them they would have been acquitted" [*Brisbane Courier*, attachment to CO 234/45, file 1934 (Dec. 1884)].
[41] CO 234/45, file 1934 (Dec. 1884).
[42] Quoted in Docker, op. cit., p. 219.

others had escaped, when, indeed, all in the colony shared some guilt for allowing the traffic to continue so long.[43] Although the Governor, Premier, and Chief Justice all favored carrying out the executions, they had to bow before the weight of public feeling. When the Governor's own Executive Council urged commuting the death sentences he was backed into a corner. "I had not believed," Griffith wrote in exasperation to the Colonial Office, "that now in any part of the Queen's dominions it should be openly contended that the life of a black human being is not as sacred as that of a white man – that popular meetings should be regarded as better judges of the law of evidence than the Chief Justice of the Supreme Court of the Colony – and that the Government, including presumably Her Majesty's Government, are responsible for the abuses of a traffic carried on with its sanction."[44] Musgrave swallowed his similar outrage and granted the commutations (and just over five years later, when the issue had receded and these three men were gone from office, all seven were released).[45] A wide gap remained between Queensland and Britain, and even between much elite and popular opinion in Queensland itself, on the use of the criminal law against white men in conflict with nonwhites.

When the Royal Commission reported in April 1885, having unprecedentedly interviewed over five hundred Islanders as well as many Queenslanders and officials, it declared that none of the voyages in recent years had recruited strictly according to law, and that if the voyage of the *Hopeful* stood in a category of its own, the use of force was far from unknown on others, while at a minimum, deception and intimidation had been regular practices.[46] Griffith responded by dismissing most

[43] Editorial, 4 Dec 1884, in attachment to CO 234/45, file 1934. The similarly "moderate" complaint voiced at a Brisbane public meeting that "it was only reasonable to urge [in favor of commutation] the lengthened period during which the trade had been countenanced, with *its natures, perils and customs*" drew underlining and exclamation marks in the margin at the Colonial Office.

[44] CO 234/45, file 1935, in Musgrave to Secretary of State, 27 Dec. 1884. Musgrave was a man of wide experience, having previously served as Governor of Newfoundland, British Columbia, Natal, South Australia, and Jamaica.

[45] Robert A. Huttenback, *Racism and Empire: White Settlers and Colored Immigrants in the British Self-Governing Colonies 1830–1910* (Ithaca, N.Y., 1972), p. 46, cites QSA Col. 410: Chief Secretary to Governor, 26 Nov. 1889; also Parnaby, op. cit., p. 96. Musgrave was able to block efforts to win their release, until his death at the beginning of 1889. See, for example, CO 234/49, Musgrave to Secretary of State, 15 Sept. 1888. See also R. B. Joyce, *Samuel Walker Griffith* (St. Lucia, Queensland, 1984), and Robert J. Cain, "The Administrative Career of Sir Anthony Musgrave," M.A. thesis, Duke University, 1965.

[46] "Report with Minutes of Evidence Taken Before the Royal Commission," Queensland Legislative Council Journals 1885, QSA.

Government Agents, ordering a large number of workers returned, and introducing legislation to more carefully regulate both recruitment and the employment on plantations of Islander laborers and, most significantly, to gradually end the labor traffic over a five-year period. These reforms were effective: the outcome of this crisis was a major improvement in working conditions on Queensland plantations, together with a reduction in labor recruitment and a marked decline in claims of abuses in such recruitment.[47] Although a shift in politics forced Griffith into a coalition Government with his National rivals, which restored the traffic for a few more years, it never achieved the scale of earlier days, and was finally abolished for good when the Australian Federation was created in 1901. In these ways, the trials of 1884 had proved a watershed for the relations between Queensland and Pacific Islanders.

IV

Whereas violence appeared as an incidental occurrence in the interactions of Europeans and Pacific Islanders, it was more fundamental to the relations of Europeans and Australian Aborigines, nowhere more so than in Queensland. Islanders were sought for their labor, but Aborigines were less useful, and chiefly stood as obstacles to settlement. Efforts to recruit Islander labor tended to degenerate into violence, but efforts to "disperse" Aborigines from their land required continual violence – a long if largely unacknowledged frontier war, in effect. If the Pacific was perceived as a region where the writ of law only weakly and insecurely ran, the war with Aborigines created an extra-legal realm within Queensland itself, in which violence became itself almost a norm. Much of the violence was professionalized, through the creation of a Native Police, commanded by whites, to "protect" settlers largely through aggressive attacks. As one apologist for frontier "excesses" wrote back to *The Times* in 1892, "the life is so rough that the slip across the line into brutality is half unconscious."[48] It has even been claimed that in the

---

[47] Mortality rates of workers peaked in 1884, and fell sharply thereafter [Doug Munro, "Patterns of Resistance and Accommodation," in *Plantation Workers: Resistance and Accommodation*, ed. Brij V. Lal et al. (Honolulu, 1993), p. 19]. Queensland was the only area of sugar production in the Empire in which conditions for laborers markedly improved after 1884 in the face of the world depression. See Mark Finnane and Clive Moore, "Kanaka Slaves or Willing Workers? Melanesian Workers and the Queensland Criminal Justice System in the 1890s," *Criminal Justice History* 13 (1992), 141–160.

[48] *The Times* special correspondent, *Letters from Queensland* (London, 1893), p. 76.

second half of the nineteenth century, Queensland "was arguably one of the most violent places on earth."[49]

Queensland settlers in general regarded Aborigines as less than human, as their "betters" often deplored. British Vice Admiral Tryon, in charge of patrolling Australasian waters in the 1880s, reflected to his superiors that "the history of Queensland, if ever written in full, will contain some pages – on which will be narrated the dealings of white men with natives – which will not be pleasant reading. It will record massacres, horrors, cruelty, and revenge, not entirely on one side, it is true; but it rarely will record efforts to compromise. Certain it is that a 'nigger' is by many scarcely regarded as a human being. The stories told, and the acts that have passed without reproof, tend to bring up a generation hardened against natives. There has been far too much shooting down in cold blood deliberately done."[50] Arthur Gordon, exasperated after years of trying to control Queensland labor traffickers, similarly observed to his longtime friend Gladstone in 1883 that "the habit of regarding natives in Queensland as vermin" had given the average Queenslander "a tone of brutality and cruelty" in his dealings with all nonwhites. "I have heard men of culture and refinement, of the greatest humanity and kindness to their fellow whites . . . talk, not only of the wholesale butchery . . . but of the individual murder of natives, exactly as they would talk of a day's sport, or of having had to kill some troublesome animal. This is not the spirit," he concluded with upper-class understatement, "in which to undertake the government of native races."[51] As Tryon noted, such crude racism was tacitly rationalized by "educated" persons whose outlooks had been shaped by a kind of social Darwinism. "There are unquestionably," he noted, "many men perfectly honourable and just in all questions in which the European race alone is concerned, who look upon the disappearance of the aborigines as inevitable, who think that the sooner this is done the better, and who care not to hear or to know dead men's tales."[52] It was accepted, even by many of those with tender consciences, that the Aborigines were a dying race, unable to maintain themselves in life's inevitable competition with more advanced races. Their rapid diminution, from European diseases and guns, together with

---

[49] Raymond Evans, in A. Dirk Moses, ed., *Genocide and Settler Society* (New York, 2004), p. 167.

[50] Rear-Admiral C. C. Penrose Fitzgerald, *Life of Vice-Admiral Sir George Tryon, K.C.B.* (London, 1897), p. 200.

[51] Quoted in Chapman, op. cit., p. 295.

[52] Fitzgerald, op. cit., p. 200.

their declining fertility, would eventually "solve" the practical and moral problems they presented to Europeans. English civilization and the "Anglo-Saxon" race, it was generally assumed, were destined to spread throughout the world, and uncivilizable races like those of Australia were destined to vanish.

One unusually clear-eyed, if ruthlessly unsentimental, settler forcefully answered humanitarian criticism of the treatment of natives that had been published in the Brisbane newspaper, *The Queenslander*, in 1880:

We all want to get on here, and we all want to get somebody else to do the work needful; and if there is any dirty work necessary we are the first to cry out against it – when we are in a position to do so. . . . I know full well that I shall hear of atrocities, of barbarities, and other disgraceful proceedings committed by the whites; but that does not touch the point at issue. The unanswerable fact remains that by overrunning this or any other country we expose the natives to the chances of suffering the rigors of guerrilla warfare – always the cruelest and worst – and, knowing that, we come here and take up our quarter with our eyes open; by our very presence in the land justifying the act of every white ruffian in the outside country. We are all savages; look beneath the thin veneer of our civilization and we are very identical with the blacks; but we have this one thing not in common – we, the invading race, have a principle hard to define, and harder to name; it is innate in us, and it is the restlessness of culture, if I dare call it so. The higher we get in the educated scale, the more we find this faculty; and if we do not show in one shape we do in another. We work for posterity, we have a history [of striving to create something new]. . . . This brings us here to wrest the lands of a weaker race from their feeble grasp, and build up a country that our children shall inherit. And this feeling is unknown to the native of Australia. . . . He has no thought of the future. . . . [H]e never seeks to improve land for those who will come after him. This justifies our presence here; this is the only plea we have in justification of it, and having once admitted it we must go the whole length, and say that the sooner we clear the weak useless race away the better.[53]

This was a bit too clear-eyed for most. More commonly, settlers preferred to see the process in softer focus, as did one "pioneer" in his memoirs:

The native is fading away before the white man like mist before the morning sun. Nothing can avert the doom that is written as plainly as was the writing on the wall at Belshazzar's feast. And to what purpose would we preserve them? What good could accrue from maintaining of a remnant of a race that it is impossible to civilize. The buffalo of America, like the Red Indian himself (the hunter and the hunted), pass over the river in front of the advancing tide of civilization.[54]

[53] Letter by "Queenslander," in *The Way We Civilise* (Brisbane, 1880), p. 28. For responses to this letter, see pp. 30–31.
[54] Edward Palmer, *Early Days in North Queensland* (Sydney, 1903), p. 209.

The imperial Government could do little about Aboriginal displacement and diminution; not only was Queensland self-governing, but it had become self-governing before very much of it had been settled, so that even the largely ineffectual efforts made on behalf of indigenous peoples earlier in New South Wales and elsewhere, before their self-government, were no longer practicable in Queensland. In 1866 Undersecretary Rogers had lamented that it was "by no means easy to exaggerate the recklessness with which blacks have been destroyed (in some cases by strychnine like foxes) in Queensland. But the Home Government can but hold up its hands. There is no effectual power to interfere in their cause."[55] Moreover, after Rogers's departure, the Colonial Office may not anymore have even desired the power to interfere, since Herbert questioned missionary hopes of "'civilising this interesting but hopeless race." As Luke Trainor has concluded, after 1871 "the Office preferred not to know what went on at the frontier."[56]

Still, as the frontier advanced and ever more of the colony was secured, attitudes in Queensland began to shift. In the middle decades of the century, many whites as well as Aborigines died in conflicts, but after 1875, one scholar of these conflicts has noted, "death caused by Aboriginal resistance was an isolated occurrence," except in the far North, a thousand miles from Brisbane.[57] Gradually, as fear faded, the concerns that already flourished in Brisbane could now be taken up further north and west. The images of hopelessly savage and irreconcilable Aborigines were now increasingly challenged by new fears of white savagery, of immigrants who rather than domesticating their new environment, allowed the wilderness and its barbarous ways to "de-civilize" them, or perhaps had already brought the criminality far from unknown in Britain to the new land. By the 1880s, "bushrangers" – lawless white men – were taking the place of indigenes as the chief public bogey, both in Queensland and in British imaginings of the Australian "bush." When the popular imperialist novelist G. H. Henty took up the topic of Australia in 1887, his novel's hero, a young widow's son who sails from England to escape an unjustly acquired shady reputation, becomes a hero by defending hard-working settler families from murderous gangs of bushrangers;

[margin annotation: lawless white men]

---

[55] Quoted in Luke Trainor, *British Imperialism and Australian Nationalism: Manipulation, Conflict and Compromise in the Late Nineteenth Century* (Cambridge, 1994), p. 83.

[56] Luke Trainor, "Sir Robert Herbert," *ODNB*.

[57] Noel Loos, *Invasion and Resistance: Aboriginal-European Relations on the North Queensland Frontier 1861–1897* (Canberra, 1982), p. 45.

Aborigines figure only secondarily in the story, as much helpmates as adversaries.[58] The very frontier struggle against the Aborigines, which had, while it was going on, often been portrayed in heroic terms, now could be reassessed as itself a dark stain on the character of those engaged in it. If plantation owners and labor recruiters had to face the charge of being modern-day slavers, frontier settlers had by the 1880s to come to terms with being called white savages.

In 1880, a series of well-researched and sensational disclosures in a Brisbane newspaper, *The Queenslander*, that had previously criticized the labor traffic, entitled "The Way We Civilize" (published at the end of the year as a book), showed in detail how settler behavior "fell far below British standards."[59] Of all the colonies, the paper's editors concluded, "we alone have descended to the 'kitchen lay' of extermination...a process which would shame us before our fellow-countrymen in every part of the British Empire." This series and the editorials that accompanied it provoked a wide range of old pioneers to write in long, detailed accounts of atrocities witnessed or told of, virtually all agreeing, either with profound regret or brazen acceptance, that a "war of extermination" had been going on. The controversy was felt across Australia, and was echoed in George W. Rusden's three-volume *History of Australia*, published in 1883. Although he was a Conservative and an enthusiast of Empire, he expressed outrage at the compounded evidence of Aborigines "left mangled and stark on the soil of Queensland." The very "air of Queensland,'" he charged, "reeks with atrocities committed and condoned."[60]

The Oaths Act had been amended in 1876 to allow Aboriginal evidence to be accepted in a court of law, but questions had remained about just how fully such evidence would be accepted.[61] To settle this, the new

---

[58] G. H. Henty, *A Final Reckoning: A Tale of Bush Life in Australia* (London, 1887).

[59] One of the correspondents to *The Queenslander* in 1880 noted that "our legislators go to a great amount of trouble in making laws and regulations for the protection of Polynesians; why not give the first owners of this continent the same consideration?" [quoted in Loos, op. cit., p. 51].

[60] See Loos, op. cit., pp. 159–160.

[61] The Liberal *Queensland Figaro*, April 1883, complained of "instances where white savages have raped young maidens and old gins – ay, and boasted of their deeds vaingloriously. E. Camm is on trial in the North for the rape of an aboriginal girl of tender years. *He will probably escape if she doesn't know the nature of an oath*" [quoted in *Race Relations in Colonial Queensland: A History of Exclusion, Exploitation and Extermination*, ed. Raymond Evans et al. (St. Lucia, Queensland, 1975; rev. ed. 1988), p. 106].

Liberal Government passed another law in 1884 making it explicit that the only requirement for an unsworn witness's evidence to be taken as seriously as if he had been sworn was that he understood "that he will be liable to punishment" if his evidence were untruthful. Only from this date was Aboriginal evidence (and that of Pacific Islanders) effectively available in trials in Queensland.[62] By this time, with the frontier evaporating into the barren interior, fear of Aborigines had faded. Many of those remaining lived harmlessly on the fringes of white society, semi-incorporated as casual laborers. As such, they began to come within the protection of the law. Significantly, from this time on, whites began to come forward as witnesses in prosecutions for crimes against Aborigines. In 1883, an unusual combination of circumstances produced the first conviction of a white Queenslander for any crime against an Aborigine.[63] At Townsville, a port of about eight thousand and seat of the Supreme Court for the Northern District of the colony, Edward Camm was found guilty and sentenced to life imprisonment for raping an Aboriginal child, Rosie. She lived as a servant with a white woman, and was playing outside her house when he enticed her away; the enticement was seen by two white women and the subsequent rape witnessed by six white children. A white doctor treated her afterwards. The trial saw the unprecedented total of ten "European" witnesses against him, including important evidence given by the doctor.[64]

In late 1884 the Griffith Government decided to undertake one of the first prosecutions of a white officer of the Native Police along with several of his native troopers, after they shot and then burned the bodies of two women, a man, and a child at Irvinebank, in the North. One of the women's sons had been working for one of the local settlers, and a large

---

[62] Mark Finnane and Jonathan Richards have described the slow growth of government investigation of Aboriginal deaths in North Queensland, with the 1880s marking a watershed during which inquests became the norm and whites began to be willing to offer evidence incriminating other whites [" 'You'll Get Nothing Out of It': The Inquest, Police and Aboriginal Deaths in Colonial Queensland," *Australian Historical Studies* 35 (2004), 84–105].

[63] In 1849, after the investigation of a military massacre of a group of Aborigines, a British soldier, William Cairns, had been convicted of common assault and sentenced to three years' imprisonment (soon reduced, on account of his youth, to six months). Cairns's conviction – itself for a much lighter offense than the facts warranted – was the last of a white man for an offense against a native until Camm's a generation later (this event was also the last military engagement of British troops in Queensland).

[64] See Highland, "A Tangle of Paradoxes," pp. 129–131; *Queensland Law Journal Reports*, vol. 1 (1881–1884), pp. 186–187: *R v Camm* (affirmed on appeal).

number of outraged whites had given evidence to the inquest, and there seemed to be the possibility of obtaining a conviction. The subsequent murder trial featured white witnesses, but their evidence was only circumstantial and the result was an acquittal. To apply "normal" criminal law to the ongoing frontier war was a dangerous step the jury was not ready to take. Public reactions were sharply divided, with many, probably most, in the North sympathetic to the defendant. The *Herberton Advertiser* ran an editorial with the title "To Shoot or Not to Shoot That is the Question," in which it argued that the Native Police needed complete freedom to ensure peace and safety for settlement and occasional "indiscretions" should be excused; indeed, earlier that same year settlers in the North had been furiously complaining of the inactivity of the Native Police against Aboriginal cattle-killings. "If we are to support the Native Police," one settler demanded, "in the name of commonsense let them do something for their money."[65] However, the Brisbane press far to the south generally took the opposite line, all the more as news of this trial was mixing with news of the "Hopeful" trial and seemed to join together to paint a picture of a grave moral crisis for the colony. The officer and his men were discharged from service, and further stories of atrocious behavior by the Native Police circulated in the state's press.[66]

Even getting as far as a trial for murder was extremely difficult. When two white men, along with an Aborigine man, were charged at a preliminary judicial hearing with the murder of three Aborigines at Townsville in 1886, they were committed for trial only for felonious shooting with intent to murder, and were acquitted even of that charge.[67] However, in early 1888, the Townsville trial of William Nichols (whom we met at the opening of this chapter) produced a conviction. Hearing testimony from a total of six European witnesses, including his closest neighbors, the jury found him guilty of manslaughter and he was sentenced to seven

---

[65] QSA, A/40310/9064: Henry Jones to Colonial Secretary Griffith, 7 May 1884. Jones sent a copy of his letter to the Cooktown newspapers, which printed it and editorialized in support. In October a petition from ten settlers in the area supporting Jones's complaints was sent to the Government. In his report on the matter, Inspector Henry Fitzgerald supported the subinspector in charge of Native Police in the Cooktown region, who had tried to practice a policy of restraint. "It is utterly hopeless," Fitzgerald lamented, "for him to expect the good feelings of the majority of his neighbours – humanity is unrecognized – their creed: extermination of the natives." Inspector H. Fitzgerald to Commissioner of Police, 5 Mar. 1885.

[66] Finnane and Richards, op. cit., p. 100; N. Loos, op. cit., p. 60; The officer's repeated efforts to be reinstated were personally blocked by Griffith [Joyce, op. cit., p. 114].

[67] QSA, A/18486, Supreme Court, Northern District, *R v Petty et al.*

years' imprisonment.[68] He was clearly not a well-liked man; a white housewife on the stand told him, "I have several times heard of your unkindness to this gin." Nichols claimed that "if this gin had belonged to anyone else no action would have been taken."[69]

Unprecedentedly, Nichols's conviction was the second of the session for a crime against an Aborigine. The day before Nichols's trial, another white man from the Thornborough vicinity, the sixty-nine-year-old James Comes, was tried for wounding with intent to murder. Angry that a horse of his had been stolen (it was not the first time), Comes had ridden to an Aboriginal encampment near his home. After unsuccessfully chasing a man there, he wheeled his horse and confronted a woman named Polly, and fired at her from about ten yards' distance. The bullet went through the thigh of her small child who was resting on her shoulder, and made two wounds in the woman's neck. Unfortunately for Comes, his act was seen by a group of whites, who rushed over and seized the gun from him. At the trial, five gave evidence and he was quickly convicted of the second charge of wounding with intent to cause grievous bodily harm. He was sentenced to three years' imprisonment, by the same Judge who had sentenced Camm a few years before. It was only Comes's age, he explained, that prevented him from awarding the maximum sentence, as a public warning "to check the lawless gross cruelty with which the race to which Polly belonged was treated."[70] The *Townsville Herald* approved of both convictions, calling the defendants "wanton and cruel cowards"; "we think," it declared, the verdicts and sentences "will have a highly deterrent effect upon those who are inclined to 'lightly esteem' the physical feelings and the lives of aborigines." At the same time, the newspaper defended the previous lack of convictions, noting that earlier cases had generally depended upon (unreliable) Aborigine evidence. In these two trials, with their profusion of European witnesses, "the evidence was very clear." Perhaps in explanation of the recent coming forth of whites to testify, it also observed that it was only very recently that colonists ceased to be in danger from Aborigines. "The colony," it concluded, now can "surely afford to adopt a humane policy" towards them.[71]

---

[68] See Gary Highland, "Aborigines, Europeans and the Criminal Law: Two Trials at the Northern Supreme Court, Townsville, April 1888," *Aboriginal History* 24 (1990), 182–196.

[69] QSA, A/18486: Supreme Court, Northern District, *R v Nichols*.

[70] Ibid.

[71] *Townsville Herald*, 14 Apr. 1888, p. 9: editorial entitled "Whites and Blacks."

Indeed, the following year another northerner, Edward Moran, was tried, this time in Brisbane, for shooting to death an Aborigine man whose woman he had stolen, on a pearl-fishing ship off Cooktown. There was an Aborigine witness but again, it was European evidence that seems to have convicted him – that of the master of a missionary ship and his wife who had observed the event and informed the police. The defense counsel told the Brisbane jury that "southerners could have no conception of the dangers run by those who mixed with blacks. Heche-de-mer fishermen and pearl shellers risked their lives among savages that fine ladies might flaunt the pearl ornaments." If he met a black there, he went on, he "would not wait to have a spear put through him, but would use his revolver at once, and he was sure the jury would do the same." But Justice Cooper (who had also presided over the earlier trials) pressed the jury, telling them that the evidence "was in one unbroken chain, going on harmoniously to one conclusion" – deliberate murder. The jury was out for two hours, and returned to find Moran guilty of manslaughter. Cooper told him that they "have taken a merciful view of your crime, and I cannot help thinking that they have taken this view because your victim was a blackfellow. . . . The path that separates your crime from murder is so narrow that reason can hardly find a foothold on it." He sentenced Moran to the harshest possible sentence, life imprisonment.[72]

Interestingly, this novel liability to serious criminal sanctions for offenses against Aboriginal people emerged at the same time as heightened agitation against Chinese immigrants. Although constituting a mere 3 percent of the colony's population, they were widely feared and resented. Only days after Nichols and Comes were sentenced, a pogrom against Chinese broke out in Brisbane, with many stores and homes destroyed, and many Chinese attacked in the streets. Such rioting spread to other towns in the colony in 1888; Normantown, near Townsville, saw a massacre of Malays and Chinese. This violence had been preceded by years of building concern about the "yellow menace." Even the respectable and comparatively liberal *Brisbane Courier*, which had declared the acquittal of the *Alfred Vittery* defendants a disgrace, called the Chinese "the most depraved people on the face of the earth."[73] Compared to the incoming Chinese, Aborigines no longer seemed much of a threat.[74]

---

[72] *Cooktown Courier* 19 Apr. 1889, p. 2.
[73] Quoted in *Radical Brisbane*, op. cit., p. 67.
[74] Unlike the "yellow peril," Aborigines were seen (whether with satisfaction or regret) to be on the road to disappearance. Duncan McNab, a Catholic missionary, described for

Of course, the age of equal justice for Aborigines had hardly arrived. As Gary Highland has noted, even in the last years of the nineteenth century, convictions in interracial cases required, as these had, certain conditions: first, the case for the prosecution had to not depend on the testimony of Aboriginal witnesses; second, the victim had to have been employed or given charity by whites; and finally, the offense had to have been committed in close proximity to white settlement.[75] Such conditions amounted to the incorporation of Aborigines into Australian society, but on terms of indefinite dependence. The "gospel of the English" was thus for Aboriginal people both a gift and an agent of dispossession.

By 1888, northern Queensland, except in its farthest fringes, was no longer a frontier region in an undeclared state of quasi-warfare, and the mind-set of its European inhabitants was correspondingly shifting. Settlers' economic and political power was secure, and the great majority of them, especially in the towns, no longer felt under threat, certainly not from Aboriginal people. With the fading of fear came a new embarrassment about violence against natives, and a readiness to punish "bad" settlers who continued to act in old ways. Men and women now stepped forward to testify against them, and jurors did not shy from convicting them (though still typically of lesser charges than they "merited" if the law had been literally applied, and with greater leniency in sentencing). Camm, Comes, Nichols, and Moran were punished with a seriousness new to Queensland, if still with leniency compared to what they might have faced if their victims had been white. Race of course continued to matter, in a way that it did not in Britain itself, but it mattered noticeably less than it had.

Class also mattered, just as in the home country. It helped the cases against all four men that they were workingmen and not quite "respectable." And gender mattered: the fact that in three of the four cases their victims were female (and that the fourth case was provoked by the defendant's seizure of a woman) further aggravated their offenses, as had certainly become true by this time back in Britain. Yet the most decisive factor in the Queensland cases appears to have been the degree of security felt by white settlers. The "frontier war" had to be won before

the Earl of Kimberley a banquet given by the Governor at Christmas time in 1880: "[T]he discourse turned on the treatment of the Aborigines and the conclusion arrived at . . . was, that there is nothing for the Aborigines but extermination" [letter, 7 Feb. 1887, quoted in *Race Relations in Colonial Queensland*, ed. R. Evans et al., pp. 79–80].

75 Highland, "A Tangle of Paradoxes," pp. 125–126.

the law could operate throughout the colony. Together with the 1884 legislation restricting the entry of Pacific Islanders and of Chinese, the end of the frontier war settled that Queensland was to be a "white man's country." Once that was settled, legal processes could begin to be accessible to nonwhites as they had not before, and the chasm between law in the metropole and on the periphery could begin to narrow. This was what Griffith had sought – a society of equal justice under law, rather than a racial caste society, even if, by a hard irony, it required creating almost a one-race society. "The permanent existence," he had warned, "of a large servile population not admitted to the franchise is not compatible with the freedom of political institutions of the colony."[76] The alternative to exclusion, he argued, was to reproduce the decadent planter society of the West Indies on the new continent of Australia. This was a resolution deeply unsatisfactory by twenty-first-century standards, but it is difficult to see what better one was possible at the time, given the fact that Queensland was governed by an elected Parliament and not by an all-powerful colonial Governor. The actual choice humane men like Griffith faced was between a multiracial caste society that would likely become increasingly repressive over time – a pattern to be followed by South Africa – and an egalitarian and libertarian society that was essentially one-race, a "white Queensland." He chose the lesser evil.

---

[76] Huttenback, op. cit., p. 47, quoting Griffith's 1884 speech in the Queensland Parliament. This was a view shared by most reformist British officials; for example, Sir William Des Voeux, whom we will meet in Fiji, wrote after his retirement an article in the *Nineteenth Century* in 1894, "Delusions About Tropical Cultivation," replying to Flora Shaw's article enthusing about Queensland plantations and the new "aristocracy" they were creating. "I confess myself unable to conceive," he wrote, "that an Australian democracy, whatever its defects, would be less desirable than a quasi-aristocracy of planters, with its necessary complement of coloured serfs. . . . Having been through the Southern States of America in 1859, with slavery at its full height; having since then had practical experience of the contract system of coloured labour in four different colonies; having learned what the laws respecting the latter may become unless watched and checked by a supreme authority, acting in the interest of employed as well as employers; having seen what such laws have actually become when the vigilance of such authority has been temporarily relaxed; having known, moreover, what under such a system may happen despite the best laws, and how these may be administered in the absence of a strong superintending control, I, after all this experience, have no hesitation in saying that at the cost of a huge community such as that above described, I should regard yellow rice fields, waving palms, and teeming banana groves as very dearly purchased."

3

Fiji, 1875–1885

The united voice of the British subjects of Her Majesty in Fiji must be heard
through the length and breadth of England . . . crying out for those sacred rights
and privileges to be extended to us today that were given to our forefathers seven
hundred years ago.

Fiji Argus, 21 May 1880

In January 1877, in the newly annexed British colony of Fiji, a planter
named Patrick Scanlon apprehended Masiomo, an indentured Solomon
Islander aged eighteen or nineteen who had run away from his employer,
a neighbor of Scanlon. Scanlon was later to claim that Masiomo had
broken into his house, armed with two spears, whereupon Scanlon in self-
defense struck him down. Masiomo was beaten severely with a heavy
stick, bound, and left on the ground outside Scanlon's kitchen overnight.
Scanlon planned to notify his neighbor the next day to reclaim the man.
Hearing his moans and seeing him bleeding, one of Scanlon's servants
asked for permission to untie his bindings and dress his wounds, which
Scanlon brusquely refused, fearing that he would then run away. Scanlon
told another servant to watch all night against an escape. "He cannot
escape," the servant replied; "he cannot walk." Scanlon did not reply to
this. In the morning Masiomo was dead.[1] The British takeover had
brought a new regime to Fiji – the *Fiji Times* was to protest later that year
that the employment of Polynesians since annexation had become surrounded by restrictive laws[2] – and, somewhat to his surprise, Scanlon
found himself arrested and charged with murder.

[1] *Fiji Times*, 21 Apr. 1877.
[2] Quoted in Bridget Brereton, *Law, Justice and Empire: The Colonial Career of John
Gorrie, 1829–1892* (Barbados, 1997), p. 141.

Long known to Europeans (with some justification)[3] as the "Cannibal Islands," Fiji was the name given to a grouping of over two hundred islands east of Australia and north of New Zealand. Until the 1830s Europeans had avoided it as too dangerous. That decade brought the first significant number of traders and also missionaries, both groups still highly cautious. The import of firearms thereafter enabled the rise of one dominant chief, Cakobau, in the 1840s. When he decided to convert to Christianity in 1854 the Methodist missionaries came into their own, and (despite such regrettable events as the killing and eating of Rev. Thomas Baker in 1867) soon became publicists for a new image of Fijians as civilizable, in contrast to the Aborigines of Australia. When the U.S. Civil War caused the price of cotton to soar, a wave of migrants from Australia and New Zealand arrived to set up cotton plantations in Fiji's promising climate, plantations that survived the postwar slump in the price of cotton, partly by taking up new crops like sugar cane. An unstable situation developed, marked by private coercive recruiting of Fijians to work plantations, reprisal attacks by Fijians on the plantations, and punitive expeditions against those reprisal attacks. The settlers identified less with Britain than with Australia and New Zealand; they were more egalitarian and more racist, and less deferential to British authority, than migrants from the United Kingdom. They would not take native authority seriously, and paid little deference to the British Consul stationed there. Worried missionaries and British officials on the spot saw annexation as the only effective way to control the ever-growing numbers of settlers.[4] Indeed, the Methodists found it easy in Fiji to reconcile Christ, commerce, and Empire, the leading lobbyist for annexation being Sir William Macarthur, an MP and a wealthy patron of Methodist missions, who also held substantial business interests in

---

[3] Even a strongly "anticolonialist" scholar like Patrick Brantlinger has concluded that the argument of some anthropologists that "cannibal talk" was merely the product of white racism is historically untenable: "Missionaries and Cannibals in Nineteenth Century Fiji," *History and Anthropology* 17 (2006), 21–38.

[4] The Consul complained in 1871 to the Colonial Secretary that "surrounded by savages and English adventurers, rogues rough and smooth, with the office continually invaded by men excited with drink and deprived of *any* of the advantages of an Established Government, I may say I am at the mercy of the mob who for the 'fun' of the thing like to show their independence by lawless acts. Last year I counted no less than 1103 fresh arrivals – mostly, if not all, British subjects. The usual proportion consisted of absconders from the neighbouring colonies and these are the very men who generally give the most trouble" [Mr. March to Lord Kimberley, 21 Apr. 1871, Bodleian Library Mss. Eng. c. 4115 (Wodehouse Papers), f. 139].

the Pacific.[5] In 1874, a reluctant Gladstone yielded to this threefold pressure, augmented by mercantile interests in Britain who saw large profit potential in Fiji and the Pacific in general. Despite Gladstone's general opposition to expansion and the fact that his Colonial Secretary, Lord Kimberley, declared himself "entirely opposed to the annexation of these islands or meddling in their affairs," legislation authorizing annexation was introduced and passed.[6] Soon after this the Liberal Government fell and its Conservative replacement took up the realization of this aim with less reluctance, sending out an emissary to obtain the necessary offer of cession from the Fijian king. As the new Colonial Secretary, Lord Carnarvon, saw the situation, it was first a question of putting overseas Britons in order: he described Fiji to the House of Lords as "a place into which English capital has overflowed, in which English settlers are resident, in which, it must be added, English lawlessness is going on."[7]

In 1875, Arthur Gordon, youngest son of the former Prime Minister Lord Aberdeen, arrived from ruling Mauritius, a large island in the Indian Ocean captured from the French in the Napoleonic wars, to govern the new colony. Gordon, well described as "an aristocrat by birth and an autocrat by inclination," quickly placed his stamp on Fiji, to the growing discomfiture of settlers and even many missionaries who had favored annexation.[8] Fiji's experience in the following years followed a pattern we have already begun to see: powerful tensions between imperial officialdom and non-official Europeans, together with lesser degrees of internal conflict within each group. In Fiji the official–non-official conflict was exceptionally clear; the officials formed an unusually cohesive group, put together by Gordon from men who had worked for him in his previous posts. Gordon was determined to avoid in Fiji the mistakes he felt

---

[5] Gordon and his successors were to find the Methodists a persistent thorn in their side in their efforts to protect Fijians from exploitation and preserve Fijian society; one of his men wrote privately in 1881 of the continuing difficulties created by "the great political and trading concern of John Wesley & Co" [J. B. Thurston to Gordon, 21 Mar. 1881, quoted in Chapman, op. cit., p. 198].

[6] Quoted in Scarr, *Fragments*, op. cit., p. 24.

[7] Hansard, Third Series, CCXVIII, col. 185 (17 July 1874). By "lawlessness" he primarily meant the labor trade.

[8] Scarr, *Fragments*, p. 24. See Chapman's biography, op. cit., and Lawrence Brown, "Inter-colonial Migration and the Refashioning of Indentured Labor: Arthur Gordon in Trinidad, Mauritius and Fiji," in *Colonial Lives Across the British Empire: Imperial Careering in the Long Nineteenth Century*, ed. David Lambert and Alan Lester (Cambridge, 2006).

had been made in Australia and New Zealand, where settlers, pouring in rapidly, had overwhelmed government efforts to restrain their rapacious desire for land and their contemptuous treatment of original inhabitants. It was not too late, Gordon told his political masters in Whitehall, to show that British rule of a multiracial land could be both effective and fair to all subjects.[9]

In many ways, Fiji was a typical colonial possession, with an indigenous population that had to be dealt with but which posed no mortal threat to British rule. Its growing population of settlers came in search of land and of cheap labor for tropical plantation agriculture, expanding to serve growing European demand. However, they were hardly an elite body, for many of them had already failed in Australia or New Zealand. A year after his arrival Gordon described them with contempt:

A few of the planters are men of energy and character. Others have energy without character, or character without energy. The majority have neither. They lead a miserable existence drinking gin when they can get it and yagona when they cannot, living with a greater or less number of okelau women, taking no trouble to make their surroundings less uncomfortable and complaining of the low price of cotton.[10]

These settlers, of course, saw themselves in a different light, indeed as the vanguard of the white race's world expansion. In their views of native Fijians, those coming from New Zealand were somewhat more accommodating than those from Australia, especially Queensland. The former had experience of dealing with natives on a not unequal footing; the Maoris, more organized and numerous than Australian indigenes, had through serious warfare forced whites to deal with them by negotiation rather than fiat.[11] Arrivals from Australia, and especially the

---

[9] The New Zealand Native Lands Acts of 1862, 1865, and 1873 had gone a long way to individualize title to customary land, and thus open it up to white purchase. After the passage of the first act, the Duke of Newcastle acknowledged that "the endeavour to keep the management of the New Zealand natives under the control of the Home Government has failed" [quoted in P. G. McHugh, *Aboriginal Societies and the Common Law* (Oxford, 2004), p. 186]. When offered the governorship, Gordon realized that Fiji was a once-in-a-lifetime opportunity, that the "prospect of *founding* a colony" presented "the greatest chance of *individual* action I have ever yet had . . . probably *the* point of my career" [Gordon to Lady Gordon, 15 July 1874, quoted in Chapman, op. cit., p. 157].

[10] Draft of an official dispatch, Gordon to Carnarvon, June–Aug. 1876 (the draft was never sent); quoted in J. W. Davidson and Deryck Scarr, *Pacific Island Portraits* (Canberra, 1970), p. 148.

[11] However, although they were forced to limit their ambitions more than were Queenslanders, New Zealand settlers were for the most part similarly racist; indeed, racism was

sizable contingent from Queensland, however, were unprepared to accommodate. Used to dealing one-sidedly with Aborigines in terms of "dispersal" or of thoroughly subordinate labor, they thought of all natives as subhumans outside the law, and ultimately doomed to disappear. Their culture was one of radical democracy (within the white race), and they saw no reason to defer to overbearing British bureaucrats.

Fiji had some special characteristics. Its newness as a colony, its small size, and its as yet small settler population all strengthened the hand of officials, as did the still-functioning structures of native society. With intermittently effective leadership and the ability to adapt to the use of guns, Fijians could not be simply overrun as Australian Aborigines had been, but on the other hand did not pose the military threat that the Maoris had in New Zealand. Gordon collected around him a group of like-minded subordinates who sought firm, authoritative control of all the Queen's subjects, white and brown – a "crown colony of a severe type," as it had been agreed Gordon would establish.[12] The annexation legislation gave Gordon sweeping powers, such as that of halting immigration or expelling any individual settler (although these were expected to be used only in extreme situations). The Governor's Legislative Council had an official majority and no elected members; four settlers, picked by the Governor, were to serve on it. If Queensland demonstrated the inability of the imperial Government to exert any real control over interracial relations in a self-governing colony, Fiji was to be a showcase of the opposite: to provide a model of how imperial Government could shape to a large extent the path of interracial relations in a new British possession.

Settlers and traders coming to Fiji, however, had their own agenda, one of racial superiority, freedom of enterprise, and the guarantee of personal rights against the dictation of a remote imperial Government and its local bureaucrats. Urging annexation in 1873, the settlers' paper, the *Fiji Times*, declared that the "autocracy" of the Fijian chief

will not go down with white men who have been accustomed to a liberal form of government. [Chief Cakobau] feels the power of the white race, and must bow to it. Already the Anglo-Saxon has firmly planted his foot here, and so certainly

an integral part of their democratic outlook, as John Stenhouse has illustrated through examining the mind and career of the radical politician Charles Southwell: "Imperialism, Atheism and Race: Charles Southwell, Old Corruption, and the Maori," *Journal of British Studies* 44 (2005), 754–774.

[12] Bridget Brereton, *Gorrie*, p. 108.

must he remain. The whites can do without the natives, but Fiji can never again be free of the white man. Her destiny is sealed, and as sure as the American Indians, the New Zealanders, the Australians have had to give way to the superior race, so surely must the Fijian. . . . Fiji must now become the home of a white race, its original inhabitants are no doubt doomed. . . . Their inability to govern a people . . . must be apparent.[13]

Settler racism was intertwined with the ideology of the "rights of freeborn Englishmen," even those who may never have seen the English sky. They felt entitled to "a liberal form of government" (for themselves), which protected their rights against both natives and Government officials. One labor recruiter, charged in a British consular court in 1871 with assault on South Sea Islanders, had denied the court's jurisdiction over what he called the "sturdy Saxon," the "indefatigable Englishman." He had demanded to be released from "the odium of this atrocious interference with the freedom of a Briton." His jury acquitted him.[14] As one frustrated official complained, the high principles of English constitutional history had degenerated in the Pacific into the claim "that an Englishman may do as he likes, meet where he likes, smash as he likes."[15]

Besides settlers and traders, there was a small number of clergy and missionaries in Fiji, chiefly Methodist, filling no simple single role and holding no single view. On the whole, those involved in spreading Christianity and in ministering to native Fijians were very critical of settlers' treatment of them; but other clergy, attached to settlements, tended to share the enthusiasm of their congregants for further white settlement and economic development. The editor of the *Fiji Times* was himself a Methodist lay preacher. As the example of Sir William McArthur demonstrates, it was not hard to see in the South Seas "commerce and Christianity" advancing hand in hand.

In the world of officialdom, policy was largely devolved to those on the spot in Fiji. Colonial Secretary Lord Carnarvon was a paternalist Tory known for benevolence to his agricultural tenants, and he strongly disapproved of the way Australian and South African settlers treated their native populations. He was happy to send Gordon, with his strong protectionist views, to run Fiji. Undersecretary Herbert was more skeptical: although preserving native law, native systems of taxation, and native

---

[13] 4 Jan. 1873; quoted in Deryck Scarr, *The Majesty of Colour: A Life of Sir John Bates Thurston*, vol. 1: *The Very Bayonet* (Canberra, 1973), p. 204.
[14] *Fiji Times*, quoted in Scarr, ibid., p. 165.
[15] John Thurston in *Fiji Argus*, 28 Jan. 1876.

councils made "rather a large pill [for the Colonial Office] to swallow"; nevertheless, Herbert told Gordon, "we have swallowed it bravely in order to give you the chance you desire of proving that you can govern the natives instead of killing them off."[16] After all, if Herbert questioned whether indigenous peoples had the capacity to flourish in the modern world, he knew Australian settlers too well to expect much forbearance from them in regard to natives; many Europeans in the South Seas, he remarked in 1879, "for a few shillings profit would readily risk the extermination of thousands by disease."[17] Also from an aristocratic family and Oxford educated, Herbert had far more in common with Gordon and his subordinates from clerical and professional families than with the unofficial commercial whites of Fiji. Yet he also disdained the idealism of Gordon and his men, and their readiness to quarrel with settlers. Herbert saw his responsibility as a far wider one than theirs, the security and well-being of the Empire as a whole, of which settlers were an often-exasperating but essential part. Settlement and the economic development it brought were also the only way to make colonies pay for themselves, which in an age of minimal home taxation and Treasury control of Government was a necessity.[18] "Do not," Herbert continued in his letter to Gordon, "check white settlement more than you can help."[19]

On the other hand, settlers had a habit of provoking violent resistance from put-upon natives, which the imperial Government was then obliged to deal with, and so a strong Governor who could keep settlers under control was appreciated in Whitehall.[20] And Fiji, a small and out-of-the-way outpost of Empire, seemed a safer place to make an "experiment" in colonial Government than more important colonies. So Gordon got permission to institute his new approach of preserving native society and protecting natives from settler domination – an approach that marked off

---

[16] Carnarvon's Liberal successor felt much the same as did the Liberal Herbert: "As to saving the natives from extermination by the natural decay of the race," Kimberley remarked in 1881, "it is an interesting experiment and should be fairly tried. I wish I could believe in the probability of success" [quoted in Joyce, op. cit., p. 27]. In this era Conservatives and Liberals did not divide on such questions as we might expect.

[17] Quoted in Joyce, op. cit., p. 28.

[18] Constraining the efforts of Gordon and his men was always the reminder from Whitehall that, as Kimberley put it in 1881, "the islands must rely on their own resources" [quoted in ibid., p. 27].

[19] Herbert to Gordon 1876, quoted in Chapman, op. cit., p. 199.

[20] "As long as Sir Arthur balanced his budget and kept the natives at peace," his biographer observed, Whitehall would be happy to allow him to "follow closely his own designs" [Chapman, p. 179].

Fiji from its neighbors Australia and New Zealand, and was an early
building block of the system of "indirect rule" that was to spread widely
in the Empire by the twentieth century.

The Whitehall indulgence shown to Gordon was underpinned by his
high social and political position, unusual for a colonial Governor.
Having been raised within the ruling elite, a relation of Carnarvon and an
old friend of Gladstone, he was able in a dispute to go over the heads of
the men in the Colonial Office to their political masters. In his previous
governorships in Trinidad and Mauritius, he had energetically pushed
through reforms in the treatment of indentured Indian plantation workers. His low opinion of European settlers had been acquired from his
experiences there. As Lady Gordon wrote to a British acquaintance from
Fiji, the settler "feels he is in a new country, is apt to look down upon his
neighbour of the aboriginal race, and prone to hold the maxim that to
get whatever he can in such circumstances is the true morality, simply
because he is the civilized white man."[21] The Fijians, on the other hand,
Gordon likened to "our Scotch rural ancestors . . . 400 years ago. Like
those Scotch, they are eminently improvable, and the problem is if I may
so express it, how to get them from the fifteenth century to the nineteenth.
I am sure in a few generations this great interval could be got over, but it
must take time. My doubt on the one hand is whether they will ever be
allowed this time and breathing space, and my effort on the other is to
secure it for them."[22]

Gordon well knew, however, that he could not ignore planter interests,
neither politically nor economically. If he were to halt the increasing
employment of Fijians on white plantations he would have to find a
substitute. Recruiting nearby South Seas Islanders was only producing
crimes and outrages, as we have seen. Here Gordon's Mauritius experience suggested a solution: indentured laborers from India, a virtually
inexhaustible source of inexpensive willing workers, treated fairly (as he
flattered himself he had brought about there by a series of reforms), could
be imported and Fijian society could continue, given the "breathing
space" to slowly adapt to the modern world. To enable Fijians to live
without working for whites, land sales would be strictly limited. Thus,
Fijian land and labor would be safeguarded from exploitation, while
economic growth could go on through existing plantations, modestly

---

[21] Lady Gordon to Mrs. Ryan, 23 Nov.–1 Dec. 1877, in Lord Stanmore, *Fiji, Records of
Private and Public Life, 1875–1880* (London, 1897–1912), vol. 2, pp. 642–643.
[22] Quoted in Chapman, op. cit., p. 69.

expanding in size, worked by Indians. Colonial self-support and economic development could be reconciled with the preservation of indigenes and their society. The imperial circle could indeed be squared. So beginning in 1879, to accompany new regulations sharply restricting the employment of Fijians and then of other Islanders came Indian "coolies" (as Indian laborers were called) to open up a new import trade.[23]

In his efforts, Gordon was backed up by a friend, a son of a clergyman with aristocratic relations named William Des Voeux. Des Voeux, first a barrister and then a career civil servant, was brought on Gordon's recommendation from the West Indies to serve as Acting Governor when Gordon took leave in Britain. Again with Gordon's backing, Des Voeux succeeded to the governorship and the Western Pacific High Commission in early 1881 when Gordon was, under protest, moved to New Zealand. Like Gordon, he had formed his views in other tropical colonies – British Guiana, St. Lucia, and Trinidad – and had already there come into conflict with plantation owners. He had first made his mark in 1869, when having been moved from his post as a stipendiary magistrate in British Guiana to be Administrator of St. Lucia, he had immediately written the Colonial Office a long indictment of the systematic mistreatment of coolies imported from India to British Guiana, bringing about a Commission of Inquiry and significant reforms. As he remarked in his memoirs, "I had learnt by experience how many Europeans hold in practice to the principle announced in the celebrated Dred Scott decision of the Supreme Court of the United States that the coloured man 'has no rights that the white man is bound to respect,' and how when a European employer is in embarrassed circumstances the chief sufferer is apt to be his coloured labourer."[24] Gordon could feel some confidence that Des Voeux would stand up to Fiji planters.

Three others, all also "Gordon men" (two of them fellow Scots), played major parts in the governing of Fiji. John Thurston was an early settler who had become appalled at the new type of men pouring in with the rush to "open up" the Islands. In 1873 he became a leading member of King Cakobau's Government, complaining to a naval friend of "the grasping and rapacity of the Europeans [in Fiji]." "We are," he even remarked

---

[23] In doing this he was unwittingly creating the conditions for later conflicts between the two communities. When independence came in the late twentieth century, the population of Fiji was evenly divided between native Fijians and descendants of imported Indian laborers, and the new nation has since been roiled by a series of alternating tumultuous elections and military coups.

[24] G. W. Des Voeux, *My Colonial Service* (London, 1903), vol. 1, p. 367.

privately a few years later, "as a race, a race of robbers and spoilers."[25] With annexation, Thurston was made Acting Governor until Gordon's arrival and soon after that Secretary of the colony. He enthusiastically enlisted in Gordon's experiment, telling his chief, when he reluctantly left to govern the larger but already-formed colony of New Zealand, that "we have a chance here of avoiding the follies and iniquities of New Zealand [in the treatment of indigenous peoples]."[26] Indeed, Thurston became, his biographer declared, "undoubtedly more hated by the settlers than any other man in Fiji" – not only for his official actions, but as a turncoat who had joined with natives and with officials against his own kind.[27] Even more than Gordon, Thurston became a student of ethnography, and expert in the ways of Fijian culture. He stayed in Fiji until his death in 1897, for his last decade as Governor.

John Gorrie was a Scot who had moved to London, and had become a barrister and a supporter of radical causes. He had been active in the Jamaica Committee's efforts to convict Governor Eyre of crimes in his brutal suppression of the 1865 rebellion there, and thereafter had taken up a colonial judicial position in Mauritius. He became there Gordon's chief lieutenant in his campaign to reform abuses in the treatment of Indian laborers. Gordon brought him to Fiji as Chief Justice; when the Western Pacific High Commission was established, Gorrie became Chief Judicial Commissioner, and when Gordon was on leave in Britain, Acting High Commissioner. More than any other official, Gordon included, Gorrie burned with a passion to right wrongs and vindicate the ideals of British law. As in Jamaica, he saw Fiji colonists as racists preoccupied with their own enrichment, and his role as the protection of the weak and the chastisement of the strong. He was less interested in preserving Fijians' way of life than in seeing that they received their full measure of British justice. During his time filling in for Gordon as Western Pacific High Commissioner, he was to create a crisis by overenthusiastically attempting to expand its authority and thereby antagonizing the Admiralty, producing a crisis that forced Gordon to return and hastily backtrack. "I don't care one brass farthing what the Admiralty say or think,"

---

[25] Thurston to Captain Hope, 28 July 1873, quoted in Scarr, *Majesty*, vol. 1, p. 229; to Gordon, 1879 (vol. 2, p. 48).

[26] Thurston to Gordon, 23 Dec. 1880 (BL OIOC Add. Mss 48204).

[27] Perhaps, it appears he hoped, not entirely "his kind": while he was siding against the other Europeans, he began to research his family pedigree; by 1876 he was using the crest he had thus found. Humanitarianism and contempt for "greed" seemed in the Victorian world to go naturally together with class snobbery.

he impoliticly wrote Gordon. "In our capacities as judges our only superiors are Her Majesty in her Privy Council by the Judicial Committee."[28] This unfortunately was not the view of the Colonial Office. As Thurston's biographer commented, "in his desire to see the law amended to what he considered it should be, [Gorrie] was invariably confused as to what it actually was."[29] It was not surprising that he frequently clashed not just with settlers but also with Thurston, and also with another of Gordon's officials, Dr. William Macgregor.

William Macgregor was first Chief Medical Officer, then Treasurer, Colonial Secretary, Acting Governor of Fiji, and finally, from 1888 to 1898, Governor of the new colony of New Guinea. The rare colonial official who came from a poor family, he rose under the patronage of his fellow Scot, who was impressed by his medical work in Mauritius and brought him to Fiji. Though readily following Gordon's policies, he was more of a pragmatist, less "sentimental" (as he saw it) about natives, and more sensitive (particularly once he served as Treasurer) to the need for the colony to pay for itself. Still, while he was more likely than Gordon to appreciate the views of white planters in disputes with their workers, he worked hard to stamp out the labor traffic between the Islands, fully sharing Gordon's contempt for Australian "man-hunters." His initial act as the first Governor of New Guinea in 1888 was to ban Queensland recruiters from the area.[30]

Inevitably then, officials and settlers clashed. Settlers found that the new British Government they had asked for, was, far from helping them, dictating to them. They complained of the lack of business sense among the overeducated officials. "All their experience," the *Fiji Times* complained on the same day that Patrick Scanlon's trial opened, "seems to have been of so highly a moral character as to induce them to look beyond the stern necessities of life, and to expend the strength of their powerful minds in sympathy with unsoaped aborigines and ungratified yearnings for their social and moral elevation. It is felt in Fiji that those gentlemen are much too good for the place."[31] Fiji needed what it called "practical

---

[28] Gorrie to Gordon, 14 Apr. 1880, in Stanmore, *Fiji*, vol. 4, p. 262.

[29] Scarr, *Majesty*, vol. 2, p. 43.

[30] As in Fiji, Macgregor sought economic development, but with as little European settlement as possible. "The development of British New Guinea," he later wrote, "requires that its population remain and work in their own country, on their own soil, and in their own climate." "British New Guinea," *Journal of the Royal Colonial Institute* 26, no. 4 (1895), 296–297.

[31] *Fiji Times*, 21 Apr. 1877, p. 2.

men" instead of unworldly philanthropists, who would facilitate and not obstruct the recruitment of needed labor from among natives and nearby Islanders. How was the new colony to develop, burdened as it was with officious and superior bureaucrats? The labor question was the most immediate point of conflict. Gordon's first major piece of legislation, a Native Labour Ordinance, was pushed through the Legislative Council by its official majority over vociferous settler protest. Planters found their employment of Fijians made virtually illegal, and their consequent turn to increased recruiting of nearby Islanders mired, as the *Fiji Times* complained, in "red tape." "Government," it soon complained, "heaps Ordinance upon Ordinance" upon us, acting more like "Czarist offici-aldom" than English public servants.[32] By the time indentured Indian laborers began to arrive at the end of the 1870s, tensions between settlers and officials had reached fever pitch. The more contentious settlers called upon their friends, families, and business associates in Britain, wrote British papers, and even agitated among Fijians, pointing out how the new Government was reinforcing the power of traditional chiefs and blocking ordinary Fijians from making money by taking employment with settlers. Gordon complained to his superiors that settlers were cynically playing a double hand, denouncing him for coddling natives while at the same time telling natives, and British humanitarians as well, that he was oppressing them. To deal with them, he asked for permission to put through addi-tional laws to empower him to censor newspapers, prosecute for sedition, and further regulate labor relations. We should be firm with settlers now, he urged, to avert future problems such as the native wars New Zealand has suffered. Taken somewhat aback by his zeal, Herbert assured him of backing but denied his requests for new laws.[33]

These clashes over labor policy led to broader conflict over govern-ment itself. The root of their problem, colonists felt, was their subor-dination to bureaucrats. Within a few years of annexation as a Crown colony, settlers began to petition for at least some steps toward self-government. Fiji's destiny, in their minds, was obviously as a part of Anglo-Australasia. To Gordon and his officials, this was both anathema and absurd; there were practically a hundred Fijians to every European in the colony, and they had no intention of allowing them to either "fade away" or become a subject race. This "Crown colony of a severe type" must continue as such.

---

[32] Ibid.
[33] Gordon to Secretary of State, 16 May 1879 [CO 83/21], and attached materials.

One of the aspects of the Crown colony form of government that particularly irked settlers, and was to play a central role in criminal justice, was the lack of a right to trial by jury. Contrary to settlers' views that they carried this right with them as a birthright, in colonies of "conquest" such as Fiji, English laws did not automatically apply; the rules of trial were set by ordinance. In Mauritius, an old plantation society, formerly French, a sentencing in 1874 by the sole English magistrate of an Englishman named Piddington to fourteen days in jail for kicking his Indian laborers created a stir among the Britons there. "As the kicker is an English engineer and the kickees Indians," wrote Gordon to Gorrie, "the white population are naturally furious. What! is a white man not to swear and kick at an Indian if he does not understand orders given as to the placing of a piece of machinery? Is it not one of the rights of a freeborn Briton to 'walk into' a stupid 'nigger'? The papers are of the opinion that '*L'incident Piddington aura peut-etre des suites graves.*'"[34] Although it led to a question in the House of Commons about the lack of jury trial in the colony, the Colonial Office refused to interfere. Gordon saw no reason to treat Europeans in the new colony of Fiji any differently than in the old one of Mauritius.

So when Patrick Scanlon was charged with the murder of a South Seas Islander worker in 1877, it was doubtful whether he was entitled by the ordinances of annexation to a jury trial. Since it was a capital offense, Chief Justice Gorrie bent over backwards and acceded to the Attorney General's opinion that he was. The Attorney General's opinion did not arise from sympathy for Scanlon; prosecuting the case, he concluded by vividly describing the beaten Masiomo, "a mere boy . . . left uncared for, to die like a dog." Scanlon's counsel argued that the man could have died from an undiagnosed disease or from additional assaults during the night by other Fijians, though he could not provide any evidence of either of these possibilities. Gorrie summed up strongly against the defendant, noting that it was clear that the victim had been beaten after being apprehended, a matter of Scanlon "taking the law into his own hands" without any justification, for "there was no necessity to take human life for the protection either of property or of life." He made a point to inform the white jury that if a verdict of murder was too much for them to swallow, they could find manslaughter. However, the jury acquitted Scanlon of any offense, finding that he acted in self-defense. Gorrie created a stir by publicly disagreeing with this verdict. Even the *Fiji Times*,

---

[34] Quoted in Brereton, *Gorrie*, p. 97.

usually a reliable voice of settler opinion, disagreed with the verdict, excoriating Scanlon and the employer whose mistreatment Masiomo had run away from as bringing all Fiji settlers into disrepute. However, in its view, Gorrie shared blame with the jury: from talking with jurors it concluded that "had they not thought that an extremely severe sentence would be passed upon the person accused, they would have found a verdict of manslaughter."[35] Gordon was upset with Gorrie for an opposite reason, convinced that the Attorney General's opinion was in error and that a jury had not been required. In interracial cases juries could not work in Fiji anymore than they would have in Mauritius, Gordon pointed out: "It is not too much to say that whatever the evidence, a jury composed of white settlers in Fiji will never find another white settler guilty of murder if the murdered man be a native." The Colonial Office agreed that a jury, while an option, had not been necessary, and a chagrined Gorrie complained that the ambiguities of the colony's founding ordinances should be clarified; otherwise, the pressures of public opinion in favor of jury trial, "the constitutional right of a thousand years," would be practically impossible for Judges to resist.[36] However, the Colonial Office took no action on his request, preferring to leave it to judicial discretion.

Meanwhile, outraged settlers bombarded the Privy Council and the Colonial Office with appeals from decisions of the Fiji courts; though these all failed, Gorrie and Gordon were concerned enough to ask for the power of appeal to be restricted (nothing was done).[37] The following year another conviction raised a fresh storm. When Harold Walker was charged with unlawful wounding of a Fijian employee who had died after a flogging by him, his counsel requested a jury trial but, when that was denied by Gorrie, did not press the constitutional arguments, presumably because it was not a capital case. Walker was convicted and given six months' imprisonment, to much public outrage. Gorrie himself complained to the Colonial Office that he was being denounced as a tyrant, and asked for the option of jury trial to be eliminated in cases involving nonwhites, so as to remove this responsibility from local officials; "in this colony," he observed, "so many of the white settlers have come from

(2) flogging

---

[35] *Fiji Times*, 28 Apr. 1877.
[36] CO 83/13, file 78, Attorney General to Secretary of State, 5 May, with enclosures, etc; also file 81; Stanmore, *Fiji*, vol. 2, pp. 631–634 (letter from Gorrie to Gordon), vol. 3, pp. 238–239 (Gordon to Secretary of State).
[37] CO 83/13, file 162: Gordon to Secretary of State, 29 Nov. 1877.

colonies where the sentiment in regard to the protection of natives is by no means healthy." He was again denied.[38]

These trials exposed the ubiquity of the practice of flogging natives, which upset officials and politicians in Britain. "The miscarriage of justice in this particular case [Scanlon's acquittal]," remarked John Bramston, now at the Colonial Office, "is a minor matter compared with the revolting inhumanity with which every white employer mentioned in these pages appears to treat his labourers, native or Polynesian." Such planters should not be allowed to employ Fijian or Polynesian laborers.[39] Lord Carnarvon, the Tory paternalist, agreed, calling it "a disgraceful case." "If we cannot have justice done in this case," he reflected, "we must endeavour to prevent a recurrence of such iniquity."[40] In 1878 Gordon requested and was granted authority to create the position of Immigration Agent and Inspector of Labour, and appointed a dedicated young man, William Anson, to the post. Anson took his job seriously enough to soon become the new focus of settler complaint, producing in 1882 a formal petition drawn up by the Planters' Association urging his removal. In contrast to similar Agents in Queensland, Anson was never "captured" by those he inspected.

The courts continued to be a scene of struggle between officials and planters. When early in 1880 the overseer for a member of the Legislative Council, J. E. Mason, was convicted of a savage assault on a seventeen-year-old Solomon Islander and sentenced to six days' imprisonment with hard labor (a sentence the magistrate, Archibald Taylor, admitted was inadequate), Mason instituted a campaign against Taylor. Outraged that "an English gentleman is put to work on the roads with Fijian prisoners," Mason not only instituted a petition for Taylor's removal, but persuaded his friends to write letters to Taylor threatening to cut off all social relations with him and his family. Taylor wrote the Chief Justice about what he called "a decided attempt to intimidate a magistrate in the discharge of his duties." Gorrie was incensed at "the supreme impertinence of these men." He told Gordon that "this is purely and simply intolerable, and the firmest action must be taken to put it down." It was: Gordon curtly dismissed the allegations of incompetence and encouragement of insubordination in the petition, and more or less ordered

[38] CO 83/17 [1878], file 96: Acting Gov. Des Voeux to Secretary of State, 10 Sept. 1878, supporting recommendation in enclosed letter of 3 Sept. from Gorrie to Des Voeux.

[39] CO 83/13, file 78, minute, 11 Aug. 1877.

[40] Ibid., 16 Aug. 1877.

Mason and his friends to withdraw their letters and apologize to Taylor. They did so.[41]

The lack of the right to a jury continued to gall Europeans in Fiji. Soon after the Mason affair the *Fiji Argus* called for a petition to the Crown to be got up, "signed by every white man, woman and child over ten years of age . . . praying for the right of Trial by Jury to be extended to British subjects in Fiji." The paper protested against the slanders made in the home country upon the character of Fiji settlers, as if they were "an abandoned set of rascals" or even "lawless brigands," not safe to trust with the duties of jurymen. Rather, it urged, "the united voice of the British subjects of Her Majesty in Fiji must be heard through the length and breadth of England . . . crying out for those sacred rights and privileges to be extended to us today that were given to our forefathers seven hundred years ago." The following month it returned to the call: "On what plea of right or justice," it asked, "are we debarred from that which has ever been regarded as an Englishman's most unassailable right and highest privilege – trial by jury? . . . [W]e have been ridden over roughshod by the Colonial Office as if we were so much dirt instead of being free subjects of Her Majesty. This state of things cannot and *shall* not last."[42] However, despite this burst of inspirational rhetoric, the petition effort seems to have fizzled.

Feelings were further stoked later in 1880, when a former Naval Lieutenant, now a planter, E. C. Chippendall, was charged with the manslaughter of a Polynesian employee by kicking. Chief Justice Gorrie followed the option of appointing three assessors, all white men, whose verdict would be nonbinding on him. The victim had not died until ten days after his kicking, and although in his summation Gorrie stressed the violence of the assault, the assessors (one of them, unbeknownst to Gorrie at the time, a friend of the defendant)[43] found him not guilty because the man would not have died if he had not already been ill with pneumonia. Gorrie accepted their verdict, but told Chippendall that "I hope it will be a warning to yourself and all others to abstain from every kind of violence towards your labourers." However, the planters were incensed that Chippendall had been put on trial at all for merely kicking a Polynesian laborer. His trial, they claimed, was the culmination of a systematic

[41] Stanmore, *Fiji*, vol. 4, pp. 190–192, 226–232 [drawing on CO 83/26, Attorney General to Secretary of State, 21 May 1881]; Brereton, *Gorrie*, p. 129.

[42] *Fiji Argus*, 21 May 1880 and 11 June 1880, editorials.

[43] Stanmore, *Fiji*, vol. 4, p. 390: Gorrie to Gordon, 29 July 1880.

policy of harassing planters. This "outrageous" case, the *Fiji Argus* complained, was far from the first attempt to falsely prosecute planters for the death of their employees. All that had happened, as the paper saw it, was that Chippendall, "one of the most kind-hearted and popular planters in Fiji," came down to the sugar mill one morning, "and seeing this boy slow at some work he was doing, gave him a kick to help him along faster." For this trivial and routine action, he was committed for trial by officials who "do not hesitate to try to ruin and damn the name and character of a fellow citizen upon the very slightest evidence." "Of course," it concluded, "the result of the trial was an honest acquittal, but when it is considered to how great expense the planter was put, owing to his unnecessary persecution by Mr. Hobday, the Crown Prosecutor, and what must have been his anxiety of mind pending the decision of the judge, we may fairly ask how long this state of things is to continue." The *Argus* here voiced the resentment felt by planters, who saw themselves as men of substance, the real workhorses of the Empire, at being continually condescended to by officials and, even worse, liable to being treated as common criminals. Indeed, the paper declared, in the present circumstances "there can be no security to a planter in Fiji. . . . His neck is in a halter as he goes about his work – his life, his liberty is endangered; and such a system as this must necessarily retard the progress of the colony."[44]

Additional trouble for officials appeared when Chippendall's father, an Anglican clergyman in England, published a pamphlet denouncing what he saw as his son's persecution and placing the blame on Governor Gordon. He persuaded a front-bench Opposition M.P. to put a question in the Commons. His son, the Rev. John Chippendall insisted, had with his labors "turned a wilderness into an Eden" while treating his workers "with invariable kindness." Even after his son's arrest, he argued, the examining magistrate wanted to dismiss the charge and it was only Gordon's personal insistence that kept the case alive. Even though he was justly acquitted, his son's name had been besmirched. "As a British subject," Rev. Chippendall declared, "my son has a right to an appeal to the Crown where he considers he has been deeply injured."[45] The Colonial Office pressed Gordon for information; he replied furiously, not only rejecting the allegations but also insisting that all such cases had to be prosecuted

---

[44] *Fiji Argus*, 30 July 1880.
[45] Rev. John Chippendall, *A Plea for Inquiry into the Conduct of Sir A Gordon . . . in the Case of Lt. E. C. Chippendall* (Manchester, 1880); see also CO 83/23, several files with correspondence on this case.

according to the law precisely because, to the Fiji whites, "a native life is looked on as a matter of infinitely small value." "The agitation," he argued, "is directed less by any feeling with regard to the merits of the case itself than by a wish to *deter* police, magistrates and law officers from taking up cases of violence against natives in future and to show them that if they dare to do their duty, they will incur popular odium, much unjust suspicion and abuse, and a great amount of trouble and annoyance." Gorrie added his exhortation to the Colonial Office to stand firm:

In a community the material success of which depends upon the introduction of native labourers from Polynesia and India, there must be no flinching from a firm carrying out of the law. Upon this the whole success of the experiment depends, and if any encouragement is given at Home to interested clamour the experiment will prove a failure alike for whites and natives. I trust therefore that Peers and Members of the House of Commons will not hastily give credit to charges against public officers, who, from the peculiar conditions of the society among which they are placed, are apt to be most bitterly assailed when most deserving of approbation.[46]

Herbert agreed to back up Gordon: "I think," he noted, " it was probably a violent and brutal assault." Moreover, he proposed that Chippendall "should at least be warned that in the recurrence of any ill treatment the question whether he should be allowed to employ imported labour should be considered." However, this suggestion was vetoed by Lord Kimberley, concerned no doubt to avoid any further provocation: "the man was acquitted," he noted, "and the kick was not *proved* to be a violent one. It would therefore not be expedient to take this opportunity of warning him. The prosecution will have been a sufficient warning."[47]

While this contretemps raged, Gordon was moved to the governorship of New Zealand, a step up in status and salary, though not in actual power, for, like Queensland, New Zealand had become self-governing. Nonetheless, he did what he could there to check the aggressiveness of the

---

[46] CO 83/23, Gordon to Kimberley, 13 Sept. 1880; Attorney General to Secretary of State, 28 Dec. 1880, enclosing Chief Justice to Attorney General, 9 Nov. The Parliamentary questioning, Gorrie privately observed to Gordon, "shows how relentless those ruffians are, and they always get some fool in the House of Commons to believe them" [Stanmore, *Fiji*, vol. 4, p. 429: Gorrie to Gordon, 11 Sept. 1880].

[47] CO 83/23, Gordon to Kimberley, 2 Oct. 1880, marginal comments. In the related conflicts between Gordon and Australian labor recruiters, O. W. Parnaby has observed that "Kimberley thought that Gordon was as biased in favor of the natives as the Australian colonists were toward the Europeans" [Parnaby, op. cit., p. 171]. It would be fair to say that Kimberley viewed his job less as backing up local officials, as Carnarvon had, and more as holding the balance between them and the local white population.

white population, making himself again very unpopular. Despite the backlash he had roused in both colonies, the Colonial Office was satisfied with him. As Lord Kimberley reflected, "[Gordon] has no doubt shown his sympathy with the coloured races at times injudiciously, but he has done good work in Fiji and it may not have been altogether without use that he has had the courage to tell some unpleasant truths to the New Zealand colonists. In this country the feeling is with him rather than with the colonists."[48] In Fiji, Gordon's policies were continued under Des Voeux, who soon became as detested by settlers as Gordon had been.[49] "Interference" with labor relations continued, as did prosecutions against violent planters.[50] A particularly dramatic case took place in 1883, after a Polynesian worker got his overseer punished for breaching the labor regulations. This so enraged his employer, the son of a certain Colonel Akers, that he personally gave the worker a whipping. Akers was summoned before the magistrate and in default of appearing was sentenced to a month's imprisonment. Rather than submit, he fled the colony – as an official remarked, in consequence "the £2000 which his father invested in the estate has gone to the dogs." Another Whitehall official, F. W. Fuller,

---

[48] Minute, 4 Sept. 1882, quoted in Chapman, op. cit., p. 262. Gordon was less satisfied with the Colonial Office; he complained to Gladstone and to Lord Chancellor Selbourne of "the almost incredible weakness of the CO [*sic*] in giving way to noisy demands" and of the Office's "great indifference . . . as to the fate of natives" [Paul Knaplund, ed., "The Gladstone-Gordon Correspondence," *Transactions of the American Philosophical Society* 51 (1961); Gordon to Selbourne, 12 Dec. 1883, Stanmore Papers, quoted in Chapman, op. cit., p. 294].

[49] In 1880 Des Voeux sent the Secretary of State for the Colonies a memorandum listing his services, and requesting a better appointment than he had yet received. In it he noted that "in all the four colonies in which I have served my strong sympathy with the subject races and the firm protection which I have afforded them – sometimes under very difficult circumstances – have gained for me many proofs of their respect and affection," while at the same he maintained the respect of representatives of the dominant race: "Memorandum re Services of G. W. Des Voeux," n.d. but from internal evidence 1880, Bodleian Library Mss. Eng. c. 4176 (Wodehouse Papers), f. 140a. In response, he was given the governorship of Fiji. See also Des Voeux, *My Colonial Service*, vol. 2, p. 54: in Fiji, he carried out the "duty of giving my utmost support to the inspectors [of immigrants and of labor conditions on plantations] in the performance of their very disagreeable and invidious task. Apart from minor causes, such as my refusal to grant largely signed petitions for remission of sentences passed upon white men convicted of outrages upon the coloured, the support thus given alienated the sympathies of the planters from an administration they had so enthusiastically welcomed on my return as Governor."

[50] Des Voeux, in op. cit., vol. 2, p. 54, gives in full his unyielding reply to an anti-Anson resolution of the Planters' Association, 1882.

noted with satisfaction, "law in Fiji knows no difference between blacks and whites."[51]

However, what the law knew depended very much upon who was administering it, and when in 1883 Chief Justice Gorrie was posted to Antigua in the West Indies and replaced by a Judge far less sympathetic to natives, the hopes of the settlers revived. Sir Henry Wrensfordley had been Chief Justice of Western Australia, and brought with him Australian attitudes of racial solidarity, which he freely pronounced in public. Settler complaints against other officials revived, and a petition campaign for either greater effective power in Fiji's Government or federation with New Zealand or an Australian colony was organized. Acting Governor Thurston passed the petition on to Whitehall, but offered settlers little hope of action, telling them that "the Government would always be willing to be guided by the views of the white inhabitants of the Colony whenever they did not affect prejudicially the interests of the coloured races who were entirely unrepresented in the Legislature."[52]

Now more hopeful of redress, a leading planter and editor of the *Fiji Times*, W. F. Parr, who had been charged with manslaughter by neglect in 1880 by Henry Anson, the dedicated Immigration Agent and Labour Inspector, instituted a civil suit against Anson. This suit quickly became the focus of public attention in the colony.[53] Although a magistrate had dismissed the manslaughter charge, Parr claimed damages to his business and reputation. Thurston informed the Colonial Office that "since the advent of Sir Henry Wrensfordley," Anson has been subjected to "libels, insults and threats" simply for conscientiously doing his duty. With Wrensfordley presiding, Parr requested a jury trial and looked forward to humiliating Anson and teaching the overmighty officials a lesson. Surprisingly, Wrensfordley refused the request, and although in court he sympathized with Parr and criticized Anson's behavior, he dismissed Parr's suit, to the great relief of the Colonial Office. Lord Derby, Colonial Secretary, observed that "Sir Henry Wrensfordley has not been wise in his language, but we may hope that this decision shows some sense of

---

[51] CO 234/43, "Polynesian Labour Traffic," 10 Aug. 1883.

[52] CO 83/36, J. B. Thurston, "Minute with reference to a petition addressed to the Queen by certain of the colonists of Fiji, praying that the colony may be either incorporated with one of the Australian colonies, or that British-born residents within the colony may be relieved from what they regard as their present humiliating position," 17 Nov. 1883; CO 83/37, Thurston to Secretary of State, 21 July 1884.

[53] The *Sydney Morning Herald* reported the case in detail and observed that it "has stirred Fijian society to its not very profound depths" [6, 7 May 1884].

responsibility." But the Chief Justice's remarks during the trial had given planters hope that they might yet win their fight, and Parr continued to demand Anson's removal and to bombard the Colonial Office and the British newspapers with his complaints about Fiji's administration. However, he got nowhere; he came to be regarded in Whitehall as a pestiferous crank.[54] Anson was not only confirmed in his position, but also promoted to a higher rank. The settlers' petition for a new form of government was summarily rejected, the petitioners being reminded that other European settlers in the Empire, for example in Ceylon, were in a similar position.

Wrensfordley, who continued to publicly criticize officials' treatment of settlers, and Governor Des Voeux engaged in a competitive campaign of complaint about each other to the Colonial Office, to the great irritation of Herbert. "Sir Henry Wrensfordley," he advised Lord Derby, "is a vain and foolish man, who has opposed the Government with the view of making himself important and popular." At the same time, he also noted, Sir William Des Voeux "is an ill-tempered man, with little knowledge of the world, and little tact in dealing with men." However, this situation could not continue, and he recommended that the Governor's demand for Wrensfordley's removal be accepted, though the Judge had been in Fiji scarcely over a year. Yet Herbert, always sensitive to competing pressures, was aware that an outright demotion "would be represented in Australia as a Government attempt to *terrorize* the judiciary." He thus proposed that a lateral transfer to another Chief Justiceship be arranged. Lord Derby shared Herbert's irritation with Wrensfordley; indeed, even more: "the difficulty," he observed, "in my view is how to justify inflicting him on any other colony." The Governor, on the other hand, he felt, though he had acted intemperately and indiscreetly, had suffered "extreme provocation. . . . I cannot agree to treat both parties as if they had been equally in the wrong." Wrensfordley's current leave for health reasons in Australia was extended, to the great disappointment of Fiji planters, and Des Voeux's advice was taken on a replacement. When Des Voeux himself was moved to the governorship of Newfoundland late the following year, his second-in-command,

---

[54] "Parr was back in England by June 1886," Thurston's biographer has noted, "a ruined man, having wasted ten years of his life and lost £10,000. The colonial government was responsible, so he said for the next twenty-odd years in letters from Lincoln's Inn Fields, the Carlton Club and the London wine merchants for whom he worked" [Scarr, *Majesty*, vol. 2, p. 136].

the "turncoat" planter Thurston, replaced him.[55] Gordon's policies were reaffirmed.

A decade of struggle had established Gordon's "experiment" in protecting an indigenous people and their society on firm footing. Backed by Whitehall, he and his officials had laid down the law to planters, labor recruiters, and other settlers. Fiji was set on its path as "a Crown colony of a severe type," with policy set by officials, and the principle (if not always the practice) of impartial justice upheld. By 1884–1885, Fiji in these respects made a sharp contrast to self-governed Queensland. And yet, what kind of a model was it for other parts of the still-expanding Empire? The path Fiji took after its 1875 annexation depended very much on the unique character and position of Arthur Gordon – a man of unusually definite ideas, strong will, and high social standing and political influence for a mere colonial Governor. Gordon had been given *carte blanche* in bringing in his own picked subordinates; here the fact that Fiji was a new (and minor) acquisition further empowered him. It was an exceptionally propitious situation to engage in a policy experiment, a situation not likely to be often matched in other colonies.

Even beyond this, one must ask what kind of a success it was. For one thing, economic development was inhibited in Fiji, with most of the land "locked up" in collective Fijian ownership. That could certainly be considered a worthwhile price to pay for the survival of an at least partly autonomous Fijian society. But that was not the only price: if indigenous Fijians were better served than the Maori in New Zealand or, without question, Aborigines in Australia, there were others who paid for this outcome. Since the Treasury demanded that all colonies be self-supporting, settlers' enterprises, though they might be interfered with and restricted, could not be allowed simply to fail. Above all, plantations of sugar, the most important crop in Fiji, required large numbers of workers, and if they were not to be Fijian, and if "manhunting" in the South Seas was not to be permitted, they had to come from elsewhere. Gordon's answer, beginning in 1879, was to import indentured laborers from India – a system he had found in operation in Mauritius, and which he thought, if suitably supervised, could solve his problem in Fiji. Between 1879 and the end of the system in 1920, more than sixty thousand Indians were thus imported into Fiji (most remaining at the expiration of their

---

[55] CO 83/36, Thurston to Secretary of State, 7 May 1884, "*Parr v Anson*," 11 Jan. 1884, "Minute with reference to a Petition . . . ," and other files; CO 83/37, Des Voeux to Secretary of State, 27 June and 25 July 1884, and other files.

indentures, though they had the right of free passage back to India). However, neither Gordon nor his subordinates seemed to feel the same affection for, or duty to, these workers, whom they saw as already deracinated from their original culture, free and rootless individuals contracting to work in a newly global labor market. Indian laborers signing indentures to work for five years or longer bore no resemblances to "noble savages"; they were not romantic in any way. Where Gordon had much preferred dining with Fijian chiefs to meeting with settlers, he had no desire to mix with, or even learn much about, this sort of non-Briton.[56] Nor did his successors. As the labor force in European enterprises became ever more completely Indian, official concern for their treatment diminished. At the same time, these enterprises became fewer and larger, and the men at their head richer, more sophisticated, and more congenial to officials. Moreover, from 1884 the overdeveloped world sugar market entered a long period of depressed prices, putting new pressure on Fiji's young plantation economy to minimize costs. Since the Treasury would cut no slack for the excuse of low world prices, protecting the profitability of their economy came for most local administrators to take precedence over protecting the laborers in it, now no longer either Fijian or Pacific Islander.

William Anson was the one official who, as Immigration Agent as well as Labor Inspector, continued to feel the same duty to prevent Indian laborers' mistreatment as he had the mistreatment of Fijians and Islanders, and within a few years Thurston and Macgregor were having to rein him in. As Macgregor (who had always been the most skeptical of the group about Gordon's experiment) explained to his former chief in 1887:

I am much grieved by the "morbid spirit" that inspires our immigration office. The ruling idea is that the employer of a black or brown man is a cheat and a conspirator. Anson cannot see that men are under a contract, and that there are reciprocal obligations. Men [planters] are persecuted, worried by inquiries, irritated by interference and that too often over such trifles. A genuine case of bad treatment is far from common here.[57]

When in 1888 Thurston, now Governor, failed to support him in his application to be promoted to Colonial Secretary, Anson resigned; his post was then abolished, its duties added to those of the Receiver General.

---

[56] See John D. Kelly, "Gaze and Grasp: Plantations, Desires and Colonial Law in Fiji," in *Sites of Desire/Economies of Pleasure: Sexualities in Asia and the Pacific* (Chicago, 1997), pp. 72–98.
[57] Quoted in Joyce, op. cit., p. 80.

The Government's attitude toward business in Fiji steadily warmed, while its attitude toward working conditions became increasingly "pragmatic." In the later years of Thurston's governorship, enforcement of protective regulation eased while restrictions on laborers (for example, penalties for absence from work) increased. By the end of the century, as one recent historian of the Indian indentured diaspora has noted, Fiji "invited odious comparisons with other Indian-importing colonies." In 1895 the Government of India concluded that "the relations between the employers and the immigrants [in Fiji] are not as satisfactory as they are in the West Indies." Similarly, the Colonial Office by then believed that Fiji was "no doubt rather worse than Mauritius and British Guiana." In 1916, just before the abolition of indenture, the Rev. C.F. Andrews, the Indian nationalist sympathizer, declared that it was in Fiji that the prosecution of laborers was most frequent, and the suicide rate in the indentured community among the highest in the world. In short, he concluded, in Fiji the indenture system existed "at its worst."[58]

In a sense, the price for Gordon's experiment in indigenous protection within a self-supporting Empire was paid by these Indians, whose labor enabled Fiji to succeed economically while allowing Fijians to keep their land and a good deal of their culture. Within this experiment, the protection of the law could be called upon by Fijians, at least as against Europeans, but far less effectively by imported Indians. It was, as compared with Queensland, a triumph of a sort for racial justice, but yet a very partial and tainted one.

---

[58] Brij V. Lal, "'Nonresistance' on Fiji Plantations: The Fiji Indian Experience," in *Plantation Workers: Resistance and Accommodation*, ed. Brij V. Lal, Doug Munro, and Edward D. Beechert (Honolulu, 1993), pp. 187, 213; see also Brij V. Lal, "Labouring Men and Nothing More: Some Problems of Indian Indenture in Fiji," in *Indentured Labour in the British Empire 1834–1920*, ed. Kay Saunders (London, 1984), pp. 126–157.

4

Trinidad and the Bahamas, 1886–1897

All you who have ears to hear and brain to understand,
Come listen to Judge Gorrie's praises the wisest in the land,
He likes the poor to get their right, the rich he does not fear;
He is the greatest blessing of this great Jubilee year.
                    First stanza of Trinidad street ballad, 1888

The exaction of excessive bail by Cook J. was contrary to the Bill of Rights, but
the defendants Gorrie and Cook actually pleaded in their defence that "The Bill
of Rights did not apply to the Islands of Trinidad or Tobago."
        Hugh H. L. Bellot, "A Judicial Scandal: Are Judges Above the Law?"
                    Westminster Review, 1896[1]

I. A CHIEF JUSTICE GOES TOO FAR

On a Sunday evening in 1888, on the outskirts of Nassau, the capital of the
British colony of the Bahamas, a black fisherman named Shadrach Gay
was set upon in the street by five men, four of them white, one "colored."
They knocked him about, tore his clothes, and insulted a woman accompanying him. Then some fishermen friends of Gay came to his assistance,
and in the melee Gay pulled off his belt and struck one of his assailants,
Jeff De Pain, on the head with it. De Pain thereupon took out a razor and
slashed Gay in the stomach, inflicting a wound of which he died in a few
hours. Before expiring, Gay identified those who had set upon him, and in
particular De Pain as the one who stabbed him after saying, "I'll kill the
son of a bitch." At the inquest the coroner's jury returned a verdict of
willful murder against De Pain, and of being accessories before the fact

[1] P. 401.

95

against five others of his friends. This apparently simple homicide was to lead within a year to the forced retirement of a Chief Justice.[2]

This murder took place in a British colony half a world away from the South Pacific, a colony both like and unlike Fiji. The colony of the Bahamas, and that of Trinidad and Tobago, which we will also consider here, consisted, like Fiji, of tropical islands, small, lightly populated, and comparatively peripheral to the larger concerns of imperial policymakers. Yet unlike Fiji, a new entrant to the Empire, Trinidad and the Bahamas had been under British rule for a long time. Trinidad had been founded by the Spanish soon after Columbus's voyages and acquired by Britain in 1797, and the Bahamas had been British since 1629. Their indigenous populations had long since been replaced by African slaves, now liberated, and above them, a minority white settler society. Trinidad, like those other sugar islands in the West Indies, Barbados and Jamaica, had once been a great fountain of wealth, of prime interest to the British Government, "precious jewels," in J. A. Froude's phrase,[3] but like them since emancipation it had entered into an economic decline; the Bahamas were never of great economic importance, but they too had stagnated in the nineteenth century. A phrase of the time had it that Englishmen "with capital went to Australia, with brains to India, with neither to the West Indies."[4]

Trinidad, a lush and, like Fiji, "languidly charming"[5] tropical island off the coast of Venezuela, had long been dominated (as Fiji was coming to be) by the cultivation of sugar.[6] When emancipation had diminished the supply of ready labor for the grueling work of raising this crop, the planters persuaded the British authorities to sanction the importation of indentured laborers from India, which began in 1845, setting a precedent that other tropical colonies, including Fiji, would follow. By 1880, 134,000 laborers, the great majority male, had been brought over, most choosing to remain when their five-year indentures expired, and in doing so transforming the social composition of the colony. Even after world

---

[2] CO 23/230, files 17768. 21384. 23573; CO 23/231: file on "Controversy between Chief Justice and Attorney General." The incident took place on Dec. 8.

[3] *The English in the West Indies* (London, 1888), p. 9.

[4] Quoted in Bridget Brereton, *Race Relations in Colonial Trinidad 1870–1900* (Cambridge, 1979), p. 34. Whereas in 1815 trade with the West Indies amounted to 17.6 percent of Britain's total overseas trade, by the early twentieth century it had fallen to less than 1 percent [Douglas M. Peers, "Britain and Empire," in *A Companion to Nineteenth-Century Britain*, ed. Chris Williams (London, 2004), p. 58].

[5] Froude, op. cit., p. 66.

[6] The petrochemical economy of today, like the Bahamas tourist industry, was not yet even imagined by anyone.

sugar prices collapsed in 1884,[7] Trinidad planters did not cease importing laborers (like Fiji but in contrast with Queensland), and the British authorities did nothing effective to prevent such importation. The resulting unemployment pressed wages ever lower. Still, the East Indian proportion of the population continued to increase: in 1891 those of Indian descent numbered about 70,000 in a population of barely 200,000, and by 1908, a few years before the end of such imports, the figure reached 102,000, about 45 percent of the total population, the great majority no longer indentured. Perhaps 20,000 of the rest were more or less "white"; the remainder were descendants of former slaves. As in Fiji, this policy stored up ethnic conflicts that would shape post-independence politics, though that is an issue for another book.

Yet if Trinidad and Fiji had obvious similarities their differences were, for the concerns of this book, even more important. Trinidad's economy was stronger; its plantations were much longer established, operated on a much larger scale, and closer to their chief markets, thus more able to weather downturns in the world market. Further, the downturn in sugar was compensated for in Trinidad by a rise in the production of cocoa, whose market was still buoyant, and which, unlike sugar, could be grown by smallholders. Compared both to Fiji and to the rest of the Caribbean, Trinidad had a good deal of unexploited land that time-expired laborers could acquire to become small proprietors, as well as opportunities for indentured laborers to escape to Venezuela very close by, a safety valve that set limits upon their exploitation. Consequently, Trinidad remained into the twentieth century an attractive destination for Indians; as an English medical man visiting from India in 1891 sanguinely noted: "Of all the colonies in the West Indies, Trinidad is the favoured home of the coolie settler, where he can easily and rapidly attain comfortable independence, and even considerable wealth with corresponding social position."[8] Another difference, however, has even more direct bearing on our story: Trinidad's white elite had developed as slave-owners,

---

[7] Gad Heuman, in *Black Experience and the Empire*, ed. Philip D. Morgan and Sean Hawkins (Oxford, 2004), p. 160: "When Germany, the world's major producer of beet sugar, doubled bounties on its sugar exports in 1883–84, the effect on the British market was dramatic. There was a massive increase in the amount of beet sugar imported into Britain and, consequently, a collapse in the sugar price."

[8] Quoted in Walton Look Lai, *Indentured Labor, Caribbean Sugar: Chinese and Indian Migrants to the British West Indies, 1838–1918* (Baltimore, 1993), p. 141. Indentured laborers in Trinidad also benefited from the tradition established during the long tenure of Dr. Henry Mitchell, Agent-General of Immigration from 1850 to 1883 [p. 81].

acquiring over a long period of time substantial wealth and habits of command; a significant number had come as refugees from the Haitian revolution. Despite emancipation, they expected to run their estates or businesses as they saw fit, and did not meekly brook "interference" from imperial officials. Although divided between older French (and a few Spanish) families and newer British ones, this elite in the course of the nineteenth century gradually merged into a single social class, quite conscious of its interests. Without a surviving indigenous society, as in Fiji, to offset them, their effective power was much greater than that of their newer South Pacific counterparts; neither former slaves nor indentured laborers lifted up from Indian villages half a world away could form much of a counterweight.[9]

Formally, Trinidad was a Crown colony, ruled without elections by a Governor, like Fiji. However, after early clashes with the imperial Government during the Napoleonic Wars and then again around Emancipation, the local planters managed to establish their dominance. The Governor's nominated Legislative Council had a majority of "unofficials," all of whom were substantial men of property, who tended to agree with each other (except on questions of religion), and Governors came to follow their lead. "The theory of the constitution," it has been observed of Trinidad then, "asserted autocracy. The practice of politics assumed an oligarchy."[10] Not that Governors much minded their limited power; sharing the society of the planters, they tended to share also their general outlook, and agreement was far more common than disagreement. This consolidation of a planter oligarchy was rudely interrupted by the appointment in 1866 of a young Arthur Gordon as Governor by a Colonial Office whose attention had been suddenly drawn to the Caribbean the previous year by the Jamaica uprising. In the next few years Gordon put through, over planter protests, a veritable blizzard of reforms: making it possible for small purchasers to buy lots of Crown land, which made up a large part of the colony; setting up the first state primary schools throughout the island; and instituting the first serious oversight of the treatment of laborers. He also strongly backed a magistrate, Thomas Shirley Warner, who was accused by planters of stirring up the laboring classes. In four short years, one or another of Gordon's measures touched

---

[9] "In the colonial setting of Trinidad," V. S. Naipaul has remarked of his birthplace, "where rights were limited, you could have done anything with these people" [*A Way in the World* (New York, 1994), p. 19].

[10] F. R. Augier (1966), quoted in Brereton, *Trinidad*, op. cit., p. 25.

most aspects of life in Trinidad.[11] Two decades later, J. J. Thomas, the foremost politically active black in the colony, looked back to the years of "that true king in Israel" as a time of great hope. To Thomas, Gordon was "a ruler both competent and eager to advance [Trinidad's] interests, not only materially, but in the nobler respects that give dignity to the existence of a community." Gordon's legacies, for Thomas, were

laws that placed the persons and belongings of the inhabitants beyond the reach of wanton aggression; the means by which honest and laborious industry could, through agriculture, benefit both itself and the general revenue. He also left an educational system that opened (to even the humblest) a free pathway to knowledge, to distinction, and, if the objects of its beneficence were worthy of the boon, to serviceableness to their native country.[12]

It did not take Gordon long, in this his first governorship, to develop a low opinion of settlers: as he complained to his friend Bishop Wilberforce, "one planter and one only takes real thought for his coolies and he is laughed at by his neighbours."[13] However, although they resented his superior attitude they could do little to block his reforms; the son of a former Prime Minister was above their reach.

But Governors were only temporary; after Gordon was promoted to the larger colony of Mauritius in 1870, the planters gradually regained control of affairs. His successor, J. R. Longden, was a far more cautious man, a careful careerist described by Thomas as "a gentleman without initiative, without courage, and, above all, with a slavish adherence to red-tape and a clerk-like dread of compromising his berth."[14] Characteristically, rather than confront income tax evaders Longden agreed to abolish the

[11] See Chapman, op. cit. pp. 45–101.

[12] *Froudacity: West Indian Fables by J. A. Froude Explained* (London, 1889), pp. 61–62, 71.

[13] Gordon to Bishop Wilberforce, 20 July 1867, quoted in Chapman, p. 83. See Gordon's criticisms of the medical care plantation owners provided for their workers (CO 295/236, file 131 [24 Nov. 1866]) and of their evasion of income taxes (CO 295/248, file 121 [20 Sept. 1869]); see also his summary memorandum on the treatment of immigrant workers (CO 295/250, file 46 [8 Apr. 1870]), in which he noted the improvements he had made and the distance yet to go, observing that too many of the planters were "needy, unprincipled and utterly unscrupulous." One particular problem he regretted not having been able to solve was the subservience of the magistrates to the planters; to address this he proposed giving the Agent General for Immigration powers to inflict fines on planters for breach of regulations, but before he could win Colonial Office assent for this he was on the way to his next posting.

[14] Thomas, op. cit., p. 62. After four years in Trinidad, Longden was promoted to the governorship of the larger colony of British Guiana, and four years after that, moved up again to run Ceylon until his retirement [H. M. Chichester, rev. Lynn Milne, "Sir James Longden," *ODNB*].

levy, leaving almost all revenue to be raised by indirect taxes on the general populace. Under his administration Gordon's measures began to be eroded; schools and hospitals received little support, sale of government land to smallholders was stopped, and when the tough-minded Agent-General for Immigration retired, Longden replaced him with an unassertive man. The drift of power back to the oligarchy continued under successive brief governorships.[15] Most West Indian Governors in this era were novices, and acted more like Longden than like Gordon. As J. A. Froude noted in 1888, these islands had "been made to serve as places where governors try their 'prentice hand and learn their business before promotion to more important situations. Whether a man has done well or done ill makes, it seems, very little difference unless he has offended prejudices or interests."[16] Most of Gordon's successors in Trinidad seem to have been most concerned to avoid offense, either at home or in the colony, and inclined to follow the lead of the most powerful local residents. Here, ironically, Gordon's very vigor had produced a reaction in a more united body of whites, helping to heal the remaining social divisions between Catholic French and Protestant British planter families and melding them into a coherent body that could more effectively protect its interests.

The handling of a homicide a year after Gordon's departure showed the return of the old order: an estate manager named Ache fiercely horse-whipped two coolie women, stopping only when an overseer pulled the whip from his hands. One of the women died. Charges were laid before a magistrate by the Inspector of Immigrants. However, the magistrate found him guilty only of a common assault, and merely fined him £5 for assault on the woman who died, and £1 for assault on the other.[17] This matter was closed, until the unhappy Inspector of Immigrants brought it to the attention of the Colonial Office, which asked Longden for an explanation. The Governor replied that the magistrate stated that the evidence was "contradictory" and "the demeanour of the witnesses unsatisfactory. He formed the opinion that the violence of the assault had

---

[15] Thomas lamented that in the decade and a half since his departure "every act of Sir Arthur Gordon's to benefit the whole population was cynically and systematically undone" [p. 64].

[16] Froude, op. cit., p. 92.

[17] By contrast, the previous year two East Indians convicted of murdering an African overseer during a dispute had been sentenced to death, a sentence which the newly arrived Governor Longden commuted to penal servitude for life [Longden to Kimberley, 3 Jan. 1871, CO 295/255, file 1 with enclosures].

been much exaggerated." This vague response led Henry Taylor, the last official surviving from the earlier more active days of the Office, to analyze the case in detail, highlighting the many failures of justice it revealed;[18] he proposed that the Secretary of State write the Governor "regretting that the laws for the protection of the immigrants should have been so loosely administered," and reminding him "that this kind of behaviour makes it very difficult to defend coolie immigration against criticisms from the Government of India," thus imperiling its continuation. Another official added the suggestion that the Office specifically threaten to not permit immigrants on any estate that was found to violate employment regulations. Herbert, now Undersecretary, refrained from commenting, and Lord Kimberley accepted Taylor's proposal, while demurring at making any threats to the employment of labor merely because of "an isolated case of brutality."[19]

For fifteen years after Gordon's departure from Trinidad, the large planters generally had their way, in court as well as in administration, for not only were Governors accommodating, but the Chief Justice through this period, Sir Joseph Needham, owned and managed what was said to be the finest cocoa estate in the island, and was thought to be more interested in the prosperity of his estate than in the judicial business of the colony.[20] Although the reform-minded G. W. Des Voeux became Acting Governor toward the end of 1877, his term lasted less than a year, as he was soon called out to Fiji. He later recalled the great pressure he felt in Trinidad to appease Europeans. Within months of arrival he found himself in a number of quarrels with planters, but was transferred away before any came to a head. Des Voeux's successors returned to the path of appeasement, allowing Gordon's land, education, and labor regulations to be eviscerated. They also shared the planters' fear (the examples of Haiti and Jamaica always in their minds) of any signs of political mobilization

---

[18] He pointed out, for example, that although the evidence of coolies "is to be taken with distrust, it is to be borne in mind that it is subject to bias from fear as well as from resentment," and that evidence of such fear was apparent in the notes of the trial and of the Inspector's investigation. He also noted that it was important as a deterrent to rebuke Ache's behavior, for it was probably unusual only by coming to light through the death of his victims; after all, Ache was described as a well-regarded person by local officials.

[19] Longden to Kimberley, 22 Feb. 1872, remarks of Taylor, 2 Apr., and Kimberley, 9 Apr., CO 295/260, file 34 and enclosures; for context, see David Vincent Trotman, *Crime in Trinidad: Conflict and Control in a Plantation Society* (Knoxville, Tenn., 1986), pp. 139–141.

[20] Brereton, *Trinidad*, p. 27.

among Africans or Indians. Such fear was heightened by a growing number of strikes by plantation workers, and came to a head in October 1884, when at a moment when sugar prices were falling and consequently wages were being reduced, an Indian festival seemed to turn into a political protest, and the Governor authorized police to shoot down a number of unarmed people.[21]

However, the political situation again changed with the appointment of Sir William Robinson in the summer of 1885. Confronted with both an economic crisis and a potential political crisis, Robinson, though a Conservative, proved to be a more active and independent Governor than any since Gordon; Thomas called him "a man of spirit and intelligence, keenly alive to the grave responsibilities resting on him," and "prompt to hear the cry of the poor."[22] Soon after Robinson's appointment, John Gorrie, who had returned from Fiji to Britain to be knighted, was appointed Chief Justice of Trinidad.[23] The Colonial Office was aware that his reformist reputation would make his appointment unpopular with the white community. Herbert, however, dismissed that concern, praising him as "a strong judge" and (perhaps concerned that Trinidad had been neglected for too long) declaring that "in the West Indies it is generally a good thing to have a Chief Justice who does not care for popularity."[24] He may have underestimated Gorrie's lack of interest in popularity among whites, or his interest in popularity among blacks, for as soon as Gorrie took his seat on the Trinidad Supreme Court in February 1886 he began to make waves.

The later 1880s were a particularly difficult time to hold office in the West Indies, for both the depressed world sugar market and the not-unrelated first stirrings of Afro-Caribbean political consciousness raised public tensions and the pressures upon its Governors. However, Gorrie was never one to give much heed to political difficulties, and with a belief that he understood the West Indies, underpinned by his work for the Jamaica Committee against Governor Eyre in 1866, and a confidence

[21] Thomas, op. cit., p. 70.

[22] Ibid., pp. 58–59.

[23] The knighthood had been strongly urged by Gordon, who argued that not only had he more than earned it, but "the unseemly violence with which he has been assailed [in Fiji] for daring to do his duty would render a mark of approval the more becoming and the more useful" [Gordon to Kimberley, 27 Feb. 1881, Bodleian Library Mss. Eng. c. 4147 (Wodehouse Papers), f. 37].

[24] Havelock to Derby, 25 June 1885, minutes by Antrobus and Herbert, 2 Nov. 1885, quoted in Brereton, *Trinidad*, p. 231.

bordering on arrogance, fed by years of largely successful action under Gordon in Mauritius and Fiji, he plunged immediately into reforming the administration of justice. But Trinidad proved to be a quite different situation from any he had previously encountered. His efforts, the growing reaction they called forth, and his ultimate defeat have been recounted in Bridget Brereton's biography of him, and this brief account is heavily indebted to her work. However, although she acknowledges her subject's lack of judicial temperament and interest in the fine points of the law (he had really wanted to be a colonial Governor rather than Judge), it must be allowed that Brereton downplayed Gorrie's lack of respect for the law, a rather serious flaw in a Judge. His admirable zeal for helping the downtrodden was to lead him to ignore legal restraints and dangerously expose him to his ever-more-enraged enemies.

Gorrie's first priority was to make the sluggish and expensive legal system in the colony more available to the wider public by speeding up procedures and making legal aid available to those who convinced him they were in need. He was strikingly effective: the number of lawsuits, particularly those *in forma pauperis*, soared, and ordinary people began in large numbers to bring their grievances, particularly against landlords and moneylenders, to court. He also actively supervised the work of magistrates, limiting their free and highly discretionary use of the Master and Servant laws to control labor. In court he sharply criticized lawyers, medical men, and even the Chief of Police for failing in their duties to the public. During one murder trial, he noted that the victim, a colored woman, would not have died had she received prompt medical care, and upbraided a doctor for his lack of interest in her survival, implying that such neglect was not uncommon (leading to a formal protest from the local medical society). He even carried on a running feud with the Attorney General, and did not hesitate to pronounce from the bench his views on current political questions. In the space of a year, there were few members of the white elite he had not offended. Outside of court as well, he spared no special interest: made chair by Robinson during his first year of a commission to review existing taxes and tariffs, Gorrie virtually single-handedly produced a report that recommended undoing many of the changes since Gordon's time, and then going further to make the burden of taxation still less regressive. Few of its recommendations were adopted, but it succeeded in frightening those of the elite who had not encountered him in court. A sense grew among planters, merchants, and professional men of being under siege, with profits evaporating, rents falling, estates selling out, and in the midst of this economic crisis being subject to a Chief Justice seemingly determined to deprive them of any way of maintaining their control of their laborers, their sharecroppers, or their debtors. Gorrie's penchant for rebuking their selfishness and callousness from the Bench was still harder to take, piling insult upon these material injuries.

In little more than a year after his arrival the Chamber of Commerce produced two petitions, with several thousand signatures, first calling for the appointment of a third Judge (to enable appeals to be heard against decisions of Gorrie), and then asking for an official enquiry into his behavior. The petitions were supported by memorials from the Trinidadian Bar and the Medical Board. These moves called forth an even larger popular counterpetition in his support, and the writing of a ballad hailing him, and he became a well-known public figure, cheered in the streets – signs of popular mobilization that only raised for his critics the specter of race and class conflict.[25] Even Governor Robinson, who initially favored reform, became exasperated with Gorrie, complaining to the Secretary of State in 1887 that "matters are coming to a head here in regard to the C.J. and we shall have a serious row before long. . . . He resembles the metaphorical 'Bull in a China Shop.' "[26] Whitehall officials privately agreed: one minuted that whether Gorrie was right or wrong on specific issues "there can be little doubt that the whole tone of his communications is impracticable and unjustifiable – and he seems to deserve a severe rebuke for traveling completely out of his own judicial line in the manner of tone of his letters." Indeed, Edward Wingfield, in charge of the West Indies desk, concluded that Gorrie was nothing less than "a violent and reckless person."[27] The Colonial Office was all too familiar with overreaching colonial Judges.[28]

Still, the Colonial Office swallowed its irritation and, recognizing the value of having a strong Chief Justice who could stand up to West Indian planters, refused an enquiry. It did create a third judgeship and, against its

---

[25] J. J. Thomas praised him in 1888 as "vigilant, fearless, and painstaking" [Thomas, op. cit., p. 109]. Two newspapers begun in the previous few years claimed to represent middle-class black Creoles, and in the late 1880s agitated for an end to the indenture system and for black political representation on the Legislative Council.

[26] Robinson to Holland, 17 Sept. 1887, CO 295/315. Robinson acknowledged, "on the other hand there is no doubt that the work of the Supreme Court has hitherto been disgracefully scamped."

[27] CO 295/321, file 105, minutes of 15 Apr. 1889. Wingfield, a product of Winchester and New College, Oxford, had been called to the Bar and had practiced for several years before becoming an Assistant Undersecretary in 1878.

[28] See Lord Kimberley's remarks to Lord Ripon, cited in the Introduction.

preferred practice, filled it with a local man, probably hoping that this would serve as a sufficient check on Gorrie to preserve the rest of the Trinidadian "china."[29] If so, such hopes were dashed, as Gorrie soon resumed not only ruling against planters in cases before him, but also trying in a variety of ways to extend his authority, which included publicly chastising men of position when they failed, in his eyes, to behave appropriately. All this made him an even greater hero to the nonwhite populace, and, simultaneously, a villain to the elite. As a leading newspaper observed in 1889, "the name of Sir John is commonly used by the working-classes to employers and planters as a threat to enforce their insolent and unreasonable demands."[30] A second set of petitions came in 1890, from planters and merchants in Tobago, which had been incorporated into the colony, but again were denied. Finally, in 1891, the stars aligned for Gorrie's opponents: a new Governor, F. N. Broome, more sympathetic to the planters than Robinson had been, and an undeniable judicial scandal (one of the other two Judges, Cook – ironically, the local man added to the bench to restrain Gorrie – had turned out to be an alcoholic and had rendered verdicts while under the influence) provided the right soil to nourish a new effort to depose Gorrie.[31] A Tobago planter who had been jailed on dubious grounds for contempt of court by Justice Cook, a jailing along with the imposition of very high bail that was upheld on appeal by Chief Justice Gorrie, instituted a suit against them both, and a Civil Rights Defense Fund was created to send him to England to pursue his action, which he did.[32] More decisively, with Governor Broome instructing the

---

[29] Wingfield observed that it was clear that "an enormous majority of the inhabitants of Trinidad appreciate Sir John Gorrie's desire to do substantial justice" [CO 295/321, file 105, minutes of 15 Apr. 1889].

[30] *Port of Spain Gazette*, 20 Mar. 1889, p. 5.

[31] For an example of Broome's attending to the interests of planters, see his acquiescence in 1894–1895 to shifting the tax burden further away from them and onto the general populace [Brereton, *Trinidad*, pp. 30–31]. "That the course adopted by Sir. F. Broome," Wingfield sourly observed after this surrender, "was the most convenient for himself there is no doubt," but it was hardly in the best interests of the Government [CO 295/363, file 210, minute of 3 July 1895].

[32] He and his supporters described themselves in a letter to the *Pall Mall Gazette* as "individuals enjoying hitherto some remnants of the rights of free men and British subjects, and bent on defending and, if possible, preserving those rights" [*Pall Mall Gazette*, 12 Dec. 1890]. On the course of this litigation, and its significance for English law, see Patrick Polden, "Doctor in Trouble: *Anderson v Gorrie* and the Extension of Judicial Immunity from Suit in the 1890s," *Legal History* 22, 3 (Dec. 2001), 37–68. The suit only ended in 1895, after Gorrie's death, when the House of Lords dismissed it in a leading ruling that buttressed judicial immunity from suit. Ironically, a clash that exposed the weak political position of colonial Judges as compared to their home

official members to abstain, the Legislative Council passed a resolution urging a formal enquiry into the administration of justice, and in particular into the conduct of the two Judges.

Governor Broome took a stronger stance against Gorrie than had his predecessor, advising that the situation in Trinidad and Tobago had become "dangerous." Moreover, Gorrie's opponents made sure to bring some English opinion to their side, including not just the *European Mail*, the newspaper of the "West India interest," but *Truth*, a London paper owned and edited by the Liberal politician Henry Labouchere, and even the *Pall Mall Gazette*, which had at first been sympathetic to Gorrie and his well-known "love of justice." By the end of the controversy the *Pall Mall Gazette* was to welcome Gorrie's replacement, observing how "the confidence of investors" had been "rudely shaken" by the unfortunate conflicts between the branches of Government in the colony.[33] A question was asked in the House of Commons, a West Indian Civil Rights Defence Committee was set up in an office near the Law Courts, and a cry was raised of colonial liberty and property under threat from judicial "tyrants," a cry that could always rouse sympathy in the House and on Fleet Street.[34] Finally the Colonial Office gave way; Lord Knutsford acknowledged that complaints about this "have been far more numerous than those which have been made in any other colony," and that some action would have to be taken.[35] A Commission consisting of two distinguished jurists, Sir William Markby, a Liberal, and Sir Frederick Pollock, a Conservative, was sent out in early 1892 to report on the administration of justice in Trinidad and Tobago.[36]

The Commissioners first investigated Justice Cook, and found that he should be removed from the Bench; he was eventually dismissed without pension. Gorrie's case was more difficult, and they ruled some of the charges against him to be without substance. However, the majority, they concluded, were indeed well founded. Although they made it clear that

colleagues, and which had led to the removal of one and the imminent removal of another, had the result of strengthening judicial immunity in England. Viewing the situation from England, Polden does not quite appreciate the difficult situation faced by colonial Judges, who may have been immune from suit but not at all from removal.

[33] *Pall Mall Gazette*, 22 Sept. 1890; 2 Dec. 1892 (the new Chief Justice, it happily noted, was apparently possessed of "common sense").

[34] See for example, *Truth*, 4 Aug. 1892, and Bellot, op. cit., 237–246, 388–406.

[35] Knutsford to Broome, 16 Dec. 1891, CO 295/334.

[36] Markby had served for some years on the Calcutta High Court and was a Reader in Indian Law at Oxford; Pollock was also at Oxford as a Professor of Jurisprudence, and was a very highly regarded barrister.

"we see no reason to doubt that Sir John Gorrie was actuated by a desire to do justice," they declared that he had on numerous occasions transgressed the limits set by a reasonable interpretation of judicial discretion and by the scope of his office: encouraging litigation, and appointing free legal representation without clear evidence of inability to pay, for example, were not, they noted, proper activities for judges. They crushingly concluded that in his desire to do substantial justice, Gorrie "perversely disregarded the explicit provisions of the Ordinances and of well-established principles of law and procedure in dealing with the rights of parties, leading to arbitrary and unjust results, and tending to destroy confidence in the administration of justice."[37] Thus armed, Governor Broome asked for the Chief Justice's resignation, but he refused and instead applied for leave to go to England to put his case personally to the authorities. By this point, however, his health had seriously deteriorated, and soon after arriving back in England he took ill and died, bringing the issue to a close. Gorrie was, the *European Mail* summed up, "an enemy-making man, especially as his lot was cast in those tropical Crown Colonies where white and coloured peoples are found together."[38] In these mixed-race colonies, a Judge determined to provide equal justice would inevitably make powerful enemies, and if he both had an imperious temper and lacked the shield that a friendly and strong Governor could provide (such as Gordon had given Gorrie in his previous posts), it was hardly surprising that his career ended in humiliating dismissal.[39]

II. A MAGISTRATE'S BRIEF TENURE

A similar story, in triplicate, was laid out in the same years in another even older West Indian colony, the Bahamas. If Trinidad was one of the most naturally favored of Britain's West Indian possessions, the Bahama islands may have been the least. They formed a territory, as one historian noted, "singularly cursed by nature." The surface of these islands was porous limestone, flat, dry, stony, and infertile. They possessed neither mineral

---

[37] From a telegram summarizing their findings, CO 295/338, file 170 (15 June 1892).

[38] *European Mail*, 13 Aug. 1892.

[39] With Gorrie gone, the Governor could comfortably rebuff Inspector of Immigration Gibbins's request of February of that year to be allowed to provide legal assistance to immigrant laborers charged with criminal offenses, since magistrates frequently would not. In May, Broome told him that would be impossible, since he was not legally qualified; the question would have to remain at the discretion of the magistrates [CO 295/338, file 160].

resources nor much natural vegetation, and agriculture was difficult. Not surprisingly, despite Columbus's landing, they were soon abandoned by Spain, and remained long unclaimed by any state. "Since they supported human life with difficulty," this historian observed, "they were destined to be settled eventually by desperate men."[40] Beginning in 1629, English pirates became their first settlers. A century later, after subduing the pirates the Crown set up an organized colony, creating an elected House of Assembly in 1729. Yet it was from the start a difficult colony: "such a headstrong set of simple, ungovernable wretches," its second Governor, Richard Fitzwilliam complained, "were never convened in legislative capacity."[41] After the American Revolution, the islands gained many fleeing Loyalists, and their slaves, and some plantations were developed. Yet the most profitable enterprise was probably "wrecking" – luring ships onto rocks with false lights, and then looting them.

By the 1880s the colony had a population of barely seventy thousand, of whom fewer than five thousand were white, the rest descended from African slaves; its economy was stagnant. In law there was no racial distinction, but the elite of merchants and landowners was almost purely white, and social life assumed a hierarchy of color. There was a significant body of "colored," usually lighter-skinned and often better off than blacks, who made up together with some whites a middling class below the white elite; some coloreds were lawyers, businessmen, or small farmers, and the Assembly had some colored members. The vast majority of blacks were laborers, kept poor by the combination of the Master and Servant laws and the prevalence of the truck system of paying in advance in kind, or sharecroppers, continually in debt. The few British officials and expatriates in the islands tended to look down upon Bahamian-born whites, even the rich, as not really gentlemen, all the more as few native whites could be sure, after generations in a multiracial society, of the "purity" of their blood; there was much reference, when British were among themselves, to the origins of the colony in piracy.[42] Such condescension was of course resented, and only strengthened the solidarity of white Creoles and their distaste for paying salaries of officials sent from overseas to fill positions that Bahamians, they agreed, should be holding.

---

[40] Michael Bloch, *The Duke of Windsor's War* (London, 1982), p. 107.
[41] Quoted in ibid., p. 111.
[42] One of the few important allies of the beleaguered Judges in the Bahamas was the Anglican Archdeacon, whose parishioners were disproportionately expatriate and official.

Politically, the colony was atypical. The Bahamas was not a Crown colony like Trinidad; it possessed a greater degree of practical self-government than any predominantly nonwhite part of the Empire other than perhaps Bermuda.[43] Its politics were frozen in the eighteenth century, with property qualifications for the franchise (raised further in 1882), plural voting, open balloting, and both bribery and intimidation accepted. In the 1840s the Crown had established a nominated Legislative Council (as it did elsewhere in the West Indies), with the ultimate goal of replacing the elected Assembly. Yet while in many colonies the "LegCo," dominated by the Governor and his appointees, became the key organ of Government, here the opposite happened: this Council fell under the sway of the leaders of the Assembly, itself "little less than a family gathering of Nassau whites, nearly all of whom are related to each other, either by blood or marriage."[44] Their leaders also came to sit on the Governor's Executive Council, which increasingly took its lead not from the Governor but from them. After the middle of the nineteenth century, the colony was in practice ruled by a caucus of white merchants and landowners known as the "Bay Street Boys" (for the main street of the capital, Nassau, where their offices were located), whose relatives filled most of the posts of Government.

In 1880 this caucus suffered a double blow, when a subsidy from the imperial Government was ended and a Canadian barrister, Henry Austin, was appointed Chief Justice, a post hitherto filled by Bahamians. The position was to remain outside Bahamian hands until 1897, and these years were to see the most serious challenge to Bay Street's control until the 1940s. In the course of it, two members of one of the ruling families, the Sandses, were to be tried for murder, and three "outsider" Judges were to be sent packing. At its close, Bay Street had triumphed and the Colonial Office ceased to concern itself with the rule of law in the Bahamas. Although he soon quarreled with the Attorney General, a member of the Bay Street clique, Austin, a conservative man lacking noticeable sympathy for the black majority, did little in his early years to endanger Bay Street interests. But late in 1884, just months before Sir William Robinson was

---

[43] Apart from white settlement colonies, in the Empire only Bermuda, Barbados, and the Bahamas had constitutions and elective assemblies; Jamaica had lost its own after the 1865 insurrection.

[44] Louis D. Powles, *The Land of the Pink Pearl, or, Recollections of Life in the Bahamas* (London, 1888), p. 41. In this Assembly, he went on, "laws are passed simply for the benefit of the family, whilst the coloured people are ground down and oppressed in a manner that is a disgrace to the British flag."

sent to govern Trinidad, an energetic new Governor arrived in the
Bahamas, and political tensions rose. It was the first governorship for
Henry Blake, who had been a resident magistrate in the Irish Constabu-
lary, and he soon was seeking ways to improve the sluggish Government
and restore some of the usual power of his new position. Like its electoral
system, the Bahamian administration of justice was eighteenth century,
based on unpaid (and unsupervised) resident magistrates.[45] It was one of
the first parts of government to draw Blake's attention. He persuaded the
Legislature in early 1886 to pass an act creating two new salaried legal
officers, to be called Stipendiary and Circuit Magistrates, who would
travel a circuit periodically around the Out-Islands to hear appeals against
the decision of the resident Justices.[46] The passage of the act raised hopes
among the populace, and a petition was drawn up at a large public
meeting in Nassau and sent to the Colonial Office complaining that
"crimes when committed by the white man, who has friends and
means . . . are to be overlooked and condoned, but crimes when committed by the poor friendless black or coloured man . . . are to be detected
and punished with the full severity of the Law." Part of the reason for
this inequity, it went on, was that "the whole machinery [of justice was]
almost exclusively confined to one class."[47] High property qualifications
restricted jury service to the well-off, and police officials and Justices of the
Peace were appointed from the even more well-off; qualified coloured men
only rarely received appointments. Blake hoped to do something about
these grievances (and the inequities of the truck and sharecropping systems as well) and wanted the new officials authorized by the Act to be
recruited from outside. He only managed to get one such appointment,
that of an English barrister, Louis Powles.[48]

---

[45] J. J. Thomas at the same time described the resident magistrates of Trinidad contemp-
tuously: "these gentry, far from being bulwarks to the weaker as against the stronger,
have, in their own persons, been the direst scourges that the poor, particularly when
coloured, have been afflicted by in aggravation of the difficulties of their lot" [*Froudacity*, p. 85].

[46] The additional cost would be small, because these magistrates would also do the work
of the Nassau police magistrate and the Justice of Common Pleas there, allowing the
abolition of those posts; however, the Legislature refused to abolish these positions, held
on patronage, and instead reduced the proposed salaries of the new officials.

[47] "Alleged Grievances of Certain Coloured Inhabitants of New Providence," enclosed in
E. B. A. Taylor to Earl Granville, no. 765, 24 June 1886, CO23/228/ Files 233–245.

[48] In his later bitter criticisms of the colony, Powles largely exempted Blake: "Shortly
after my first circuit," he later recalled, "I had many conversations with Governor
Blake upon the condition of the coloured race in the colony, and I am convinced that

Educated at Harrow and Oxford, a member of the Inner Temple for twenty-one years, Powles was highly qualified.[49] However, in less than a year he was forced to resign on spurious "health" grounds. A mere magistrate, if the senior one in the colony, he was in a more vulnerable position than a Chief Justice, and his abbreviated tenure is a testament to that fact. As had just happened with Gorrie in Trinidad, Powles's first circuit, in November 1886, produced an upsurge of litigation and attempted litigation: "as soon as they heard I was in the settlement," he later recalled, "people flocked to me with cases they wanted tried. They were all matters which ought to have been settled but which I had no power to try, and probably never would be settled at all because the parties were all too poor to go to the Chief Justice's court in Nassau." Some of these matters were appeals from decisions of the magistrates, a development that soon made them his enemies. Powles, again like Gorrie, incensed local employers (who often were the magistrates) by criticizing the truck system, which Governor Blake had tried to reform. A measure Blake had gotten the Legislature to pass in 1885 placed limits on the truck system, but, Powles recalled, "all the time I was in the Bahamas this law virtually remained a dead letter."[50]

The most explosive issue for Powles's position turned out, not surprisingly, to be a case of interracial violence. Several months into his service, fed up by the frequency of domestic violence, Powles announced in the Nassau Police Court that he would send all persons he convicted of striking a woman to prison without the option of a fine, except in "very extenuating circumstances." Soon after this announcement, he sentenced three black men for this offense to various terms of imprisonment, to general approbation. But then he did the same to a white man. James Lightbourn had publicly beaten his black female servant, Susan Hopkins, and three "respectable and quite disinterested" black people witnessed the assault and gave evidence; there were no witnesses for the defense. As merely common assault, the charge under Bahamian law did not require a jury trial, and Powles found Lightbourn guilty and sentenced him to a month's imprisonment. Outrage followed, and an appeal to Chief Justice Austin was organized, one organizer urging that "the Lightbourn case

no man was ever more *sincerely anxious* to benefit them than he was, at that time" [*Pink Pearl*, p. 100].

[49] Lord Chief Justice Coleridge had personally recommended him to Lord Granville, the Secretary of State [CO 23/229, file 541].

[50] Powles, op. cit., pp. 53, 87.

touches us all. Why, I have twice kicked a coloured girl from the top of the house to the bottom myself." The lack of jury trial in such matters was widely lamented.[51]

As Trinidad's Governor was at the same time discovering with Gorrie, discretion was not Powles's strong suit. Governor Blake advised him not to discuss the case, but, convinced that Lightbourn had perjured himself, and finding out after the trial that the man was a Methodist (his brother-in-law was a Methodist minister), Powles exclaimed that he would not believe a Methodist on oath. This careless remark was seized upon, and he was denounced as a religious bigot incapable of giving Lightbourn a fair trial. The dangerous issue of race could now be avoided. Instead, old resentments against Anglican "persecution," dormant since the Church had been disestablished in the Bahamas in 1868, could be revived – and, indeed, anti-Catholicism, for Powles, whose closest friend in the colony was the Anglican Archdeacon, was himself a Roman Catholic. The *Nassau Times* declared that "the effect of Mr Powles's intolerance is really to deprive Methodists of their civil rights," and called for his dismissal, a call soon seconded by a petition signed by all the Methodist ministers in the colony.[52] A counterpetition in support of Powles from black and colored inhabitants (like those in Trinidad for Gorrie) probably only worsened his position, by appearing to bear out white charges that he was heightening racial divisions.[53] Whites in the Caribbean had not forgotten the Jamaica insurrection of 1865; the imperial Government's plans after 1881 to reduce expenditures by removing troops from the West Indies had been stubbornly resisted in the Bahamas (as in some other colonies), with Blake reminding the military authorities in 1885 that "there is a strong feeling on the part of the black and coloured people against the white population of Nassau."[54] Once Powles was felt to be stoking this feeling, even Chief Justice Austin halted his feuding with Attorney General Ormond Malcolm long enough to join him in supporting Powles's removal. After the nonwhite petition the Governor also abandoned him, concluding that his continued presence would be likely to develop "a colour question much to be deprecated."[55] In just a few months, Blake

[51] Ibid., pp. 307–311.
[52] Editorial, 2 Apr. 1887; CO 23/229.
[53] CO 23/229, files 288–292.
[54] Blake to Col. Frederick Stanley, 8 Aug. 1885, CO 23/227, files 10–15, and 19 Sept. 1885 (files 167–9).
[55] Blake to E. B. A. Taylor, 11 Apr. 1887, CO 23/229, file 247. Apart from his professional duties, Powles had encouraged a colored member of the Assembly, James

wrote the Colonial Office, Powles had "done mischief that it will take years to undo."[56] In June 1887 he offered him three month's medical leave with half pay, to be followed by resignation on health grounds, making it clear that the alternative was a formal request for his dismissal. Reluctantly, Powles took the offer, and a local doctor certified his "nervous exhaustion."[57] A second petition from "coloured inhabitants" asking for his replacement to be either another Englishman or a coloured attorney was ignored; he was quickly succeeded by a white Bahamian.[58] After his resignation, Lightbourn's appeal was heard by Chief Justice Austin, who quashed the conviction, not on any legal point but simply because in reviewing the evidence he found the black prosecution witnesses unconvincing.

III. THE SANDS BOYS GET IN TROUBLE

However, Austin himself was soon to become a similar target. His downfall was initiated by a murder trial, the second within two years involving young men from the same elite family. In December 1886, the newly arrived Powles had witnessed a near riot in Nassau, after one of these young men, Charles Sands, shot to death a black policeman. Sands was rescued from a spontaneous mob that might have beaten him to death, and charged with murder. "The way the whites talked of this habitually," Powles recalled, "was, 'that the man was only a nigger, and it was a pity a few more were not shot.'" Such attitudes explain the anger of the crowd. As Powles went on, "A member of the New York Yacht Club, who knows the Bahamas thoroughly, once said to me, 'I was here the day Sands was arrested, and I never shall forget it as long as I live! No one who saw that crowd could doubt that there was an undercurrent of race-hatred with which the White Conches will have to reckon sooner or later.'"[59]

Carmichael Smith, in his efforts to start a weekly newspaper, which began in March 1887, under the title of "The Freeman." This paper ran repeated editorials in Powles's defense, to no avail.

[56] Blake to Henry Holland, 25 June 1887, CO 23/229, files 236–7.

[57] However, it was clear on all sides that he was being "run out," as a headline in the *New York Herald* put it ["SLAVERY IN FREEDOM: An English Judge Run Out of the Bahamas for Protecting the Blacks" (this cutting had been sent to the Colonial Office, and is in CO 23/229, file 363)].

[58] CO 23/229, file 108.

[59] *Pink Pearl*, pp. 113–114. Governor Ambrose Shea recalled this event in trying to retain imperial troops in the colony: "The present Police," he wrote the Secretary of State, "are equal to the ordinary routine duty, but they all but failed on an occasion of about three

Sands's insanity plea (he apparently had a history of disturbed behavior) was ratified by his jury, which included two coloured men, with Austin concurring. However, we may never know for sure about his mental state; his former teacher, Archdeacon Wakefield, did not think him insane, but he was not called to give evidence by the prosecutor, Attorney General Malcolm (who was the defendant's uncle by marriage).[60] Since there were no facilities intended for an insane prisoner in the Bahamas, the Sands family tried to persuade Governor Blake to have him moved to a private asylum in the United States, or else a similar facility in England, offering to pay all costs. Blake, backed by the Colonial Office, rejected this. Finally, he was sent to Jamaica, where there was a prison with a wing for the insane. How long he remained incarcerated is unclear; rumors in the Bahamas in the early 1890s told of his being seen working as a clerk in Jamaica.

Almost exactly two years later another Sands boy, Frank, was involved in a killing, that of Shadrach Gay with which this chapter opened. Frank was one of the five charged with being accessories in that killing. By this time not only was Chief Justice Austin not on speaking terms with the Attorney General, whose use of his office to favor his private interests deeply offended Austin,[61] but he was also alienated from the entire Bay Street establishment and no longer willing to accommodate them. He had expressed his concern, when the local Savings Bank had failed, that improper behavior by its managers was being hushed up. Following that, in a salvage case, he had been assured that his salary, paid by the Legislature, would be increased if he ruled in favor of Bay Street against the New York insurers; he refused the offer, and ruled against.[62] From this point on, Bay Street was looking for a way to end his tenure. The tensions between them came to a head in the aftermath of Shadrach Gay's death.

---

years ago when an attempt was made by a coloured mob to 'rescue' a white prisoner who had shot a black Policeman. . . . The incident has made a deep impression in this community" [Shea to Knutsford, 22 Nov. 1888, CO 23/230, file 105].

[60] Blake to Stanhope, 11 Dec. 1886, CO 23/228, file 119; Blake to Holland, 4 Mar. and 25 Mar. 1887, Holland to Blake, 25 Mar. and 28 May 1887; and Taylor to Holland, 14 Oct. 1887, CO 23/229. Sands did not leave for Jamaica until May 1888 [CO 333/11; ADM 53/15317].

[61] One action that the Attorney General did not forget was his stopping Malcolm from receiving fees from the Admiralty Court.

[62] "Lucile" case, late Feb. 1889 [per Austin's account in his privately published pamphlet, *Ten Years Chief Justice of the Bahamas, 1880–1890* (copy in CO 23/235, file 163)].

IV. TWO CHIEF JUSTICES LOSE THEIR JOBS

Confronted with another nephew (and several of his friends) involved in a killing, Attorney General Malcolm found a way out: as soon as the coroner's jury returned a murder finding against five men, he instructed the presiding magistrate, T. A. Thompson, also a relative of his (and thus also of Sands), to separate the case into two proceedings; all the assailants except De Pain, who had delivered the fatal razor thrust, were charged only with "affray," a misdemeanor, while De Pain alone was charged with murder. Moreover, the affray trial was held first, and in it Malcolm, conducting the prosecution, took care to keep witnesses from saying anything that linked the fight to its fatal outcome.

This crafty handling of Gay's killing stoked a judicial explosion. In charging the jury in the affray trial, Austin told them that even the seemingly incomplete evidence heard strongly suggested that the prisoners should have been charged not with affray but with aiding and abetting De Pain in the murder. At the close of his charge the Attorney General indignantly rose to ask whether the Chief Justice was suggesting that he had neglected his duty. The Judge refused the challenge, and sharply asked the Attorney General to sit down. The jury did not take long to acquit the prisoners, an outcome that enabled them to serve as defense witnesses the following week when De Pain went on trial for murder. There Malcolm began his opening of the case by attempting to vindicate his course of action in regard to the others involved, citing legal authorities. Austin let him go on in this vein, and then at the close of the trial unwisely replied, prefacing his charge to the jury with a lengthy disquisition on the duties of the Attorney General and arguing, citing a long series of rulings on the subject of accessories, that the men who were tried for affray should have been in the dock in this trial. The jury found De Pain guilty of manslaughter but not of murder, a verdict the Judge deplored. He then ensured his unpopularity with the white population by sentencing De Pain to the maximum possible penalty, penal servitude for life.

Austin's enemies (who now included the new Governor, Ambrose Shea, a Newfoundland businessman and politician, who had replaced Blake in the summer of 1887)[63] saw that they had their opportunity to dispose of

---

[63] Shea was not a typical colonial Governor. He had gone into politics from a business career and had become the Speaker of the Newfoundland Legislative Assembly. Representing the colony on various diplomatic missions seems to have given him an interest in colonial government in a warmer clime.

him, for he had already irreparably damaged his standing with the Colonial Office through an incident the year before. In July 1888, a black prisoner, Matthew Taylor, upon being convicted of burglary, had attacked the Chief Justice with a stick seized from a table in the court-room. Aiming at the Judge's head, he hit only his arm raised in defense; however, he kept trying and had to be pulled away, not before drawing blood. A week later, still seething, Austin summarily sentenced him for contempt of court to thirty lashes and life imprisonment. Governor Shea immediately queried the Colonial Office about this sentence; there it was called "of course utterly illegal"; one official wryly noted, "the Judge seems to think he may inflict any punishment for contempt of court – it is fortunate that he did not sentence the man to be hung." The sentence was annulled. Moreover, the Governor was told to inform Austin that "should any similar grave miscarriage occur again it may have very serious con-sequences for the Chief Justice."[64] Bay Street made sure its friends in England were informed, and several questions were raised in the House of Commons by Radical members objecting to the use of flogging for con-tempt of court and to the excesses of this colonial Chief Justice.[65]

Knowing that the Chief Justice was on probation in Whitehall, Attorney General Malcolm did not let his public rebuke in the De Pain trial rest, but demanded a retraction of what he called the slanderous charge that he had suppressed evidence. Shea backed him up, asking Austin to support his "charges" so that the Colonial Office could decide their merit or publicly withdraw them. Austin equivocated, and Shea sent the matter to Whitehall, making sure to emphasize the Judge's increasing deafness and irascibility with age. However, the Colonial Office responded that both men had acted unwisely, but also that "it may be necessary to hold an inquiry" into "the most serious feature in this case" – the allegation that relevant facts that were known to the Attorney General were suppressed.[66] To prevent this, Shea convened a court of his own: by having a bill rushed through the Assembly allowing him to administer oaths and issue summons to appear before the Governor and Executive Council. This body (which Austin later called a "totally incompetent body to decide a question of law" and *The Freeman* labeled a "Star Chamber") then took evidence for several days, including that from a protesting Austin and from other witnesses. While this inquiry

---

[64] CO 23/230, files 93 and 94.
[65] Ibid. *The Times* headed its description of the parliamentary questions by Radical members Fowler and Pickersgill "Flogging in the Bahamas" [16 Mar. 1889].
[66] Knutsford to Shea, 27 Mar. 1889, CO 23/231, file 38.

was being held, Austin was being privately urged to back down and come to an arrangement with the Governor; he refused.[67] Despite some striking evidence supporting Austin's position (one witness in the audience during the affray trial observed that "if I had been a stranger in Court I should have thought the Attorney General was DEFENDING INSTEAD OF PROSECUTING"), it concluded (not surprisingly) that the Chief Justice had misconducted himself, and was "deserving of the severest censure." A one-sidedly edited version of the proceedings was sent to the Colonial Office,[68] and Shea himself left for England to personally lobby for Austin's removal.

After hearing in person from Shea, the Colonial Office was, if nothing else, convinced that this situation could not continue, and threw its support to the Governor. The Secretary of State gave him a letter to take back to the colony declaring, "after what has occurred in this case, and in the case of Thomas Taylor, his further continuance in the office which he holds has become very undesirable in the public interest." Seizing upon Austin's growing deafness, he suggested that the Assembly might be willing to grant the Chief Justice a pension if he retired on grounds of infirmity.[69] Faced with the possible alternative of being dismissed without a pension, Austin surrendered in November and accepted the Assembly's pension, to take effect upon his successor's arrival, upon which he went home to Montreal to write a pamphlet detailing his grievances. He was

---

[67] *The Freeman*, 7 May 1889. In his pamphlet, Austin recalled an anonymous letter placed under his door the night before the Enquiry closed – "I believe it was written by Judge Camplejohn (the Coroner) – one of the parties interested. It said, 'Take advice of one who knows, who feels for you, who condemns in a great measure the course you have adopted, ask a private interview with the Governor, without loss of time. He is a good man, be prepared to make some concession. You are lost if you go on. Malcolm may get *hurt* – but you ruined.' " "On the same day," he went on, "Thompson [the Magistrate in the case] called at my house. . . . He had never called upon me in ten years. He said he came from Government House; that he came to see me in a friendly way – to ask me to withdraw the case against Mr. Malcolm. . . . 'You know the Governor's influence at the Colonial Office. You will be ruined.' "

[68] For example, one man called by the Chief Justice, Charles A. Demerett, recounted his experiences as a witness in the affray trial: "I was *interrupted* and *checked* by the Attorney General several times in giving my evidence. He said, 'I don't want this,' 'I don't want that,' when I was examined, when I answered. I wanted to tell more. . . . After the evidence at the Police Court I was threatened by Tom Sands, one of the brothers of the defendant, Frank Sands. . . . Tom Sands called out, 'You white son of a bitch, if you give evidence against my brother, you will have your guts cut out.' W. R. Kemp heard this; he also told me not to go eastward as my life had been threatened by one of the Sands. The elder brother Sands said he would do anything for me he could [if I didn't testify]." This evidence was not entered in the minutes of the proceedings [per Austin, *Ten Years Chief Justice of the Bahamas*, CO 23/235, file 163].

[69] Knutsford to Shea, 30 Sept. 1889, CO 23/231, ff. 486–7.

not without local supporters, and upon his retirement in the early summer of 1890 he was presented with a memorial signed by thirty-two ministers of religion, and another signed by over six hundred Nassau citizens, praising his career and regretting his retirement. The two chief newspapers in the colony, however, refused to print these memorials, instead writing editorials heaping scorn upon the departing judge. At the Colonial Office, he was to be remembered as "a hopeless incompetent judge."[70]

One might have expected Austin's successor to be more cautious, but, quite the contrary, the English barrister Roger Yelverton was cut more on the lines of a Powles than an Austin. An energetic and reform-minded man, jealous of the high prerogatives of a Judge, he immediately set himself to eliminating a backlog of cases by establishing more frequent sittings, and seeking ways to make the legal system in the colony work more effectively.[71] This did not make him popular on Bay Street, for whom the system already worked quite effectively. A decisive ruling came in the "El Dorado" case, heard in Admiralty Court in January 1892. A steamer wrecked upon one of the Out-Islands had been, in Yelverton's judgment, "swamped upon by some of the natives dishonestly." His ruling against them and for the foreign ship owners, and even more, his subsequent action appointing Deputy Marshals throughout the Out-Islands responsible to Admiralty Court for the proper conduct of "so-called salvors" within their districts "put an end to such conduct," he later observed with satisfaction. It also put an end to the business elite's tolerance for this Judge. That spring Yelverton went further, and blocked the leader of the Assembly, R. H. Sawyer, from using Government agents to advance his land claims against a group of colored and black small proprietors in the Out-Islands.[72] Yelverton was increasingly planting himself as a barrier between Government business and private interests, and in the process arousing ever-greater dislike. That spring the Bahamas papers

---

[70] Wingfield minute, 24 Oct. 1892, re Austin's request for a review of his case, CO 23/235, file 163. Austin's 1892 pamphlet was not appreciated at the Colonial Office; Wingfield remarked in 1895 that he "did not improve his case by public violent pamphlets attacking Sir Angus Shea and the Imperial Government" [minute, 19 Aug. 1895, CO 23/242].

[71] IN THE MATTER OF THE RELEASE BY THE GOVERNOR OF THE BAHAMAS OF ALFRED E. MOSELEY. NOTES BY THE CHIEF JUSTICE OF THE COLONY. published by Spottiswoode & Co. Printers, New-street Square, London, 1892, p. 22 [written by Yelverton and sent by him to Privy Council, received 15 Dec. 1892] , copy in CO 23/236.

[72] See affidavits re this matter in IN THE MATTER OF . . . MOSELEY. NOTES BY THE CHIEF JUSTICE, CO 23/236.

began to attack him, and at the same time stories detailing his arrogance and abuse of his authority began to appear in the English press.

The hostilities came to a head at the beginning of May when the *Nassau Guardian*, the colony's leading paper, published an anonymous letter from "Colonist" making fun of Yelverton. The Chief Justice demanded that the editor reveal the author of what he considered defamatory and seditious writing. The editor, Alfred Moseley, closely related to the leaders of the Assembly, refused, and Yelverton ordered him jailed for contempt of court. Again a Judge had overreached. Governor Shea immediately telegraphed the Colonial Office, asking their permission to use his delegated prerogative powers to release Moseley. Obtaining assent, he released Moseley, over the protests of the Chief Justice, less than two days after his committal, and Bay Street put on a public demonstration (with free food and drink) to celebrate his release. Moseley, speaking to loud cheers at the demonstration, declared that "victory had been secured for the freedom of the press and the people." Governor Shea then wrote the Colonial Office to complain about Yelverton, noting that among other things he had come to see himself as "protector of the rights of the coloured population," an unneeded role that could only end badly. "The race question," Shea warned, "is pregnant with trouble and, if urged into activity, the issues would be calamitous."[73]

Yelverton also wrote to the Colonial Office, and Wingfield concluded that although the Governor was justified in releasing Moseley, he could have avoided confrontation by negotiation: "I am afraid it is not unlikely to be true that Sir Angus Shea is too much influenced by the white natives." Since neither party was ready to back down, the only thing to do was to submit the Moseley issue (in which the Colonial Office had already backed up Shea) to the Judicial Committee of the Privy Council.[74] A hearing was set for December, and with the Governor having secured his reconfirmation in his post for another term of five years, this time it was the Chief Justice who traveled to England.[75] Austin, inspired to press for a reconsideration of his own treatment, offered his support, as did Powles; both provided letters for the Colonial Office and Privy Council denouncing, as Austin put it, the "cabal against the administration of

[73] Shea to Knutsford, 9 June and 20 June 1892, CO 23/234, files 362–70. He noted that the Chief Justice was threatening to upset the "maintenance of a wholesome restraint over the out-island population" [9 June].

[74] Wingfield minute, 6 July 1892, CO 23/234, files 255–257.

[75] *Glasgow Herald*, 5 May 1892, p. 7.

justice" that ran the colony.[76] "I think," Austin concluded, "the only thing to do is to make it a *Crown* colony again!"[77] A friend from the Bahamas urged Yelverton to seek support from among all the colonial Judges; it was ultimately an issue that threatened the independence of them all, as "recent events in Trinidad" have shown. "Don't be beaten," he concluded.[78] Yelverton certainly gave it his best, listing in his pamphlet and in letters to the Colonial Office all the misdeeds that had taken place in recent years, as fruit of a rotten tree. The treatment of Gay's murder was typical: "the system," he wrote, "which . . . allowed of the indecent spectacle of the Attorney General of the Colony prosecuting his wife's nephew for a minor offence when a man's body had been fatally ripped open by a knife possibly wielded by Sands, is corrupt to the core."[79]

Yelverton's contempt for the "corrupt" Government of the colony was colored by a good deal of class (and race) snobbery: the piratical and otherwise dubious origins of the island's elite was a theme in his private correspondence; as his friend Archdeacon Wakefield complained to him, the colony was run by "the offspring of blackguard whites." In an article published in the English press Yelverton sneeringly described Malcolm as a "half-caste." Austin, writing supportingly to Yelverton that year, recalled how "Malcolm had the audacity once to tell me he was one of the Malcolms of Scotland! I know him to be a son of a bastard in Nassau, and that 'Drimmie'[80] (which always amused me) is his mother's name, an Ethiopian he had *shut* up in his own house. When I was there, she never showed." A frequent topic among Englishmen in the West Indies was the laughable aristocratic airs put on by "old families" when their origins were rarely free from illicit interracial liaisons, and here Austin, Yelverton, and Wakefield were typical.[81]

Yelverton published his charges as a pamphlet, and wrote a long letter on the case to the *Pall Mall Gazette*. Bay Street joined in the fray, and a pamphlet and press articles critical of him also appeared in England, adding to the unseemliness of the quarrel in the eyes of imperial officials.

---

[76] Austin to Secretary of State Ripon, 10 Oct. 1892, requesting a review of his case, CO 23/235, file 163.

[77] Austin to Yelverton, 12 Aug. 1892, included in pamphlet sent to Privy Council; copy in CO 23/236.

[78] Anon. to Yelverton, 20 July 1892, included in pamphlet sent to Privy Council.

[79] Yelverton to Secretary of State, 28 Nov. 1892, CO 23/236.

[80] This was Malcolm's middle name.

[81] Austin to Yelverton, 12 Aug. 1892, included in pamphlet sent to Privy Council; copy in CO 23/236.

Yelverton's statement submitted to the Privy Council declared that in addition to himself, two other Chief Justices – not only Austin but also Chief Justice Burnside, of Ceylon, who had formerly been Attorney General of the Bahamas – and the former Circuit Justice, Powles, were all "prepared to testify before your Lordships, or before any Royal Commission, that the Government of the Bahamas has been and is corrupt" and that "it is only by the firm and thoroughly fair administration of justice by Englishmen unrelated to the native families that the present most unsatisfactory state of things can be remedied."[82] However, the Privy Council turned down the offer as beyond the scope of its remit, and confined its attention to the specific issue of Moseley's jailing and release. Its attitude was indicated in the course of the hearing by unfriendly remarks to Yelverton about the near-libelous remarks he had published about various public officials in the colony. After a month it issued a decision not only that the Governor did have the undoubted authority to release Moseley (as the Colonial Office had ruled), but also that his refusal to reveal the author of the objectionable letter did not constitute contempt of court, and thus the Chief Justice had erred in the first place.[83]

With Yelverton thus rebuffed and humiliated, Shea now moved to obtain his dismissal. Even before the Privy Council had issued its decision, he argued that Yelverton should not return to the colony, his wholesale attacks (and even more, his publishing them) having made it impossible for him to serve impartially. The Colonial Office was receptive to this argument, for it saw his denunciations as bringing the Government itself into discredit. Such "casting [of] wholesale aspersions" only served to raise questions among officials about his own discretion; as one clerk observed, "Mr. Yelverton's genealogical trees (which he has watered with so much ink) require pruning."[84] As soon as the Privy Council decision was announced, the Legislative Council and House of Assembly passed a joint resolution against Yelverton's return, arguing that "public confidence" in him had been destroyed.

Yelverton did not go quietly, however, particularly since, as he and Austin had hoped, while the conflict over his imprisonment of Moseley

[82] Yelverton to Privy Council, with pamphlet, CO 23/236. "The Bay Street gang," Burnside wrote to Yelverton" have driven every honest man out of the place, and they'll drive you out too, unless you can persuade Downing Street that the judges of the colonies are not outlaws" [IN THE MATTER OF . . . MOSELEY. NOTES BY THE CHIEF JUSTICE, CO 23/236].

[83] *The Times*, 3 Feb. 1893, p. 15 (the hearing had been held on Dec. 15–16, 1892).

[84] H. W. Just minute, 25 Jan. 1893, CO 23/236.

had raged, Gladstone had returned to office. Yelverton wrote to the new Liberal Colonial Secretary, Lord Ripon, reiterating his request for an official investigation, and simultaneously had an M.P. friend put down a question calling for a full enquiry into his charges concerning the administration of the colony. Shea turned back this second threat of an enquiry by calling on his political ace in the hole, no one less than the rising power in the Conservative Party, Joseph Chamberlain. He had met Chamberlain in Montreal in the summer of 1890, and the two former businessmen now in Government had hit it off personally. Shea had given him what Chamberlain described to his wife as "a romantic account of the resurrection of his colony . . . due to the discovery . . . that a weed peculiar to the place would give the best quality fibre for hemp."[85] This was just when Chamberlain was beginning to turn toward what was to be the focus of the rest of his political life, the economic development of the Empire, and he was in a receptive state for Shea's pitch – receptive personally as well, for his family finances were beginning to pinch, and he was on the lookout for new investment opportunities. Shea urged him to get in on the ground floor by growing the "weed," sisal, in the Bahamas. A few months later, Chamberlain's personal finances became seriously squeezed by a crash of Argentine securities, and he turned to Shea's offer. Eager no doubt to have Chamberlain in his debt, Shea arranged to sell him Government land at what he claimed was a special price, and spend Government money building a wharf to serve it. Chamberlain bought ten thousand acres on Andros in 1891 and put his younger son Neville in charge. While Shea's battle with Yelverton was going on, Neville was in the Bahamas, sending his father the views of his fellow landowners. The investment proved a mistake; by 1897 Chamberlain had to liquidate at a heavy loss.[86]

Shea's political investment in the future Colonial Secretary paid off handsomely, however. With Shea's position in danger in 1893, Chamberlain stepped forward to stop Yelverton. He first wrote to Charles Buxton, the Liberal Parliamentary Undersecretary at the Colonial Office, passing on the aspersions on the character of the Chief Justice that Neville and Governor Shea had forwarded to him, and accusing him of trying to stir up racial animosity in a colony where the races had "for the last twenty years at least lived in perfect harmony."[87] When the question

---

[85] Joseph to Mary Chamberlain, 27 Sept. 1890, quoted in Peter Marsh, *Joseph Chamberlain: Entrepreneur in Politics* (New Haven, Conn., 1994), p. 324.

[86] David Dilks, *Neville Chamberlain*, vol. 1: 1869–1929 (Cambridge, 1984), pp. 71–72.

[87] Chamberlain to Buxton, 3 Sept. 1893, CO 23/236.

was put in the House of Commons a few days later, he intervened with a biting speech. He cited the refusal of the Privy Council to entertain Yelverton's charges:

Lord Herschell would not permit the Chief Justice's notes to remain on record in the Judicial Committee of the Privy Council, on the ground that it was impossible to allow that Court to be made the vehicle for disseminating the scandalous allegations against a great number of persons in the colony which they contained, and he himself would now take his part in preventing the Committee of the House of Commons from being used for the same purpose.

Claiming direct knowledge from "a relative of his" there, he praised the work of Governor Shea in reviving a moribund economy, and denounced the malicious efforts of a vindictive man to besmirch his name. Chamberlain then went on to do what he could to besmirch Yelverton, portraying him as an eccentric and egomaniacal figure, obsessively spreading "disgraceful calumnies and insinuations" against seemingly everyone holding any authority in the Bahamas. "The Bahamas," he declared, "had been most unfortunate in its Chief Justices. (Hear, hear) They were appointed by this country, and he wondered what genius of discord presided over their appointment. (Laughter) The late Chief Justice had got into hot water over a particular case of murder, and was retired upon a pension which the colony still paid." Yet the next appointment was even worse. "Mr. Yelverton," he observed, "swaggered about as Chief Justice," obsessed with his high position. When a harmless letter appeared in a local paper "in which his conduct was criticized in a humorous manner," he reacted in a monarchical fashion, setting off the sequence of events that led to the present situation. After being rebuked by the Judicial Committee of the Privy Council, he resumed having "calumnies" against the Governor published in the press, and now sought to involve the House of Commons in his destructive efforts. Dismissing the notion of an enquiry, Chamberlain asked the House "whether the Chief Justice, after having provoked, insulted, and libeled the inhabitants of the colony, could be allowed to return to it in an official capacity." He sat down to strong applause from the benches behind him.[88]

The man who had been called in 1888 "the best debater in the House"[89] thus killed the possibility of an enquiry. Chamberlain's speech was followed by a shorter one by a Radical backbencher expatiating on the

---

[88] *The Times*, 9 Sept 1893, p. 8.
[89] By the seasoned parliamentary correspondent Henry Lucey, quoted in Marsh, op. cit., p. 308.

excessive powers of committal possessed by Judges in Crown colonies, which had led to "substantial injustice" being done. This M. P. called for "a general Act with regard to every Crown colony, providing against the arbitrary power of committal for contempt of Court." "The Trinidad and Tobago Commission" of the previous year, he went on, "showed that we required more supervision in our Crown colonies in respect of the Judges than the Colonial Office at present gave." A defensive Buxton agreed that "there was a considerable abuse of judicial power in some of their colonies. . . . [T]he Chief Justices had an undue idea of their powers." However, he deflected calls for legislation, or specific administrative changes, such as periodic visitations. As for the Bahamas, "he would ask the Committee to leave the responsibility of the government of this colony in the hands of the Colonial Office. Any specific accusation would always receive careful attention. The colony was improving in many respects, and he hoped there would be no recurrence of scandals in the future."[90]

Yelverton's fate was now sealed. The Colonial Office was aware that the Government of the Bahamas was far from ideal: "We know," minuted one official, "that the abuses have existed and Mr. Yelverton has not conciliated the local clique. From the way they hate him nothing is more probable than that he has stood in their way." Another agreed that though much of what he claimed might well be true, Yelverton's unfitness was nonetheless clear: "The islands are no doubt as bad as he says, but by his own rashness or want of discretion . . . he has made them too hot to hold him."[91] The Colonial Office now asked the Privy Council to decide whether Yelverton should be removed from his position. At the hearing of its Judicial Committee, Yelverton vainly raised the general issue of the protection of judicial independence in the Empire, while the Judges did little to hide their exasperation with his behavior. "How could you," asked Lord Coleridge, "write such a letter as [the one published in the *Pall Mall Gazette*, which accused the Governor and other officials of corruption and perversion of justice] and expect to be sent back to the Bahamas afterwards?"[92] When the hearing ended, and it was clear what the Committee's formal answer would be, he was asked for his resignation, under threat of being dismissed; he unwillingly complied, and a new Chief Justice was immediately appointed, even before the Privy Council issued

[90] *The Times*, 9 Sept 1893, p. 9.
[91] H. W. Just minute, Oct. 1893, and R. W. [?] minute, 1 Nov. 1893, CO 23/236.
[92] *The Times*, 7 Dec. 1893, p. 5.

its ruling.[93] When that came, it was as expected, an endorsement of the appropriateness, if he had not resigned, of his dismissal.[94]

Three outside judicial officials had been gotten rid of in the space of a half decade, under both Conservative and Liberal Governments. While Archdeacon Wakefield bleakly wondered whether "it is quite impossible to rule an English Colony on upright principles," the Bahamas business elite and their friends in England congratulated themselves that they had turned back "judicial tyranny."[95] Although Governor Shea was asked to retire in late 1893 on grounds of age (he had just turned seventy-five, unusually old for a colonial Governor), his successor, happy to leave his post in the cold and windswept Falklands, raised no waves. All that was left now was for Bay Street to recapture the chief judicial post for one of its own. Although Buxton in his placatory remarks in the House of Commons had made a gesture toward acknowledging something of Yelverton's complaints by "deplor[ing] that in the past judicial posts in these small colonies had been filled up by relatives of those in power," and assuring the House that they "intended in future to put in outsiders rather than those in the island," this intention was not held to. Wingfield had observed in 1893 that "it would be a very good thing to get [Attorney General Malcolm] away from the Bahamas," but they were not able to find a chief justiceship that paid sufficiently well to meet his expectations (at least as well as the Bahamas). Two years later, when it appeared that Yelverton's successor might be moved up to Jamaica, Malcolm applied to be appointed his replacement. Wingfield opposed this, arguing for an appointment from outside: "it would not be advisable," he wrote, "to appoint Mr. Malcolm Chief Justice . . . where he is related by blood or marriage to so many of the small community." However, the Legislature that year cleverly reduced the future salary for the post, further diminishing its appeal to non-Bahamians, and when in 1897 the vacancy did come about, Malcolm, strongly recommended by Governor Haynes-Smith, was given the appointment.[96]

---

[93] He went out making it clear that he had not jumped but had been pushed, and warning that "the independence of the Judges in the smaller colonies is seriously endangered by the present attitude of the Colonial Office towards them" [letter, *The Times*, 1 Jan. 1894, p. 12]. He returned to his practice at the English Bar.

[94] 7 Mar. 1894, CO 23/240.

[95] Wakefield to Yelverton, in pamphlet, CO 23/236; the "Bay Street" view was presented regularly in the pages of the *Nassau Guardian*.

[96] Malcolm to Secretary of State, 25 Nov. 1895, minute by Wingfield, CO 23/242; Secretary of State to Malcolm, Oct. 1897, CO 23/247. A year after Malcolm's

Bay Street had won its decisive victory over interfering Judges, as the Trinidad planters had in the same years, and neither was to be seriously challenged again until the 1930s. In sharp contrast to the new colony of Fiji, where strong-minded officials were able to dominate a relatively small number of white planters and traders, the old colonies of the West Indies, with their long-entrenched white elites, formed in the time of slavery, presented a far less favorable field for such officials, and it was not surprising that they became increasingly rare.[97] Administrative and judicial positions in the West Indies in the late nineteenth and early twentieth centuries were normally either left to local men or treated as mere stepping-stones to more challenging and prestigious posts in Asia and Africa.

Underneath the surface security of white Creole rule in the Caribbean, however, lay a continuing awareness of the large black and colored majority in these colonies. The invocation by Shea and Chamberlain of the specter of race conflict was not merely tactical; genuine anxiety fueled a decade-long delaying action in the Bahamas against the withdrawal of troops, and the spending of considerable money in recruiting a replacement force of special police from other islands. Such fears were not all that different from the fears of Austin and Yelverton, except that for the latter it was Bay Street's misrule, not the "agitation" of Judges like themselves, that would bring on the troubles. As Archdeacon Wakefield wrote to Yelverton, "in a country semi-civilised, with an excitable people like the negroes, anything bringing high officials [he meant here Chief Justices]

---

appointment, the Assembly rescinded the salary cut; an outraged Colonial Office objected, but eventually allowed it.

[97] The Caribbean colonies were particularly difficult for "independent-minded" judges. In 1869, Chief Justice Joseph Beaumont of British Guiana had been ousted after six years' tenure in a conflict that began in a clash with the Governor over his favoritism to planters, and came to a head in a remarkably similar fashion to Austin's, when the Chief Justice imprisoned the editor of the colony's largest newspaper for contempt of court. William des Voeux was a stipendiary magistrate strongly sympathetic to Beaumont, and this experience shaped his lifelong dislike of English settlers. H. L. Hall, in his semi-official history of the Colonial Office, noted that Justice Beaumont's "sympathy with the Chinese immigrants" led him into "unwise acts . . . and resulted in a case before the Privy Council" [op. cit., p. 142]. See also John McLaren, "The Perils of Judicial Tenure in Britain's Caribbean Colonies in the Post-Emancipation Era, 1830–1870," paper to The British World Conference, Bristol, 14 July 2007. Yet another combative West Indian Judge was Alan Ker (like Gorrie a Scot), a member of the Jamaican High Court from 1860 to his death in 1885 and throughout a sharp critic of the system's favoritism to whites; if Ker was never removed, he also was never, despite his seniority, appointed Chief Justice. See Rande Kostal, *A Jurisprudence of Power: Victorian Empire and the Rule of Law* (Oxford, 2005), p. 96.

into contempt is not only mean but fraught with actual danger. . . . I only fear lest some day the down-trodden and discontented, who at present are silent, should make their voices suddenly heard in a very unpleasant way."[98] He was even more explicit a few months later, frustrated with the rebuff given Yelverton by the Privy Council over Moseley: "The bigwigs of the English Law Courts," he wrote, "have no idea of the insolence of Colonials, neither can they see what an evil effect the unchecked abuse of the Chief Justice by the 'upper classes' has upon the coloured people who are nine out of ten of the population. An attack which would provoke nothing more than a hearty laugh in England has, for the upholding of authority, to be dealt promptly with among semi-civilised races. A joke can pass among people who have come to years of discretion but woe betide the unhappy boy at school who tries it on with his master; and what are the Bahamans, as but children?"[99]

The race question in the West Indies was always at the back of white minds, both of local whites resisting the interference of "ignorant" and "self-righteous" officials with their dominance, and of such officials, English visitors, and imperial bureaucrats in London worried over the arrogance of Creoles toward their nonwhite populations. As long as things remained reasonably quiet, however, the local white elites generally could have their way; these islands in their nineteenth-century decline had become too peripheral to broader British interests to be worth sustained attention from the metropole. The situation was, however, quite different with the largest and most important British possession, the proverbial "jewel in the imperial crown," India.

---

[98] Wakefield to Yelverton, in IN THE MATTER OF. . . MOSELEY. NOTES BY THE CHIEF JUSTICE, CO 23/236.
[99] Wakefield to Yelverton, 20 Feb. 1893, CO 23/236.

5

India: The Setting

[T]he British Power in India is like a vast bridge over which an enormous multitude of human beings are passing, and will (I trust) for ages to come continue to pass, from a dreary land, in which brute violence in its roughest form had worked its will for centuries – a land of cruel wars, ghastly superstitions, wasting plague and famine – on their way to a country of which, not being a prophet, I will not try to draw a picture, but which is at least orderly, peaceful, and industrious, and which for aught we know to the contrary, may be the cradle of changes comparable to those which have formed the imperishable legacy to mankind of the Roman Empire. The bridge was not built without desperate struggles and costly sacrifices. *Strike away either of its piers and it will fall*, and what are they? *One of its piers is military power: the other is justice*, by which I mean a firm and constant determination on the part of the English to promote impartially and by all lawful means, what they (the English) regard as the lasting good of the natives of India. Neither force nor justice will suffice by itself.

James Fitzjames Stephen (Legal Adviser to the Government
of India, 1869–1873) 1878[1]

At two in the morning on November 7, 1889, four soldiers of the East Kent regiment stationed at Dum Dum, then a few miles outside Calcutta, restricted by regulations in their ability to buy liquor from nearby stores, set out in search of "toddy" (an alcoholic drink made from the sap of the palm tree). Breaking into a shop, they proceeded to drink up what they found, and went on in search of more. They roused a villager sleeping on his veranda and demanded toddy. Not receiving a satisfactory reply, they dragged him into a nearby ditch, and when he continued to insist that he had none, one of them shot him. The villager crawled back to his house, where he died that night.

---

[1] "Manchester on India," *The Times*, 4 Jan. 1878, p. 3 [my italics].

This incident, by no means without precedent in British India, eventually led to a trial and a murder conviction of the soldier, Thomas O'Hara, which was then overturned on appeal. It caused a good deal of trouble for the Government, both in India and in Britain itself, its repercussions reaching into Parliament. The controversy surrounding it disrupted the smooth everyday operation of British rule, for it threw into public question the ideology that provided the strongest justification for British domination – the claim that Britain had brought to India the "rule of law." It also brought the glare of public attention, in India and, to a lesser degree, in Britain itself, onto the ongoing problem of private European violence against "natives" in India. Such violence was a particularly difficult problem for the British rulers of India. India possessed an extensive, growing, and ever-more-assertive native press, and a rapidly increasing body of indigenous professionals trained in English law. Such violence was resented, and extreme cases, when lives were lost, were widely publicized in the city or province in which they took place, and sometimes across the subcontinent, even reaching Britain.

"The main cause of the unpopularity of English rule" in India, the Radical *Westminster Review* argued in 1868, "the one most difficult to counteract, and at the same time the most extended in its operation, is the extreme antipathy which the English residents manifest for the people of the country." "Nigger talk," it complained, was ubiquitous among the lower class of European. "A 'nigger' is a thing to be beaten with a stick. A stick is to be valued according to its capacity for *beating* a nigger. The swarms of Europeans, again, who have been let loose upon the country, without any official control or sense of responsibility, to aid in the construction of railways and other public works, are perhaps the most powerful agents which could be devised for bringing the English name into utter discredit."[2] In a similar vein, an Indian newspaper later recalled that Sir Richard Temple, Lieutenant Governor of Bengal in the 1870s, used to say "that the greatest difficulty which the administrators of this country had to meet with was that involved in keeping their own countrymen under proper control, and that if the English were ever to lose India, it would be through the vanity and high-handed conduct of their own countrymen."[3] Most of this conduct, even when violent, was of a barely noticed everyday character: in 1892, an important visitor from

---

[2] "The Character of British Rule in India," *Westminster Review* 15 (Jan. and April 1868), 9–10.

[3] BL OIOC L/R/5/32 Pt. 1, p. 187: *Bangavasi*, 5 Mar. 1906.

England remarked disapprovingly to the Viceroy that he had seen in several hotels "printed notices requesting visitors not to beat the hotel servants."[4] Beyond quotidian blows were the serious instances of deaths resulting from individual violence. The specific issue of unpunished killing was highlighted in an Indian newspaper cartoon in 1878 (one of the "seditious" items cited within the Government as justifying a press censorship law) showing a European standing over a dead Indian while a European doctor gives a perfunctory exonerating post-mortem; the perpetrator is calmly smoking a cigar.[5] As the cartoon suggested, many cases of violent death at the hands of Europeans never even reached the criminal courts. For example, eighty-one shooting "accidents" by Europeans resulting in the deaths of Indians were recorded between 1880 and 1900.[6] Instances of nonfatal injury usually received even less attention from the authorities. Even in fatalities criminal trials were the exception, and such convictions as there were more often than not involved only fines.

India of course was the heart of the Empire, with a population larger than all the rest put together. The heart of India was Bengal, and its capital, Calcutta, the capital also of the Raj until 1911. Consequently, it was the most desirable posting, staffed with the most successful officials and Judges. What happened in Bengal was guaranteed the attention of the central Government of India. Similarly, Calcutta boasted the largest group of Indian lawyers and newspaper editors, and events in this city and province were likely to be more publicized than similar events elsewhere in India. For these reasons, our examination of the tensions of the "rule of law" in India will pay particular attention to Bengal. India was unlike other British possessions in more than size. It was neither a settlement colony nor a Crown colony, but in a political category of its own. From 1858 it had its own department in Whitehall, the India Office,

---

[4] Lord Radstock to Lansdowne, 18 June 1892. When he spoke about it to one of the Indian hotel keepers, the man replied, "'They all do it, and then they are surprised there is a mutiny.'" Radstock also reported a conversation with a young officer, who "seemed quite surprised when I told him coolies in the hills were not obliged to work for him. . . . I think many look on them as only serfs, whom they can order about as they like; and surely it would be well that this delusion should be once and for all dispelled" [BL OIOC M/3/103 (Lansdowne Papers)]. In the same year the Liberal M.P. Sir Harry Verney, long involved with Indian affairs, asked his friend W. W. Hunter "what gives the [Indian] press-writing against us so much power? The want of consideration on the part of our countrymen towards the natives" [letter, 15 Feb. 1892, quoted in Francis H. Shrine, *Life of Sir William Wilson Hunter* (London, 1901), p. 417].

[5] BL OIOC Lytton Papers, Mss Eur. E 218, 146.

[6] Sumit Sarkar, *Modern India, 1885–1927* (London, 1983), p. 22.

generally thought of as "rather superior in importance" to the Colonial Office.[7] Its chief administrator, the Viceroy, exercised unprecedentedly extensive powers (even if ultimately subordinate to the Secretary for India), and was drawn (unlike mere colonial Governors) from the ranks of major aristocratic politicians. British India also had its own civil service, more prestigious and more difficult to enter than ordinary colonial service.

India was also socially distinct from the rest of the Empire. In the late nineteenth century it held an enormous native population, several times the population of Britain itself, and in addition a comparatively large British military force – one-third of all Britons under arms – and a substantial "European" population of about 150,000, plus at least an equal number of mixed-race "Eurasians." It was a complex mix to rule. The non-official members of the British community in India, as William Gladstone privately lamented, were all too ready to "assume a superiority over their fellow-citizens and fellow-subjects" of the Crown.[8] At the same time, their assumption of superiority was tinged by an underlying fear: vastly outnumbered by natives, and keeping fresh memories and fantasies of the 1857 Rebellion, Europeans felt surrounded by an endless India, and were primed to react strongly to the merest hint of threat. This sense of insecurity was only enhanced by their self-segregation from Indians other than servants. As their numbers grew, Anglo-Indians developed a self-contained society of their own, which at every point of contact with Indians emphasized its difference. Even British soldiers were kept separate from the larger numbers of Indian soldiers, as well as from the civilian population. Yet separation increased ignorance, and ignorance fostered anxieties. As a consequence, even in the late-nineteenth-century heyday of British power on the subcontinent, when the Raj was at its peak of organization and prestige, without serious internal challenge, a sense of its precariousness was widespread among Europeans. Lord Roberts, the military commander, characteristically emphasized in 1884 "the smallness of the force we have at our disposal," and one inspector of police observed in 1894 that "in India we walk atop a slumbering volcano. The truth of it is now and again brought home to us with startling vividness,

---

[7] *Journal of John Wodehouse, First Earl of Kimberley*, ed. A. Hawkins and J. Powell (London, 1997), p. 334 (11 Dec. 1882).

[8] Letter to his son, Harry, 6–8 Feb. 1884, quoted in C. Brad Faught, "An Imperial Prime Minister? W. E. Gladstone and India, 1880–1885," *Journal of the Historical Society* 6 (2006), 573.

and an incident here or there reveals to us, for the moment, the glow of the molten mass under the crust upon which we walk so blithely."[9]

Among non-official Europeans perhaps even more, the sense of personal security depended on the maintenance of what was called "European prestige" – the confidence that Indians would unthinkingly obey European commands. Any challenge to this assumption was deeply threatening. Everyday face-to-face interaction was loaded with emotional freight, as deferential responses on the part of Indians became necessary for Europeans to feel at ease. The result was an almost pathological fear of native "insolence."[10] Such "sensitivity to the slightest hint of a challenge to their dignity or authority," as E. M. Collingham has pointed out, meant that Anglo-Indians "frequently met any act which suggested insolence with physical violence."[11] In this way, violence was embedded in the social structure of the Raj. This was especially true for British soldiers – armed and trained in violence – who became well-known for their dangerousness.

Even at its height, therefore, the Raj had its rooted tensions. And in the late nineteenth century two connected developments only intensified them. The first was a growing assertiveness by non-official Anglo-Indians, as their numbers grew, toward both native Indians and British officials. Against the latter, complaints about social snobbery and high-handedness (a development we have seen at this time in other colonies as well) were more frequently voiced. The erosion of deference to officials made its mark in India, as elsewhere, in criminal justice. Here the hardening sense of racial solidarity increased the willingness of Anglo-Indian jurors to ignore prosecution evidence and even judicial directions, making the treatment of European violence against non-Europeans more lenient.[12]

---

[9] Lord Roberts, quoted in Kaushik Roy, "Spare the Rod, Spoil the Soldier? Crime and Punishment in the Army of India, 1860–1913," *Journal of the Society for Army Historical Research* 84 (2006), 9; T.C. Arthur, *Reminiscences of an Indian Police Official* (London, 1894), p. v.

[10] Anglo-Indian sensitivity to any symbolic threats to European physical dominance continued well into the twentieth century: in 1910 the Governor of Madras urged the Viceroy to prohibit interracial showings of the "cinematographs" of a prize fight in which a Negro contender defeated his white opponent [Lawley to Lord Minto, 13 July 1910, quoted in Stephen Koss, *Morley at the India Office*, p. 126n].

[11] Collingham, op. cit.. A similar point was made by John Michael Compton, "British Government and Society in the Presidency of Bengal, c. 1858–1880," D.Phil. thesis, Oxford, 1968.

[12] See Raymond Cocks, "Social Roles and Legal Rights: Three Women in Early Nineteenth-Century India," *Journal of Legal History* 22 (2002), 77–106; Elizabeth Kolsky, "Codification and the Rule of Colonial Difference: Criminal Procedure in British India,"

However, following in the wake of this rise in Anglo-Indian assertion was a new collective consciousness among the elite minority of educated Indians, which began to produce its own novel assertiveness. In the later nineteenth century, such Indians were discovering that as British subjects they too were supposed to have rights, and learning from the example of the Anglo-Indian community methods of publicizing their grievances and demanding rectification. The growth of the Anglo-Indian press was followed by a much larger growth of an Indian press, in both English and vernacular languages.[13] Rapidly increasing numbers of Indian lawyers were similarly learning from British models.[14] The promises made after the suppression of the Rebellion of one law and equal opportunities for all began to be publicly invoked, and their ongoing non-fulfillment to be sharply criticized. This failure was made all the more visible for Indians by the fact that for legal relations between Indians themselves, which vastly outweighed in daily importance interracial legal relations, British rule had in fact had radical consequences. Where caste and other group distinctions had once largely determined legal relations, the Raj brought a new element of equality between man and man (and sometimes even between man and woman). This broad change only threw into sharper relief, for the urban and the educated minority who came into regular contact with Europeans, the lack of real legal equality between the races. The officials of the Raj thus found themselves confronted by two increasingly restive communities, white and native, whose demands regularly were at loggerheads; to satisfy one was to inflame the other. Efforts from above to move toward realizing some of the 1858 promises to Indians, most notably by Lord Ripon in the early 1880s, evoked fierce Anglo-Indian reaction, like the "white mutiny" that forced the amending of the 1883 Ilbert Bill, which had been conceived as a moderate measure

---

Law and History Review 23 (2005), 631–684; Jordanna Bailkin, "The Boot and the Spleen: When Was Murder Possible in British India?" *Comparative Studies in Society and History* 48 (2006), 462–493.

[13] Margarita Barns, The *Indian Press: A History of the Growth of Public Opinion in India (London*, 1930); Umesh Chaturvedi, "The Image of British Administration of Justice as Reflected in the Hindi Press in the Last Quarter of the Nineteenth Century," *Quarterly Review of Historical Studies* (Calcutta), 10 (1970), 202–208; Rajah Kanta Ray, *Social Conflict and Political Unrest in Bengal 1875–1927* (Delhi, 1984); Anindita Ghosh, *Power in Print: Popular Publishing and the Politics of Language and Culture in a Colonial Society, 1778–1905* (Oxford, 2006).

[14] This growth continued through our period. "Nowadays," Sir Lawrence Jenkins, newly appointed Chief Justice of the Calcutta High Court, remarked to his close friend Secretary for India John Morley in 1909, "India is crammed full of trained lawyers" [Jenkins to Morley, 3 June 1909, BL OIOC Mss Eur. D573/46 (Morley Collection)].

to open more judicial and administrative positions to qualified Indians. The possibility raised by the Bill of Indian magistrates deciding, without juries, the fate of European defendants was not to be allowed, and after many tumultuous public meetings and petitions, in which Magna Carta and the Glorious Revolution were frequently invoked, even the Viceroy was forced to retreat. Yet such backsliding came with a high price in Indian alienation, in this case the creation of the Indian National Congress. The criminal justice system in general hereafter became a political battleground, every case of interracial violence a tinderbox for official concerns, Anglo-Indian anxieties, and Indian grievances.

There were a large number of "players," direct and indirect, in these struggles. Of the greatest ultimate but usually the least immediate importance was Parliament and behind it, the British press and public. There was always a gap in outlook between the politically conscious public in Britain and the unofficial Anglo-Indian community, as there was for all nonwhite colonies.[15] However, until the twentieth century this gap made little difference to the governance of the Raj, as of other colonies, since little was known of these faraway places and few, beyond relatives and friends of those out there, cared a great deal. This was all the more true as the India Office in its first half-century viewed its chief task as shielding the Government of India from the ignorant meddling of Parliament or British pressure groups.[16] That Government itself similarly saw its duty as keeping potential scandals or embarrassments out of public view. Even a Viceroy like Lord Curzon, himself attacked for disregarding this duty by ordering collective punishment for army regiments whose violence against natives had escaped legal sanctioning, could describe to the Secretary of State for India in 1903 several cases of soldiers who had

---

[15] The gap is apparent in the minimal response evoked, despite the strong backing of *The Times*, by Anglo-Indian efforts to mobilize home public opinion in their support on the Ilbert Bill [Edwin Hirschmann, *"White Mutiny": The Ilbert Bill Crisis in India and the Genesis of the Indian National Congress* (New Delhi, 1980)].

[16] Godley wrote in his memoirs that, starting as a Gladstonian, he had learned "humility" in dealing with India: "The difference between the East and the West is profound and all-pervading. . . . My experience leads me to say that no opinion about Indian administration is worth the paper on which it is written, except in so far as it is, directly or indirectly, founded upon and supported by the opinions of those Englishmen who have spent the best years of their life in actual contact with the people of that country" [Lord Kilbracken (Sir Arthur Godley), *Reminiscences*, op. cit., p. 185]. As he remarked to a member of the Council of India in 1904, "most of us, who are concerned with the Government of India, have a wholesome dread of the interference of the House of Commons" [quoted in Kaminsky, op. cit., p. 105]. Oddly, given this belief, he himself never visited India.

killed natives either accidentally or in an unclear dispute and noting that "none of these cases are known to the public. They are more or less successfully kept out of the newspapers, and no one, except at head-quarters, where of course the soldiers never say a word about the subject, has any knowledge of the state of things that goes on from one end of India to the other, and of the terrible injustice that prevails."[17]

Yet Curzon's viceroyalty marked a significant change in this policy of scandal control, and the appointment in 1906 of an assertive and reformist Liberal Secretary for India was to push this change further. Meanwhile, the British public's awareness of Indian affairs grew, slowly at first and then with mounting speed, in the years leading up to the First World War. The development of the telegraph had led to the creation of international news agencies, led by Reuters in 1870, and from then on the coverage of Indian news in British papers steadily increased. Indian papers eventually began to attempt to influence British public opinion: the number of Indian papers with London offices grew from eight in 1901 to forty-seven in 1914, and a rising proportion of these were Indian-owned.[18] The Liberal electoral victory in 1906 sharply increased the number of Members interested in the colonial government of non-Europeans, and bolstered that body with a number of reform-minded former Indian Civil Servants, who could ask knowledgeable and pene-trating questions of Ministers.

The Government of India, created after the 1857 Rebellion led to the dissolution of the East India Company, was by 1900 made up of a few dozen High Court Judges, just over a thousand members of the Indian Civil Service, a couple thousand members of the Imperial Police Service, of markedly lower status than the ICS men or the Judges, and several hundred thousand Indian clerks, policemen, and other lower

[17] Curzon to Hamilton, 29 Jan. 1903 [BL OIOC (Curzon Papers)]. Later that year he wrote in a similar vein to the Lieutenant Governor of Bengal: "Consideration for the good name of the British in India," he observed, prevented the Indian government from "making such a statement of the real facts – as regards outrages, collisions, verdicts of juries, and the administration of justice between European and Native – as will make every Englishman in the country hang his head with shame. . . . During all this time [that he had been Viceroy] I have never dared to let the real facts be known – either about the ninth lancers' case or about these cases in general – from the national discredit that they would involve" [Curzon to Bourdillon, 20 Sept. 1903, Mss Eur. F. 111.208, no. 71 (Curzon Papers)].

[18] Chandrika Kaul, *Reporting the Raj: The British Press and India c. 1880–1922* (Manchester, 2003). To ward off this danger, the Government of India stepped up its efforts to cultivate the British press.

officials.[19] In accordance with British constitutional precept, District Police Superintendents were subordinate to the District Magistrates of the ICS, just as the highest police official in each province, the Inspector-General of Police, answered directly to the Governor or Lieutenant Governor.[20] Thus it is not surprising that they were less desirable positions, paying somewhat less and drawn from Europeans with less education and generally from a lower social background than the members of the ICS. In the early decades especially, and in sharp contrast to the ICS, many Indian Police Service men had grown up in India. At this time entrance to the IPS was chiefly through personal connections; even after examinations to be taken in England were instituted in 1893, these were less demanding than those which had been created a generation earlier for the ICS, and sometimes ICS exam-takers who failed to win admittance instead were accepted into the Police Service. An early historian of the Indian police described the typical European recruit as an "amiable detrimental, the younger son, or the sporting public schoolboy, too lazy or too stupid for the Army, but prepared to go anywhere or do anything which did not involve prolonged drudgery."[21] This may not have been quite fair; it would appear that after 1893 at least, the ability of new recruits rose substantially.[22] Still, this difference was reinforced, David Campion has suggested, by "a siege mentality that had been hammered into the British mind following the carnage of 1857. . . . [T]he police were the sentinels on the wall, the guardians at the gate, the buffer that helped preserve the physical and psychological insularity of the British ruling class in their cantonments, clubs, and hill stations. The police interacted with the local population on a daily basis and, marked by the stain of their profession, they occupied a distinctly lower social and economic place in Anglo-Indian

---

[19] For example, in the North-Western Provinces and Oudh in 1887, 58 British police officials supervised 22,000 policemen of varying ranks (almost all of the latter were Indian, except a small number of Eurasians, given the title of "reserve inspectors," whose remit was to deal with Europeans) [David Campion, "Watchmen of the Raj: The United Provinces Police, 1870–1931 and the Dilemmas of Colonial Policing in British India," Ph.D. diss., University of Virginia 2002, pp. 42–44].

[20] District Magistrates were also known as "District Officer" or "Collector." In some provinces the chief administrator's title was Governor, in others Lieutenant-Governor. Although the DSP was formally subordinate to the DM, Campion has noted that "the precise division of their responsibilities was never fully delineated, either on paper or in reality, and their overlapping job descriptions often created tension" [Campion, op. cit., p. 39].

[21] J.C. Curry, *The Indian Police* (London, 1931), p. 55.

[22] Campion, op. cit., p. 79.

society."[23] On the other hand, in contrast to the educated gentlemen of the ICS, the IPS men felt themselves to be more in contact with the gritty realities of crime and punishment and the practical challenges of maintaining order and British authority. Such sentiments often led them to be less than vigorous in impressing upon their men what magistrates and Judges considered proper respect for judicial due process, leading to a good deal of friction between the two. Both their family backgrounds and their daily routines inclined IPS men to sympathize much more than did the ICS with businessmen, planters, and other Anglo-Indians, and to share the Anglo-Indian touchiness about condescension from the "heaven-born" men of the ICS.[24]

On the other hand, the judiciary, drawn both from the ICS and from the English and Indian bar, tended to differ from the ICS in the opposite way, even more committed to high ideals (in this case the law and the principles of the English Constitution) and even less acquainted with the hardening day-to-day realities of ruling another people in disregard of their wishes. In India, as elsewhere in the Empire, the law was very much a part of the governmental machine. At the lower levels, it was usually the same person, the District Magistrate, who both administered and judged (very much like the English Justice of the Peace of a century earlier). And even at the highest level, where a clear separation of functions existed, Judges in India could never forget that they were an integral part of an alien administration, whose writ rested ultimately upon military force. Yet even those Judges who were ICS members were not necessarily representative of their Service, for they had been earlier separated from their fellows by the choice of a judicial career path, and over time developed a distinct *esprit de corps*. The position of the higher judiciary in India had its ambiguities. Like other colonial Judges, High Court Judges in India served not for life but only "during good behavior" and were transferable and even dismissible by the India Office (although, as elsewhere in the Empire, the judiciary's prestige ensured that the latter action was an

---

[23] "Their social and educational background," Campion continued, "combined with their marginal earning prospects, made them 'small beer' in the Anglo-Indian marriage market. This effectively excluded them from the high-class social circles filled by the Oxbridge educated civil servants, magistrates, and their wives." In line with this lower status, the European police "were disproportionately drawn from Britain's Celtic periphery as Scotsmen and Irish Catholics filled their ranks" [pp. 97–98].

[24] All the more as they became targets of the scorn of often better-educated Indian lawyers, editors, and politicians. See also Louis Tracy, *Meeting the Sun: Some Anglo-Indian Snapshots* (Allahabad, 1898), p. 76, recounting an engineer's complaints of the large gap in pay and pension between the covenanted and uncovenanted Service (which included police officers).

unusual one, not lightly to be undertaken). Yet, also as elsewhere, the nature of their work often brought them into conflict with the Executive, to the endangerment of their reputation among Europeans but its enhancement among Indians.[25] As a result of the High Court's ability to overrule District Magistrates and Sessions Judges and sometimes even higher executive officials, an ability exercised with greater frequency in Bengal than elsewhere, William Hunter observed in 1888 that "the manner in which [the High Court of Calcutta] discharges its duties has caused it to be regarded with veneration by the people of India as the noblest manifestation of British justice."[26] Such veneration was not much reciprocated: Justice C. D. Field of the Calcutta High Court spoke for many of his colleagues when he observed in 1883 that most Indians "do not make a habit of speaking the truth."[27]

Another major player in India was the British Army. As a legacy of the Rebellion, it was unusually large: in the late nineteenth century over a third of all active-duty British soldiers, about seventy-five thousand, were stationed in India.[28] After economic prosperity at home had forced the Government in 1870 to shorten the term of enlistment, their average age steadily fell; by the 1890s more than half of the "other ranks" were under the age of twenty-five.[29] This change – combined with the

[25] This tension emerged almost at the start of British rule, with the establishment of a Supreme Court for Bengal in 1774. By 1781 British inhabitants of Calcutta were collectively petitioning Parliament for relief from the expenses, confusion, and rulings of the Court; among these "oppressive" rulings were some penalizing them for using corporal punishment on their Indian servants and workers. When officials also complained of judicial interference, Parliament soon cut back the Court's authority [see Robert Travers, *Ideology and Empire in Eighteenth-Century India: The British in Bengal* (Cambridge, 2007)]. This sort of tension remained as a potential, however, leaping to the forefront at moments of political crisis.

[26] In support of Hunter's claim one might note that a couple of years before he made it, a Bengali newspaper observed that "it is from the High Court that natives expect most help against their ill-treatment by Anglo-Indians" [*Ananda Bazar Patrika*, 3 Aug. 1885 (all citations from Indian newspapers are taken from the weekly *Reports on Native Newspapers*, BL OIOC L/R/5; all newspapers are located in Bengal unless otherwise noted)].

[27] Hirschmann, op. cit., p. 122.

[28] Andrew Porter, *Atlas of British Overseas Expansion* (London, 1994), pp. 118–121; J. K. Dunlop, *The Development of the British Army 1899–1914* (London, 1938), Appendix C.

[29] Those under twenty-five "increased from 33% of the British Army in India in 1877 to 55% by 1898," Mark Harrison has pointed out [*Public Health in British India: Anglo-Indian Preventive Medicine, 1859–1914* (Cambridge, 1994), p. 63]; see also Philippa Levine, *Prostitution, Race and Politics: Policing Venereal Disease in the British Empire* (London, 2003), p. 273.

continuing non-provision for married enlisted men bringing their wives with them overseas – was inevitably going to present disciplinary problems. By the time of the O'Hara case, youth, singleness, and boredom had nurtured frequent drunkenness and outbursts of violence, with Lord Roberts and others bemoaning the absence of older soldiers to exercise a restraining influence on younger ones.[30] Thus, a substantial body of European troops, which was felt necessary to underpin the rule of law, was at the same time a permanent threat to it. Soldiers were a perennial source of disorder, and in particular of violence directed at Indians. Out of the 199 cases of Europeans attacking natives formally reported in 1901, 146 were committed by members of the army.[31] Class and ethnic prejudice reinforced the concerns of civilian officials: European soldiers were drawn from the lower classes at home, and a disproportionate (if diminishing) number of them were Irish, like O'Hara.[32] Such men were not unlikely back in the U.K. to become criminal problems; in India, their behavior created political problems. Among soldiers, treated with little respect by their white superiors, the racism common to Europeans in India was present in an exaggerated form, enhanced by a sense of corporate solidarity, and not offset by the restraints of civilian or official life. Like Kipling's 1887 imaginative creation, Terence Mulvaney, many of them were, as one critic has put it, "pugnacious, lecherous, sentimental, often drunk."[33] They generally found India, despite its heat and diseases, "undoubtedly the best country for 'soldiering' in," as one observer noted in 1899, because of the position their nationality gave them. "The humblest trooper," this observer explained, "is a white sahib. Obsequious natives wait on him hand and foot" – an experience sharply contrasting with

[30] Roy, op. cit., p. 13.

[31] Collingham, op. cit., p. 143; BL OIOC L/P&J/6/781, File 3445: "Return Showing the Number of Assaults Committed by Europeans on Natives, and by Natives on Europeans in the Five Years 1901–1905." Wacha complained to Naoroji on 30 Oct. 1891 that "European murders of Natives are daily on the increase. *Soldiers* chiefly are the brutal offenders. . . . [They are] always acquitted on some plea or another" [Sumit Sarkar, op. cit., p. 22].

[32] Edward M. Spiers, *The Late Victorian Army, 1868–1902*, p. 131: In 1830 Ireland and Scotland provided over half the noncommissioned officers and men in the British Army, although the Irish proportion fell to 28% in 1870 and to 13% by 1898.

[33] Terence Denman, "'Ethnic Soldiers Pure and Simple'? The Irish in the Late Victorian Army," *War in History* 3 (1996), 253–273. *The Times* editorialized about Mulvaney as early as March 1890 (coincidentally, just when O'Hara was being tried). It found him "a truly attaching creature from his strength and his little weaknesses" [*The Times*, 25 Mar. 1890].

their life back home.[34] Having grown up forced to obey the commands of others, they were hardly prepared to exercise their race-given power tactfully. When deference from natives was slow in coming, they might react explosively. Armed, not infrequently drunk (despite official efforts to restrict sales of liquor), and often on the prowl for sex, they were a growing menace to public security and to political relations with the vast Indian population, without whose acquiescence British rule could hardly be sustained.[35]

If many British soldiers posed a political challenge to the legitimacy of the Raj's rule of law, so too did many non-military and non-official Europeans. The Anglo-Indian community reached its numerical peak of about 170,000 in 1900, and it had its own interests not necessarily in harmony with that of British officials and Judges or for that matter Whitehall or Westminster.[36] This community's political strength was mounting with its numbers, aided by the Home Government's comparative lack of interest in India in these years. It spanned a wide social range, from affluent businessmen and professionals down to the disreputable semi- or unemployed. Among the latter, some of them former soldiers or seamen, were many who were violence-prone and a challenge both to law and order and to racial hierarchy. As early as 1863, an Indian paper could turn back the rhetoric of the civilizing mission upon the ruling race: "the lower class of Europeans," observed the *Hindu Patriot*, "ought to be taught their moral and religious obligations."[37] They were a constant source of worry to the Government of India, which passed various measures to regulate their behavior and encourage their departure from India.[38] While the official might deplore the conduct of the vulgar Britons, Francis Hutchins pointed out that "he was trapped by the realization that

[34] Horace Wyndham, *The Queen's Service; or the Real 'Tommy Atkins'* (London, 1899), p. 118.
[35] Even the Prince of Wales (and future King Edward VII), during his visit in 1875–1876, had complained of the "rough and ready manner" in which soldiers treated the Queen's Indian subjects, especially the habit of referring to them as "niggers" [Bryan Farewell, *Armies of the Raj: From Mutiny to Independence* (London, 1989), p. 59]. [See Spiers, op. cit., on the low public opinion of soldiers and consequent difficulties in recruiting; see also the discussion in Compton, op. cit.]
[36] Francis Hutchins, *The Illusion of Permanence: British Imperialism in India* (Princeton, 1967), p. 111; on this society, see Dane Kennedy, *The Magic Mountains: Hill Stations and the British Raj* (Berkeley, 1996).
[37] *Hindu Patriot* [Calcutta], 18 May 1863.
[38] See Kenneth Ballhatchet, *Race, Sex and Class Under the Raj: Imperial Attitudes and Policies and Their Critics, 1793–1905* (New York, 1980); Damayanti Datta, "The Europeans of Calcutta, 1858–1883," Ph.D. thesis, Cambridge, 1995.

if he sacrificed the vulgar specimens among his countrymen by holding them up to ridicule, he was jeopardizing his own position," which ultimately rested on the kind of race "prestige" the vulgar Britons were fond of invoking. Nor was it only the bottom of Anglo-Indian society that could be a problem. It was a society at all levels more male, more youthful, and more violent than Britain itself (where these years saw a marked and prolonged decline in interpersonal violence). A trial of one newspaper owner for a serious assault on an officer just a month after O'Hara's murder trial revealed socially respectable Englishmen in India resorting to physical force against each other a good deal more readily than such persons would have at home.[39]

One form of European business was especially likely to create situations of interracial violence – planting. Plantations of first indigo and then tea, rapidly expanding in the later nineteenth century to meet growing European and American demand, were located in relatively sparsely populated highland areas of Assam, in the interior of Bengal province, distant from the cities of Calcutta or Dacca. By 1890 there were approximately seven hundred British tea-planters in Assam, who, together with another hundred or so indigo planters and their agents in Calcutta, formed a social world of their own.[40] These planters exercised a great deal of control over their workers, most of whom were recruited elsewhere on contracts of indenture. As a sympathetic English visitor, George Barker, observed in 1887, coolies were "lazy and required a lot of looking after." Assam, he approvingly noted, was "the last remaining district where any sort of respect is shown for the Europeans; in all other parts of India the black man is as good as the white, a fact that is speedily brought home to the newcomer. It is here, in Assam, that nearly all the old rights of servility that were exacted by Europeans in the days of the East India Company are still in existence, and flourish to the general better feeling amongst the whole community. Here no heavy *babu* swaggers past with his umbrella up, jostling you on the way, but with courtly mien, on seeing

[39] *Navavibhakar Sadharani*, 24 Feb. 1890: the defendant was Managing Proprietor of the *Pioneer*; he attacked a Capt. Hearsey, was found guilty, and fined.

[40] Tea production in Assam grew from 6 million to 75 million lbs. from 1872 to 1900 [Rana P. Behal, "Power Structure, Discipline, and Labour in Assam Tea Plantations Under Colonial Rule," *International Review of Social History* 51 (2006), 143]. A useful comparative study of plantation indenture is Prabhu P. Mohapatra, "Assam and the West Indies, 1860–1920: Immobilizing Plantation Labor," in *Masters, Servants, and Magistrates in Britain and the Empire*, ed. Douglas Hay and Paul Craven (Chapel Hill and London, 2004), pp. 455–480.

your pony coming along, furls up the umbrella, steps on one side, and salutes with a profound *salaam*."[41] Barker's satisfied view was, however, only one face of British opinion on proper relations between Europeans and Indians. The same year his book appeared, William Stobie critically described for the readers of the influential *Fortnightly Review* a recent unpunished death by gross mistreatment of an indigo plantation coolie.[42]

Even under these conditions, Assam planters, most of whom were either salaried managers or small capitalists dependent upon borrowed money, did not feel secure economically, particularly as in the 1890s the world price of tea entered a long decline. Thereafter, tea planting ceased to be, from the vantage point of the metropole, a very enriching occupation. A 1904 letter from a nephew of Henry Gladstone, a partner in a Calcutta managing agency and one of the Victorian statesman's sons, to his uncle brings that out well:

I failed [William Wickham wrote] to get a scholarship at Winchester . . . failed to get a scholarship at Oxford. Got a second in Mods and a third in Greats. Failed twice for the civil service and after being taken into business got kicked out. *It looks as though roughing it in Canada or that hope of the destitute and the failure tea planting, ought to be the last resort*. . . . I don't feel much like going straight into politics as you suggest. Is Egypt any use or is that too full up?[43]

After the early boom years had passed, these enterprises faced large obstacles, ranging from uncertain property tenure to primitive transport facilities to a reluctant and often-hostile labor force, all in a context of an ever more competitive world market, as new areas of tea cultivation were opened around the world.[44] As a result, planters continued to expand production to maintain their income while doing everything they could to hold down costs; in the absence of any major technical breakthroughs, this largely meant pressing down on their laborers as far as they could get away with, not only in terms of wages but also in the conditions of work. The period from the 1880s to the end of the century saw labor

---

[41] George Barker, *A Tea Planter's Life in Assam* (Calcutta, 1887), p. 138.

[42] "An Incident of Real Life in Bengal," *Fortnightly Review* 42 N.S. (1887), 329–341. There was a police inquiry, but a rather perfunctory one which found no reason to bring any charges.

[43] 30 Mar. 1904, quoted in Maria Misra, *Business, Race and Politics in British India c. 1850–1960* (Oxford, 1999), p. 49 [my italics].

[44] Most pressing was competition from the British colony of Ceylon, where tea cultivation rose from a mere 14,000 acres in 1880 to 235,000 acres in 1890 [Roland Wenzlhuemer, "Indian Labour Immigration and British Labour Policy in Nineteenth-Century Ceylon," *Modern Asian Studies* 41 (2007), 575–602]. See also Ananda Ramamurthy, *Imperial Persuaders: Images of Africa and Asia in British Advertising* (Manchester, 2003).

exploitation mount to a peak, and thus not surprisingly also saw an increase in Indian criticism and Government concern, and a consequent heightening of tensions between planters and higher officials.

Far from Calcutta, planters felt increasingly vulnerable not only financially but also physically. A peasant uprising in 1891, followed by a wave of robberies in 1892, caused widespread panic among the isolated tea "gardens." Their organization, the Indian Tea Association, pressed for additional Government security measures, but were rebuffed, the Chief Commissioner telling them that if planters established tea gardens in volatile border areas they did so at their own risk.[45] Such official inaction only added to planters' anxieties. The leading Anglo-Indian newspaper in Bengal, the *Englishman*, rather hysterically reported in 1893, in striking contrast to Barker's comforting picture just a few years before, that in Assam "Europeans are insulted, abused and jeered at by the lowest type of natives and if they retaliate, they are set upon by a mob."[46] Even if their own push for ever-greater control and productivity was helping provoke such outbursts from below, they nonetheless only intensified the pressure planters felt to maintain their authority over their workers. The legal powers they had been granted to maintain day-to-day control of their workers, including the private power of arrest, although far greater than would be legal in Britain, were in their own eyes never adequate.[47] They saw themselves not as the tyrannical individuals making their own law that Indian critics complained of, but as often-beleaguered private agents of the larger British authority, taking on the burden of acting where that authority reached only fragilely, having often to ignore the unrealistic letter of the law in order to uphold its spirit.

These various groups of official and non-official Europeans made the system of criminal justice, itself one of the reasons for Britons' pride in their Empire and specifically in their Indian Raj, into an arena for carrying on their struggles for their interests and for their values. Such struggles naturally involved the large native population in which they were immersed, and who had their own interests and values. Indeed it was in the adjudication of crimes between Europeans and Indians that all these struggles were most fully developed, and consequently most illuminating

---

[45] Raymond K. Renford, *The Non-Official British in India to 1920* (Delhi, 1987), p. 68.
[46] Cited in Ray, op. cit., p. 28.
[47] Louis Tracy sympathetically quoted one Colonel on Indians: "once slacken authority, give them the chance of loot, invite them to participate in a general upsetting of all law and order, and the spots of the leopard jolly soon show through" [Tracy, op. cit., p. 111].

legal system = arena for
struggles among racial groups

of the inner tensions of Empire. The vastness of India's population in relation to the numbers of Britons made collaboration essential to British rule. It has often been noted that the Raj was for the most part run by Indians, and only supervised by Britons. The terms of the bargain, as Anil Seal has put it, was that District Commissioners (or, as they were also called, Collectors) "could depend on the collection of revenue, provided they did not ask too officiously who paid it," and "they might take public order for granted, provided that they themselves did not play too obtrusive a part in enforcing it."[48] The educated Indian clerks, magistrates, lawyers, and other professionals administering the Raj, along with their peers in business, made up, particularly in Bengal, a growing class of "Europeanized" Indians who increasingly sought to make use of British law and Government to advance their own aims, and those, as they saw them, of their countrymen. Rather than rejecting the Raj as simply an alien imposition, the rising Indian educated and business classes sought for many years to work within it, to make use of its promises and its potential; it was well into the twentieth century before these groups went over to outright opposition to British rule. Yet, of course, along with large hopes their daily experiences were "fraught with a great deal of humiliation and frustrations."[49] Such contradictions led them to place increasing pressure upon the Raj.

In their administration of the law, high British officials in India found themselves by the last decade of the nineteenth century caught between two intensifying political pressures – one from many of the leading natives, and the other from most of their fellow Europeans. By the 1890s, the spread of the Indian press was giving significant or sensational criminal trials a public in the millions: as one vernacular paper claimed in 1893, "newspapers now go everywhere. . . . [E]ven peasants and labourers talk of and criticize criminal trials."[50] The newspapers themselves gave the lead to such criticism. "In their efforts to capture a circulation, and with it a revenue from advertisers," Anil Seal has pointed

---

[48] "Imperialism and Nationalism in India," in *Locality, Province and Nation: Essays on Indian Politics 1870 to 1940*, ed. John Gallagher, Gordon Johnson, and Anil Seal (Cambridge, 1973), p. 8.

[49] Tapa Raychaudhuri, *Perceptions, Emotions, Sensibilities: Essays on India's Colonial and Post-Colonial Experiences* (Delhi, 1999), p. 19: "Indian national consciousness developed initially alongside a great enthusiasm for British rule in India. The colonial projection that the British conquest was the best thing that had ever happened to India was widely accepted until the 1890s."

[50] *Sahachar*, 8 Nov. 1893.

out, "editors soon found that exaggerated attacks on government, the reporting of incidents with overtones of racial injustice, were what their readers wanted."[51] The English-language *Hindoo Patriot* denounced as early as 1876, during the first widely publicized case since the repression of the Rebellion of a European's killing of an Indian, "the violence which the rampant Anglo-Saxon in this country every now and then uses towards the weak native."[52] This case of Robert Fuller, an English pleader at Agra, who was merely fined a small amount for the killing of his servant, and whose case was referred to the Allahabad High Court, which increased the fine but did no more, led to what the Viscount, Lord Dufferin, called a "foul torrent of abuse" in the new native-owned press.[53] This torrent led the Government to pass in 1878 a measure to censor the Indian press, but it was repealed three years later; press censorship did not return to India until 1908, after a wave of bombings and assassinations had created a new situation. In the interim of comparative press freedom from 1881 to 1908 the "Native Press," in the words of one Lieutenant Governor of Bengal, grew "year by year more reckless in its mode of writing about the Government, Government officers, and Government measures."[54] A characteristic assertion was, as the great writer Rabindranath Tagore claimed in a Bengali paper in 1904, that "no British murderer [of an Indian] had ever been sentenced to capital punishment by an English judge or jury."[55] Although strictly speaking this was false – a good number had indeed been so sentenced, and many of them hanged, during the previous century – it could seem true to his readers, for the last such sentence had been a quarter century before, in 1880. There was no question, as we shall see, that in this realm justice was far from equal.

While the administration of justice could set Indians and Europeans at odds, it also brought tensions among Europeans to the surface. The civilian and military establishments did not necessarily agree in this sphere. Already divided by clashing value systems that led Civilians to look down their noses at unintelligent military officers, and officers to despise effete Civilians, the two groups could easily be set at odds by the misbehavior of soldiers like O'Hara. The soldiers' superiors resisted their surrender to civilian authority. Except for felonies committed within 120

---

[51] *The Emergence of Indian Nationalism* (Cambridge, 1968), p. 143.

[52] 3 Apr. 1876: "The Saheb and the Nigger."

[53] Dufferin to Kimberley, 17 May 1886: BL OIOC Dufferin Papers 19 (reel 517). See also Uma Dasgupta, *The Rise of an Indian Public* (Calcutta, 1977), pp. 255–259.

[54] Sir Alexander Mackenzie, quoted in Barns, op. cit., p. 304.

[55] Sumit Sarkar, op. cit., pp. 190–191.

miles of a Presidency town (Calcutta, Bombay, or Madras), the accepted practice was for soldiers to be tried by courts-martial. Such military courts could be severe: In 1868, for instance, a corporal and a private were found guilty by court-martial of striking and wounding a Bengali from whom they stole nearly Rs. 2,000. The corporal was given five years' penal servitude, the private four years'.[56] More frequently, however, out of concern for morale in the ranks, military authorities would overlook instances of abuse, even killings, of Indians that had not become public issues.[57] Clashes with civilian authority over such cases were not uncommon: outside these towns, magistrates retained the right to take up any unfelonious case at their discretion, and sometimes did. In 1869 one Private Flynn knocked out a Government *chaprassi* (native assistant to an official) and was convicted of assault and fined by the Justice of the Peace at Landour, who ordered the recalcitrant commanding officer to imprison him unless the fine was paid. The Commander-in-Chief of Bengal appealed to the provincial Government, asking that, whatever the strictly

---

[56] Compton, op. cit., p. 248.

[57] A revealing example was given by Frank Richards in his memoirs of service as a private in India at the turn of the century. He recalled "a certain married sergeant of thirteen or fourteen years' service who, one day . . . went out for a gharri-ride and brought it to a sudden stop by shooting the gharri driver dead with a revolver. The affair caused a mild sensation. The Sergeant always carried this revolver about with him, but had never threatened anyone with it or shown any murderous inclinations. He was a reserved man and respected by all ranks. Nor could anyone come forward, when the case was being inquired into, and give any evidence that the heat had been causing him to behave queerly of late. But the Commanding Officer allowed him the benefit of the doubt and had him confined in a small padded cell in hospital, where he was kept under observation. The gharri wallah's widow came to the hospital to get justice done her. They explained to her there that the man who had shot her husband was a madman and that nothing could be done, except perhaps to give her compensation. They gave her ten rupees, which was a matter of thirteen shillings, and it is said that she went away well satisfied and smiling. We never discovered whether this compensation came out of the Sergeant's pocket or out of the Canteen funds. In any case, the excitement had completely died down a day or two later when the Sergeant officially recovered his reason, left the padded cell for the convalescent ward, and was soon afterwards invalided home to England with his wife and children. The truth never came out. . . . The general opinion was that the Sergeant's nerves were in a bad state after the heat of the summer and that the gharri wallah must have demanded more money for the ride than what it was worth and given the Sergeant cheek when he refused; and that, with a revolver in his belt, the temptation to make a stern example of this cheeky gharri wallah to warn all cheeky gharri wallahs of the future proved too much for the Sergeant – he drew the revolver and ended the argument. So it was reckoned a good deed; for, as I have said, the Sergeant was not known as a bully or an unjust man, but was respected by all; and the gharri-drivers of Agra were certainly the limit" [*Old Soldier Sahib* (London, 1936), pp. 213–214].

legal position was, magistrates be instructed to conform to the "usual practice" of regarding breaches of the peace committed by soldiers as prejudicial to military discipline and hence matters for commanding officers or courts-martial. While the Government rejected this appeal, it was clear from the replies of senior officials that they believed punishment by commanding officers to be best, in part because of the lack of non-military prisons "suitable for Europeans."[58]

A greater tension than that between the civilian and military branches of Government was the tension between the Government itself, in particular the Indian Civil Service, and the body of non-official Europeans in India. Toward the latter, the Civilians displayed a combination of class snobbery and moral condescension. In India, Civilians constituted a social and moral aristocracy. Crucial to the self-image of civil servants was a view of themselves as acting without personal interest, seeking the larger interests of the Indian population. Their low opinion of their fellow countrymen in India for commercial reasons, to trade, bank, or plant, was reinforced by their own social origins: coming very disproportionately from clerical and other professional backgrounds, they regarded Anglo-Indian businessmen as a social cut below themselves. The genuinely aristocratic Viceroy, Lord Mayo, spoke for his subordinates more broadly when he remarked disdainfully but privately in 1870 that, unlike civil servants, these mere "birds of passage" had simply come to India "to get as much money out of the Blacks as they can, and . . . go home as soon as possible."[59] The almost-violent Anglo-Indian reaction in 1883 against the Ilbert Bill showed how sensitive most of the white inhabitants of India were to the dangers of a system of justice that might place some of them in the power of Indians. This revolt depressed A. C. Lyall, Lieutenant Governor of the North West Provinces, who wrote to his friend James Fitzjames Stephen, back in England on the High Court, that "what I mainly fear is that the violent abuse and unrestrained arrogance of the Anglo-Indian, who is now fairly on rampage, shall end by seriously provoking the Natives. . . . The political veil which the Government has always thrown over the delicate relations between the two races is rudely rent in twain, and we have a mob shaking their fists in the face of the whole Native population, and behaving in print exactly like a mob."[60]

[58] Compton, p. 69.
[59] Mayo to Argyll, 9 Nov. 1870, BL OIOC (Mayo Papers 41).
[60] Quoted in Hirschmann, op. cit. p. 102.

Anglo-Indians, for their part, bitterly resented such official characterizations of them as selfish, arrogant, and easily roused to violence. Like
Australian and Fiji settlers, they saw themselves quite differently, as
contributing to both the greatness of Britain and the well-being of natives
by "developing the resources of the country" and in so doing helping to
spread progress and civilization. They expected support, not criticism,
from British officials. One group of Anglo-Indians in particular, as we
have noted, was prone to clash with both Indians and officials – planters.
What civil servants saw as planters exceeding the bounds of the authority
granted them, they saw as necessary efforts to preserve the order without
which their enterprises could not be carried on, and the ultimate universal
benefits of "developing the resources of the country" realized. As George
Barker had told his readers, "the planters have had but little recognition
of the great work that they are performing for the State."[61] When, rather
than recognition, they received from officials only criticism and fresh
regulations restricting their existing powers, they felt genuinely aggrieved.
As one bit of verse widely quoted by planters had it,

> Now if a native's only charged with any serious crime,
> Do all you can to let *him* off, at most with a simple fine.
> But the white man must be sent to jail, for that's the modern mode
> In which our magistrates now-a-days read "The Indian Penal Code."[62]

However inaccurate as an account of the actual workings of criminal
justice in India – and it was inaccurate – such verse tells much about how
planters saw it.

As tea planting became a major economic activity in the later years of
the century, the expanding Indian press began to highlight the abusive
treatment of plantation workers. Exploitative labor contracts and
sometimes-brutal discipline on plantations led to growing numbers of
incidents of "desertion," riot, and assault, now likely to be publicized by
both Indian and Anglo-Indian newspapers. Officials (pressed in opposing
ways by planters and educated Indians) found themselves increasingly
drawn into the controversies on these cases. Plantation managers, Lord
Curzon privately complained in 1903, "are drawn from a most inferior

---

[61] He continued: "it is now high time that the Indian Government took to heart the fact that
they should do everything in their power to assist planters in their undertaking, instead
of, as at present, hindering by many absurdly vexatious regulations their enterprise, or
taking no notice of their repeated efforts to obtain redress for existing grievances"
[Barker, op. cit., p. 230].

[62] *Tirhoot Rhymes. By 'Maori'* (Calcutta, 1873), pp. 45–47 [quoted in Bailkin, op. cit.].

class of Englishmen and Scotchmen; they do not know the language; they have a profound contempt for the Native, and they are sometimes guilty of serious acts of lust and oppression."[63] Measures passed in 1889 and 1893 made a modest difference in ameliorating the condition of laborers, but the opposition of planters, who could now point to growing pressure from world competition, blocked more thoroughgoing reform. Government officials could never forget that colonies, India included, needed at least to pay their own way. After the turn of the century, however, new officials returned to the issue, and, at the price of sharpened conflict with planters, pushed through larger changes that even native critics acknowledged markedly improved the situation of "coolies."[64]

This is not to say that the relations between government officials and planters were always hostile. Indeed, at the local level they were often quite friendly. The longer magistrates and Police Superintendents stayed in a posting, the more they would be co-opted into planter society; planters, after all, were usually the only other white men in the district. Local officials in Assam thus frequently came to share the planters' sense of isolation amid the large native population.[65] These men – especially the police officials, but often also the magistrates – tended to sympathize with the difficulties that planters encountered in dealing with Indians. In such situations, the line of division when a controversial crime occurred would fall between these planters and local officials, on the one hand, and the higher officials in the Bengal Government or, indeed, the Government of India, particularly the judicial officials, on the other.

The most important tension within the Raj for the operation of criminal justice was that between the executive and judicial branches of Government. "There are few Indian Provinces," Michael O'Dwyer, a tough Anglo-Irishman who was Lieutenant Governor of the Punjab between 1912 and 1919, observed in his memoirs, "which have not at one time or another been disturbed by friction between the Executive and the Judiciary."[66] Many executive officials expressed, privately at the time and

---

[63] Curzon to Hamilton, 5 Aug. 1903, BL OIOC Mss Eur. F 111/156 (Curzon Papers).

[64] See Chapter 6.

[65] As an "Ex-Civilian" noted in 1878, "Planters . . . made the district much more pleasant for the European official when moving about in camp; but the [official] was always obliged to be on his guard against creating wrong impressions in the minds of the natives" [*Life in the Mofussil* (London, 1878), vol. 1, p. 251]. Bradford Spangenberg has pointed out how concern with the progress of one's career tended to make officials avoid creating a "fuss" over the treatment of native workers as over other issues (op. cit.).

[66] *India As I Knew It, 1885–1925* (London, 1926), p. 234. He went on to complain that the control of crime when he took over the Punjab was hampered by "the tendency of

sometimes publicly in retirement, deep irritation with the obstacles
thrown in the path of administration by lawyers and Judges. John
Beames, a long-serving Bengal official in the later nineteenth century,
complained in his memoirs that the biggest problem in India was not
passing a law, but actually putting it into effect. For

the native lawyers are as sharp as needles and very soon tear the heart out of [the
piece of legislation passed]. . . . So then cases are instituted in the courts, and
appealed and appealed till they reach the High Court. That august tribunal
always considers itself the legally constituted interpreter of all laws, and proceeds
to put an interpretation of its own on section after section. These interpretations
are embodied in the decisions of the Court, and these decisions are printed and
published as "rulings." So that before long there are two laws, the actual Statute
as passed by the legislative body, and the mass of rulings thereon as pronounced
by the judicial body. The lawyers are very proud of this; they call the former
"substantive law," and the latter "adjective law," and very much prefer the
latter, as their own creation. Now inasmuch as in arriving at their decision the
judges carefully avoid taking into consideration the circumstances which led to
the making of the law, and examine not what the legislature meant to lay down
but what the words of the Act really import, it not infrequently happens that
their decisions turn out to be the very opposite of what the law was intended to
mean. Then a new law has to be passed to rectify the error.[67]

As we shall see, many High Court Judges, conscious of following in an
unbroken line from seventeenth-century predecessors, perceived themselves as the chief check on the executive power, and freely cited English
precedents as authoritative.[68] Executive officials, not surprisingly, tended
to resent being checked, and often became exasperated with judicial
rhetoric that to their minds failed to appreciate that India was not
England. From the executive point of view, the Judges were all too prone
to let serious criminals (usually Indian, of course) escape out of excessive
concern with "legal technicalities," a concern perhaps all very well back
in Britain but impractical in the subcontinent, where the welfare of

---

the Courts – the personnel of which was 90% Indian – to take too technical and narrow
a view of evidence (a fact which led to the acquittal or discharge of thousands of
criminals), and to inflict in the small proportion of cases convicted inadequate
sentences" [p. 236].

[67] John Beames, *Memoirs of a Bengal Civilian* (written 1896; published London, 1961),
p. 244.

[68] Sir P. P. Hutchins, a Member of the Viceroy's Council, annoyed by the Calcutta Chief
Justice's charge to the jury in the prosecution of an Indian newspaper, complained to the
Viscount, Lord Lansdowne, in 1891, "I fear Barrister Judges are apt to go too much by
what they remember of English practice instead of consulting their Codes" [BL OIOC
Lansdowne Papers, V, 25 Aug. 1891].

hundreds of millions and the survival of British rule depended on the firm maintenance of authority. This conflict of constitutional and criminal law principle was exacerbated in India by personal career rivalries. High Court Judges in the subcontinent were either barristers appointed by the Home Government and sharing neither similar experiences nor an *esprit de corps* with executive officers of the Indian Civil Service, or members of that Civil Service who had taken the judicial route.[69] That route, however, was of decidedly lower prestige than the executive route, and tended to be avoided by the most ambitious of the civilians. Thus, judicial members of the ICS labored under something of a stigma of inferiority, which they naturally resented. The result was to prevent the *esprit de corps* of the ICS from reaching very forcefully into the judicial branch, and rather to reinforce what executive officials described as judicial "touchiness" about their powers and prerogatives.[70] For their part, Judges saw executive officials continually attempting to confine their role and circumvent their rulings. In January 1892, for example, the Government of Bengal criticized the Calcutta High Court after it acquitted an Indian charged with attempted murder of a European by noting that "the description of the facts given by the Commissioner of Police throws doubts on the propriety of the acquittal." In heated response, the Court formally complained to the Viceroy's office: "In England, the efficiency of the Police is gauged by the results of their efforts in Court. In India, the efficiency of the Courts should not be judged by their agreement with, or dissent from, the Police."[71]

Ongoing tension between the two branches of Government burst into the open later that year when Bengal's Lieutenant Governor, Charles Elliott, who had become steadily more unhappy about a long-declining

---

[69] By an 1861 law, at least one-third of High Court Judges were drawn from the ICS and at least another third had to be barristers (the final third could be either, or neither).

[70] Philip Woodruff [Philip Mason], in his book *The Men Who Ruled India*, vol. 2: *The Guardians* (London, 1954), expressed the view held by the ICS, to which he had belonged, when he observed [p. 23], "those judges who were or became great jurists were apt to be unsuccessful as District Judges. The letter of the law was so important to them that they were apt to forget the spirit, and they were, moreover, so astute in applying the law to the facts that they sometimes neglected to ascertain what the facts were." On tensions between Civilians who chose the executive path and those taking the judicial, see Spangenberg, op. cit., pp. 111–142. He noted that as a result of its lesser attraction for the ambitious careerists, "the mavericks and eccentrics of the I.C.S. were usually found in the judiciary" [p. 117].

[71] BL OIOC Home Judicial Proceedings, no. 297, letter of 25 Jan. 1892. On the Calcutta High Court, the most important in India, see Mahua Sarkar, *Justice in a Gothic Edifice: The Calcutta High Court and Colonial Rule in Bengal* (Calcutta, 1997).

rate of criminal convictions, issued a Notification announcing his intention to remove the most serious offenses, including riot and murder, from jury trial.[72] Elliott attributed this decline to obstacles thrown up by the existing legal system, which to his mind followed English models unthinkingly, failing to appreciate the great differences between India and England.[73] Such obstacles included strict evidentiary rules, overlenient rights of appeal, and, most of all, trial by jury, which though it did not exist in most of India, had become entrenched in the major Presidency cities and had gradually been extended to adjoining rural areas. Hindu culture, Elliott argued, made Indian juries too lenient to persons of high caste or social standing, and in general they were notoriously open to influence and outright bribery. Trial by jury was also the "obstacle" that was most within his power to restrict, and he intended to do just that. Elliott's Notification unleashed a storm of protest. Political Indians, who had been for years pressing for an *expansion* of trial by jury, predictably to a man denounced it as a major step toward despotism, and not only passed resolutions at large public meetings and submitted a petition to the India Office, but also lobbied Members of Parliament and leading British papers. There they evoked more sympathy than Elliott had ever anticipated, for trial by jury was seen, virtually across the political spectrum, as one of the most fundamental principles of the English constitution.[74] Lord Kimberley, now Secretary of State for India, could "hardly remember any matter which has excited so much feeling here except, perhaps, the Ilbert Bill. . . . [T]he unanimity with which the Press,

[72] In Bengal, conviction rates for property crime had not changed significantly, but for crimes of violence they had (and it was this category from which Elliott sought to remove jury trial): with the total number of cases changing little, a conviction rate that had been 53.4% in 1879 had fallen to 38.6% by 1892 [Annual Returns of Bengal Criminal Statistics, BL OIOC, V/24/2201 and 2202]. It is unlikely however that jury trial had much to do with this, as criminal conviction rates had fallen even more in other parts of India where jury trial was rare: in the United Provinces, the percentage of convictions in all criminal cases had decreased even more, from 74.8% in 1875 to 43.6% in 1892 [Campion, op. cit., p. 155].

[73] David Washbrook has noted that Elliott soon fell out with the large Western-educated Indian population of Calcutta, "who had developed a lively public opinion and a press often critical of British rule. Having served 'up-country' most of his life, Elliott was not used to being subject to public comment and reacted strongly" [David Washbrook, "Sir Charles Elliott," *ODNB*].

[74] Just a few years earlier, *The Times* had observed, after an argument conducted in its pages about its deficiencies particularly in civil litigation, that "trial by jury is still in possession" of English public opinion. Until that changed, "any attempt to limit a man's right to a jury will surely excite vehement resistance in the name of liberty" [*The Times*, 4 Sept. 1890, p. 9].

quite independent of politics, has condemned the measure is very remarkable," he warned Lord Lansdowne, the Viceroy.[75] Moreover, the opposition in India was not confined to natives. The High Court of Bengal itself quite unusually publicly criticized the Notification, as did the presiding Judge of the Assam Valley District, the location of perhaps the bitterest racial feelings in all India. As a result, the Judges became popular heroes, lauded in the Indian press.[76] Even some Anglo-Indians – particularly lawyers and newspaper editors – abandoned the Lieutenant Governor, worried that this change, although it did not disturb the existing right of *Europeans* to trial by jury, would set a dangerous precedent.[77] A common anxiety about the growth of "despotic" Government could, at least momentarily, unite Indians and Europeans in India in defense of Judges and juries.

Kimberley instructed Lansdowne to lower the temperature by referring the issue to a Commission for further study; this Commission, headed by Justice Henry Prinsep of the Calcutta High Court, predictably reported in 1893 against change, and the Lieutenant Governor, knowing when he was beaten, withdrew the Notification.[78] The conflict, however, went on; a few months later the High Court sent a long letter to the Viceroy to be forwarded to the Secretary of State complaining that the Lieutenant Governor had responded to his defeat over jury trial by applying fresh

[75] Kimberley to Lansdowne, 5 Jan. 1893, BL OIOC LP C.558/6/1. Writing to Gladstone a year later, Kimberley called the appointment of Lansdowne as Viceroy his "one great blunder" [letter, 21 Jan. 1894, in *Liberal by Principle*, op. cit., p. 214].

[76] Henry Prinsep, unpublished memoirs (1912), OIOC p. 438. The barrister members of the High Court had already demonstrated their resistance to tampering with trial by jury by refusing to make use of a provision in Stephen's Code of Criminal Procedure that allowed the High Court to overturn a jury verdict it found clearly in error [Prinsep, p. 407].

[77] Elliott took note of this; he wrote Lansdowne: "Your Excellency will have seen the agitation about the *Jury* Resolution. I cannot admit that a single argument has been adduced against my action; it has been pure interpolation. But I have been surprised to find how much the non-official Calcutta Englishman sympathises with the feeling. The belief that the Executive Government is inclined to be despotic is ingrained in them" [24 Nov. 1892, BL OIOC M/3/103 (Lansdowne Papers)].

[78] BL OIOC L/P&J/6/342, File 570: Telegram from Viceroy to India Office, 25 Mar. 1893, summarizing Juries Commission report. He then returned to England on leave for most of the rest of the year. However, he did not retract his hard-line views; his temporary replacement, the more liberal A. P. MacDonnell, remarked to Lansdowne that Elliott wrote him letters "maintaining that I should be governing on Continental rather than on English methods" [13 July 1893, BL OIOC Mss Eur. D 558/25]. In the twentieth century, with the growth of local and regional self-government, jury trials were extended to more areas of India; ironically, however, in 1960 the now-independent Government of India abolished trial by jury, as too susceptible to media influence and to corruption (both complaints made by Elliott).

pressure upon magistrates and police to obtain more convictions, which was causing police to fabricate evidence and torture suspects for confessions.[79] The Indian press rushed to support the Judges: after all, one paper noted, "in England the judiciary has always been independent of the executive, and every reader of history knows how much blood this independence cost England in the past."[80] The India Office, on the other hand, was unhappy with this unseemly quarrel; as its Permanent Secretary, Arthur Godley, observed to Lord Kimberley, it was "a pity the High Court Judges should have written this letter. There is a great deal of truth in what they say – but they should have let the matter rest, as no good purpose could be served by continuing the controversy."[81] Kimberley forced at least a public cessation of this quarrel. The Viceroy was instructed to make it clear that Bengal officials were not to publish any criticisms of Judges or juries, and for their part Judges were to confine themselves strictly to the cases before them.[82] The public clash, if not its underlying causes, subsided. However, as Justice Prinsep later recalled in his unpublished memoirs, "constant friction" continued throughout his period of service between the Court and the Government of Bengal.[83]

[79] BL OIOC L/P&J/6/351, File 1241: 6 June 1893.

[80] *Hitavadi*, 31 Aug. 1893, BL OIOC L/R/5/19.

[81] The High Court's complaint was taken up in Parliament by some Radical members, causing Godley to point out to Kimberley that "there is not the smallest doubt that this belief [that their promotions depend greatly on the percentage of convictions in criminal cases dealt with by them] has always been entertained by native magistrates and the police. But attention has now been officially called to the matter by the correspondence and the Government of Bengal has disowned all connection with, or approval of, anything of the kind" [BL OIOC L/P&J/6/351, File 1310: 7 July 1893].

[82] BL OIOC L/P&J/6/338, File 217: Kimberley to Lansdowne, 1 June 1893.

[83] "As a Judicial Officer," Prinsep went on, "I may be regarded as biased, but I can confidently appeal to official records to show the provocation was always on the part of the Local Government prompted by an irresistible inclination to interfere with the undoubted prerogative of the High Court – the maintenance of the Judicial independence of all Courts even of the lowest grade in all judicial matters. Since my early days as a Judge of the High Court, we have had a succession of Lieutenants-General of Bengal who with one exception have too openly shown their hostility to any judicial independence. What can be expected from such an example to their subordinate Executive officers who resented the power given by the law to correct them whenever they transgressed it? They held that the patriarchal system of Government in the early days of our rule should be maintained and restored, forgetting that by legislation, descending often into minute details, the Government had established the reign of law, that the past was dead beyond recall, and that they should unite with Judicial officers in working for the public weal, the loadstone of all modern Government" [unpublished memoirs]. Unsurprisingly, not long after public remarks along these lines Prinsep was turned down for the position of Judicial Secretary in the India Office. Administrative irritation with High Court Judges' interpretation of their "independence" continued into the twentieth century. Lord Hardinge, Viscount at

This conflict between executive and judiciary by no means made the latter a consistent champion of Indians against Europeans; much depended upon the attitudes of individual Judges. On the Calcutta High Court, for instance, in 1903 Justice Sale, a favorite of the Anglo-Indian community, strained accepted legal procedures to quash the conviction of a planter for causing grievous hurt in the death of one of his laborers, while a few months later, dealt with an appeal from other tea plantation laborers against a one-year prison sentence for assaulting their manager by enhancing their sentences to three years.[84] However, the judiciary normally had less of an interest than the executive in seeing defendants, whether Indians (as in the great majority of cases) or Europeans (in unusual circumstances), convicted. It consequently often became the target of the frustration felt by members of the executive when defendants went free. Since most criminal trials were directed against Indians, the independence of the courts in general worked in their favor. Judicial independence most notably made possible numerous acquittals of nationalist "agitators" or "terrorists" in the succeeding years, but as the case of Private O'Hara demonstrates, it also could serve as a shield for Europeans whom the executive was seeking to convict for abusing natives.

Thus, criminal justice in British India, as in other parts of the Empire, was inevitably political. In particular, interracial homicide trials formed a perennial arena of contestation between Indians and Britons, and between different groups of Britons. By the end of the nineteenth century this arena was coming under mounting pressure from many sides.

the time, complained in 1911 to Secretary for India Crewe that Justice Fletcher of the Calcutta High Court, who was being considered for appointment to the chief justiceship of the Northwest Province, was "one of those legal people who have a mistaken idea that it is the duty of the High Court to trample as much as possible on the Executive" [Hardinge to Crewe, 11 Jan. 1911: Cambridge University Library, Hardinge Papers, vol. 2, file 10].

[84] BL OIOC L/PJ/5/29. Part 1, p. 970; Part 2, p. 338.

6

India: In the Legal Arena, 1889–1922

Every British magistrate in India is in a false position when he has to try a case in which European and native interests clash. In theory he is administering an impartial system of justice; in practice he is part of a huge machine which exists to protect British interests, and he has often got to choose between sacrificing his integrity and damaging his career. . . . Nevertheless, owing to the exceptionally high traditions of the Indian Civil Service, the law in India is administered far more fairly than might be expected.

George Orwell, 1938[1]

The arena of criminal justice in India was structured by a Code first drafted in the 1840s by Thomas Macaulay, though only enacted (with revisions) in 1860. The Indian Penal Code was shaped on the model of England's criminal law, cleansed of many technicalities and obscurities that had accumulated over the centuries, and with additions and deletions to accommodate Indian conditions, like specific provision for the greater incidence of infanticide and "dacoity" (robbery by groups). As extended and modified by Fitzjames Stephen's 1872 Criminal Procedure and Evidence Acts, the Code contained provisions that both favored and restrained state power. On the one hand, it facilitated prosecution by doing away with some burdensome procedural requirements inherited from earlier English times. It also responded to the scarcity of British officials by leaving a larger role for (Indian) police, who were under less effective supervision than their counterparts in England. In trial procedure, its most obvious difference from England was the limited role it allowed for juries: where they were employed – in the Presidency cities – their verdicts did not require unanimity, and their use was not extended to most of the

---

[1] Unsigned review of Maurice Collis, *Trials in Burma*, *The Listener*, 9 Mar. 1938.

"mofussil," the vast area outside those few cities. Moreover, the higher courts possessed, as they did not in England, a reserve power to review jury verdicts. Thus, the great majority of trials of Indians took place either by magistrate alone, or by magistrate or Judge with the aid of assessors, whose decision the justice was not bound to accept, and even in jury trials the jury's verdict was not absolutely the last word. All of this should have made successful prosecution easier.

On the other hand, the Code differed from its English model in being less severe on acts of violence. Whereas in England, the law assumed a homicide to be murder until established otherwise, in India after 1862 the burden of proving that a homicide was criminal was placed more fully on the prosecution.[2] In England in the later nineteenth century, the scope of the right of self-defense and the definition of that degree of provocation that would reduce a homicide below murder were being restricted, narrowing two major avenues of defense. In India there was no sign of these developments. Indeed, the Code explicitly differed from English law in expressing the right of self-defense in wider terms than was being done in England, and in accepting words and gestures as capable of offering that degree of provocation that would reduce murder to culpable homicide, a much less serious offense. In a land in which considerations of honor played, for both the indigenous and the European population, a good deal larger role than in England, such allowances could diminish culpability for a great deal of lethal violence.[3] As a result, under the Code it was more difficult than in England, and perhaps more difficult than it had been previously in British India, to convict anyone, European or Indian, of the capital offense of murder, or even of manslaughter.[4] Thus, while at the lower levels of justice the Code probably eased the work of administrators, at the level of the High Courts it could readily frustrate them. And not only at this higher level: it may be significant that despite the

---

[2] George Claus Rankin, *Background to Indian Law* (Cambridge, 1946), p. 211.

[3] On the English restriction of self-defense and provocation, see Martin J. Wiener, *Men of Blood*. On the relevant provisions of the Indian Penal Code, see John D. Mayne, *The Criminal Law of India* (Madras, 1896), pp. 602–608. On the general workings of the Code in cases of interracial homicide, see Jordanna Bailkin, op. cit., and Elizabeth Kolsky, "Crime and Punishment on the Tea Plantations of Colonial India," in *Modern Histories of Crime and Punishment*, ed. Markus Dirk Dubber and Lindsay Farmer (Stanford, 2007).

[4] Mayne (op. cit., pp. 620–621) shows that the Code also made wide allowance for deaths caused by "rash and negligent acts," generally categorizing them as falling below the level of culpable homicide (many of his examples – all involving Indian defendants with Indian victims – would likely by his time have been considered manslaughter in England).

apparent advantages the Code gave to all prosecutions, the proportion of prosecutions of crimes of violence ending in conviction gradually *fell* in the decades following its institution; it was this fall that Elliott had hoped to reverse with his Notification cutting back the use of juries. If the proportion of criminal trials ending in conviction is taken as an indicator of the everyday repressive strength of the state (as it has been for British history),[5] then contrary to the impression given by most scholarship this strength was *diminishing* in British India in the last three decades of the nineteenth century.

The Code was of course just one factor; others may have been even more influential in producing this decline: one was a growing judicial suspicion of police-induced confessions; another was a rise in the number of trained Indian lawyers. Many of the most articulate members of the Indian National Congress began their careers primarily as defense lawyers and honed their skills in rhetoric and politics, as well as their critical view of the colonial Government, by arguing against the police in district courts across India, particularly in Bengal. Astute *vakils* could easily identify the errors and mishandling of investigations and get much of the evidence upon which the police had staked their case dismissed. As the Code became a template for criminal law in other British colonies, and the number of native lawyers grew, these conflicting effects were generalized, and contentious trials, especially of cases of serious violence, seem to have become more frequent.[6] Even before the Code went into effect, some Anglo-Indians questioned its practicality. "It is one of England's proudest boasts," wrote a returned Anglo-Indian in Charles Dickens's periodical, *Household Words*, "that wherever her flag is unfurled, there she carries the blessings of liberal institutions; she conquers but to set free. The same justice which is provided for the proudest son of Albion, is sent forth across the waters to attend on the meanest swarthy subject of Her Majesty in distant India." However, "in one way or the other it proves rather the reverse of an unmitigated blessing to those for whose expected benefit

---

[5] See V. A. C. Gatrell, "Crime, Authority, and the Policeman-State, 1750–1950," in *The Cambridge Social History of Britain, 1750–1950*, ed. F. M. L. Thompson (Cambridge, 1990), vol. 3, 243–310. In Britain in the same years the conviction rate was rising.

[6] As Lieutenant Governor Elliott complained of one distinguished and progressive Bengali lawyer, a leader of the Indian National Congress, "his practice has been of the character which I venture to think at once dishonorable and remunerative; he runs about the country protecting criminals from deserved punishment by technical flaws and objections, and he is therefore a favorite with the large class of papers which are always glad to see a prosecution break down and a criminal escape" [BL OIOC Mss Eur. D 558/23, 16 Oct. 1892].

it was wafted over the seas." Indians, he explained, perverted English law through widespread bribery and extortion, perjury, and overlitigiousness. He concluded by posing the question whether Asian subjects were capable of making English justice work.[7]

Ironically, given these complaints, the clearest beneficiaries of the decline in convictions appear to have been Europeans, at least when they were charged with offenses against Indians. Despite repeated professions of formal equality before the law, Europeans had always possessed advantages in the legal arena, both formal and informal. Magistrates were limited in their ability to sentence "European British" subjects (as they were not in regard to Indians) to a maximum of three months' imprisonment; Sessions Judges were limited to a maximum of one year, and only High Court Judges, sitting in the major cities, could impose anything more severe upon them. Europeans were also entitled, when tried by juries, to a majority-white jury. Apart from such legal differences, Europeans possessed both the money to buy skilled counsel and, even more important, the racial sympathy of the white magistrates, Judges, and, when they were defendants, their white jurors. Concern to maintain the prestige of the ruling race mean that "the general rule was that when a European assaulted an Indian he pleaded guilty, stating the provocation, and was let off with a fine."[8] This racial inequality seems to have increased in the second half of the nineteenth century, with the growth in the European community's political strength. This strength ensured the institution of the specific protections of the Code and the 1872 Acts, and the favorable resolution of the Ilbert Bill crisis, formalizing the guarantee of a majority-white jury for Europeans.[9] However, racial inequality in the criminal courts appears to have peaked in the early 1890s, and from then on began a slow retreat, diminishing if never completely disappearing down to Independence.

A number of publicized cases show the lineaments of the system at its most unequal, shaped by racial difference and also, if not so crucially, by that of class. In Calcutta in early 1890 two Britons stood trial for the murders of Indians – Thomas O'Hara, a soldier we have briefly met in the

---

[7] John Capper [Anon.], "Law in the East," *Household Words* 5 (1852), 347. The author was a former Ceylon tea plantation manager and newspaper editor [identified by Anne Lohrli, *Index to Household Words* (Toronto, 1973)].

[8] Compton, op. cit., p. 252.

[9] Bailkin, op. cit., similarly argues that treatment of European perpetrators became more favorable in this period (although she fails to notice the reversal in this trend explored in this chapter).

preceding chapter, and Duncan King, a young gentleman trader. O'Hara, with his fellow soldiers out one night without leave and drunk, had without provocation shot a villager in the semirural area just outside of the city. That two of the four soldiers were arrested over a month later was somewhat surprising, since the day after the killing an Indian witness had been unable (or unwilling) to identify them in a regimental lineup, and the matter seemed closed. However, the widespread press reports were highly embarrassing, and it was observed in the Indian press that both the Lieutenant Governor of Bengal and the Viceroy "took a personal interest" in the case.[10] On orders from above, the local British magistrate continued to investigate. He succeeded in identifying the culprits and received authorization to offer pardons to two, who had not taken part in the killing, on condition of giving full evidence in court. Armed with their statements, he committed the other two to the Sessions of the Calcutta High Court.

They were tried in February 1890, one for murder and the other for abetting. Their jury – made up not merely of a European majority, as was their right, but of eight Europeans and only one Indian – acquitted the second but unexpectedly convicted the first, Thomas O'Hara, of murder, following the lead of the Judge, Sir John Norris, who summed up strongly against him.[11] Murder was a crime that in British India as in Britain itself then carried only one penalty, that of death. The verdict created a public sensation among both Indians and Anglo-Indians;[12] the military authorities together with some "friends" of O'Hara got the opinion of the

---

[10] The *Hindoo Patriot* doubted whether, without this interest, "the culprit would have been brought to justice" [24 Feb. 1890]. The Lieutenant Governor at the time, Sir Stuart Bayley, had been appointed a few years before, when tensions were still high over the 1883–1884 Anglo-Indian "revolt" against the proposed Ilbert Bill. "His administration," it was noted in the *ODNB*, "was an unspectacular one in which he concentrated on damping down racial animosity. . . . He tried in a quiet, uninflammatory way to increase the participation of Indians in low-level public affairs by extending both the system of honorary magistrates and the application of the elective principle in local self-government. He also attempted to facilitate the advancement of Indians in government service, but again in a muted and gradual fashion" [P. C. Lyon, revised by Katherine Prior].

[11] Norris was no liberal; he had spoken out against the Ilbert Bill, and had become notorious when he sentenced a popular Indian editor to jail for sedition. He seems to have been severe on all defendants before him, regardless of race.

[12] Since the "Mutiny" six Europeans had hanged for the murder of Indians, all but one of them soldiers, but only one, a sailor who had the poor judgment to kill a policeman, more recently than 1867; the increasing size and influence of the Anglo-Indian community was making this outcome ever less likely [Compton, op. cit., pp. 274–275; Bailkin, op. cit.; the *Indian Daily News*, 24 July 1880, described this last execution].

Advocate General of Bengal that the trial Judge had committed some serious procedural errors, most importantly that he had allowed the jury to consider the evidence of a third soldier without establishing whether or not he was legally an accomplice. A rehearing was ordered before the full bench of the High Court, which found that indeed the Judge should have declared the witness an accomplice, whose testimony should require further corroboration. It then quashed O'Hara's conviction. Indians demanded a new trial, but it was not called. Instead, all four soldiers were tried by a military court for breach of regimental law (chiefly for being out without leave) and given brief terms of imprisonment.[13]

Most of the Anglo-Indian press (that is, the press produced and read by the European residents in India) denounced the prisoners; *The Englishman*, Bengal's leading such paper, went on to "regret that a technical error by the trial judge should have allowed O'Hara to escape"; a correspondent even suggested that the men should at least still be tried for theft.[14] However, the paper, like others in the European community, passed over the possibility of a new murder trial; the Indian press expressed not regret but outrage. O'Hara, *Navavibhakar Sadharani* had noted after his conviction, had "shot down an innocent man like a dog." With the quashing of his conviction, "all natives, high and low," *Sahachar* declared, "have ceased to feel themselves safe in the presence of Europeans." And *Al Punch* published a cartoon in which the sword of justice and the serpent of unlawful murder with a soldier's hat on its head are weighed in a balance, and the serpent is found turning the scale. The female figure of Justice is pale and worn out.[15] Another Indian paper prophesied that "if the sympathies of the people of India are ever alienated from English rule, the alienation will be due to this very circumstance" of belief in judicial racial bias.[16] Even the self-consciously "moderate" English-language *Hindoo Patriot* complained that Indians could hardly help but "be confirmed in the ignorant conviction that

---

[13] BL OIOC Mss Eur. D 558/18: File 195, p. 160 (Lansdowne Papers); L/PJ/6/272, Files 461, 498, 672; Mss Eur. E 243, Files 20, 30 (Cross Papers). When complaints of serious violence by soldiers against natives were handled by the Army at this time, the most severe results might be a month's confinement to the regimental jail.

[14] *The Englishman*, 13 Mar. 1890, p. 4 (editorial). It declared that "the original verdict had appeared most proper – an atrocious crime had been solved, its perpetrator brought to justice"; "All the newspapers, including even the *Pioneer* and the *Englishman* [the two 'strongest' Anglo-Indian papers] are saying that a great wrong has been committed, and that the perpetrator of a brutal murder has gone unpunished" [*Sahachar*, 19 Mar.].

[15] *Navavibhakar Sadharani*, 24 Feb. 1890; *Sahachar*, 19 Mar.; *Al Punch*, 21 Apr.

[16] *Burdwan Sanjivani*, 18 Mar. 1890.

Europeans are above the law and British-born subjects may murder 'black bastards' with impunity." It resisted this conclusion: "We feel persuaded," it went on, "that Lord Lansdowne will not allow the case to rest where it does."[17] But he did. Complaints reached Britain, and censorious accounts published in the London press led to a question in the House of Commons. Even then, officials gave their usual response to such enquiries, that no interference could be made with the normal course of the law.[18] However, when the issue resurfaced in Britain a few months later, leading to a threat to bring it up in the House of Lords, the Viceroy's office ordered the victim's widow to be given a generous pension; there the matter ended.[19]

One month later a young businessman, Duncan King, came before Justice Norris charged with the murder of an Indian. He had set out in Calcutta, with a few friends at midnight, apparently drunk, to hunt rats (according to him). They got into a street quarrel and were pursued by an angry crowd. To escape, he claimed, they broke into a strange house, fatally stabbing a servant in the process. A Bengali newspaper, *Sanjivani*, reported that "King thrust his sword through the opening in the door, and . . . the *durwan* who stood behind it resisting the culprit and his associates in their attempt to force their way into the house was killed by the stroke." His excellent defense counsel, paid for by a fund raised by his fellow European traders, argued that the fatal act was both accidental and self-defense (because he was fleeing pursuers). Norris treated King much more leniently than he had the soldier O'Hara, giving him the benefit of

---

[17] *Hindoo Patriot*, 17 Mar. 1890 [editorial]. "The Hon. Gen Chesney, the military member of the Supreme Council," it observed, "also displayed great interest in the case and was present at the first day's Full Bench hearing. It is probably at the instance of the hon. General that the four soldiers are now under military arrest awaiting trial for breach of regimental law. But the prevailing idea is that they will get off with a few 'cuts' and no retribution will follow poor Selim's violent death." *Sakti* observed (18 Mar.) that "Europeans who commit crimes in this country almost always escaped unscathed; and when they are convicted they live in a princely style in the Nainital or in the Jubbulpore Jail." In O'Hara's case, "the mountain has given birth to a mouse. The culprit is apprehended with much ado, he is brought to trial, and he is sentenced to be hanged." But in the end, he is given a mere slap on the wrist. "After the discharge of O'Hara by the High Court, oppression by the soldiery is calculated to become simply intolerable."

[18] BL OIOC L/PJ/6/272, File 498. The *Morning Post*, a leading London newspaper, reported that when, after his discharge, O'Hara was going back to his regiment, he received an ovation from many Europeans at Allahabad [reported in *Sahachar*, 19 Mar. 1890].

[19] BL OIOC, Mss Eur. E 243/30 (Cross Papers).

the doubt, and also making a point of his youth (although he was not significantly younger than O'Hara). The Judge told the jury the offense did not in his view amount to murder, and King was convicted of "causing grievous hurt" and sentenced to one year's imprisonment.

As the Indian paper complained, killing with a deadly weapon someone defending his master's house from strangers breaking in was rarely considered either accidental or self-defense when the person charged was Indian. It noted the power of money (familiar in Britain also) to buy superior counsel. "No one can doubt," it declared, "that if the widow of the *durwan* had been represented at the trial by an able counsel like Mr. Gasper, the Justice's doubts and surmises [about the degree of criminality of King's actions] would have been met." Moreover, there were particularly imperial aspects to the case: "in a place like Calcutta," it argued, "King was under no necessity of taking a sword-stick with him when he left his house." If he had done so in London, it justifiably pointed out, the court would have had no sympathy for him.[20] Another native paper contrasted the light sentence awarded King with the ten years given at the same Sessions to an Indian who had killed under much greater provocation, and asked "if such partiality as has been shown to King be shown by a Judge of the High Court, what wonder that similar things shall take place in the mofussil."[21]

If class made a difference as between O'Hara and King, racial distinction between Europeans and Indians was still more evident in these cases, and certainly more politically dangerous. O'Hara's murder conviction was exceptional: British soldiers, who constituted the large majority of Europeans charged over the death of Indians in these years, were usually merely fined for assault ("causing harm"), and not infrequently won outright acquittals. Their defenses were either accident, self-defense, or temporary insanity. When Indians died from a soldier's kicks it was more often than not viewed as accidental: the defendant lacked intent to kill, and Indians tended to have diseased spleens, far more likely to burst and cause death than European spleens. One such case, where a soldier had given a laborer who had fallen asleep at his job several kicks that proved fatal, produced a parliamentary question in 1893, but, it was replied, there were no grounds for objection, for "the medical evidence showed that the cause of death was rupture of the spleen, which was in such a state that the slightest blow might have broken it; and there were

[20] *Sanjivani,* 22 Feb. 1890.
[21] *Sar Sudhanidhi,* 24 Feb. 1890.

no external marks of violence." Given this interpretation of the act, the magistrate convicted the soldier simply of voluntarily causing hurt and sentenced him to pay a fine of Rs. 100, or in default, to three weeks' "rigourous imprisonment" (the equivalent under the Indian Code of hard labor). The fine was paid and awarded as compensation to the relatives of the deceased.[22]

Soldiers of higher rank than Private O'Hara usually fared better at trial. In 1893, in a somewhat similar situation to King's, a magistrate ruled the fatal shooting of a Bengali by an Army surgeon, Captain Pearse, in the act of forcing his way into the victim's house an accident, and dismissed the case; after Indian protests, a fresh inquiry was ordered, which led to a new charge of culpable homicide (equivalent to manslaughter) and a trial before the High Court. The Government, however, decided not to prosecute, and Pearse was immediately freed.[23] In February 1894 in Madras, twenty-four-year-old Lance-Corporal Ernest Ashford was charged with culpable homicide for the shooting of a villager who had interfered with his "dealings" with two native women of the man's household. Upon complaint by the wounded man, who said he had been protecting the two women from sexual assault, the Commanding Officer of the encampment had the 117 men in the regiment march past him, in single file, but he was (not surprisingly) unable to identify anyone. Nothing further took place until several days later, when the villager died of his wounds, and a local Indian newspaper denounced the killing and the lack of official concern. Only after the newspaper attacked did the civil Government intervene, and by offering immunity to soldiers who would come forward identified Ashford as the perpetrator and filed charges. As was usual in such cases, a subscription raised money to hire a skilled defense team, which claimed that the victim was a pimp and, supported by a group of friends, had come at Ashford with a knife (which had not been recovered). The trial concluded with an acquittal, as the jury of five Europeans and four Indians accepted the argument of self-defense.[24] Again, the Indian press

---

[22] BL OIOC L/PJ/360, File 2170 (Nov. 1893).

[23] Ram Gopal Sanyal, *The Record of Criminal Cases, as Between Europeans and Natives, for the Last Hundred Years* (Calcutta, 1896), p. 145; BL OIOC L/PJ/6/369, File 464; *The Pioneer Mail*, 22 Feb. 1894: "The Fulta Shooting Case." This was one of three acquittals of Europeans complained of by the Radical M.P. W. Caine in the House of Commons in early 1894.

[24] *Madras Times*, 8 and 15 Feb. 1894; The Anglo-Indian *Madras Times* argued that the trial had revealed the deceased "in his true character. . . . On the whole substantial justice appears to have been done, but we are by no means assured that Indian journalists will concur in this opinion" [10 Feb.]. It was right: the Indian-owned *Standard*

denounced the verdict. Again, also, a question was asked in the House of Commons by a Radical M.P., who called it "the Dum Dum/O'Hara case over again," but the India Office replied that the regular course of justice could not be interfered with.[25]

After soldiers, the group of Europeans most likely to appear in court charged with the death of Indians were men associated with plantations. Such cases became more frequent with the expansion of tea cultivation. In 1884, Charles Webb, a recruitment agent for a tea garden, found himself charged with "wrongful confinement" of a female laborer and "hurt" (assault) against her and her husband; she died several days later, although a European doctor certified that it was from natural causes and Webb was not charged with her death. He appears to have had the woman, a new recruit, seized, and kept her in his cabin overnight for sexual gratification (one suspects this was not the first time he did this sort of thing). However, the charge of rape was almost never brought against Europeans, "wrongful confinement" usually serving as a very mild substitute. A number of planters sat in court in support of Webb, and even though he had twice before been fined for assaults, the magistrate again merely fined him Rs. 100, ordering him to pay an additional Rs. 200 to the woman's husband as compensation. The District Judge was most unhappy with this (perhaps in part because the Indian press had immediately attacked the sentence), and sent the case to the High Court, urging enhancement of punishment. However, at the High Court no one appeared for the prosecution. Consequently, although the two Judges sharply criticized the magistrate for his failure to take evidence from several key Indian witnesses and for not sending the case in the first place to a higher court empowered to award harsher penalties, they concluded that the evidence on hand was insufficient to justify altering the sentence. One of the Judges, the severe Norris, wanted to retry the case, but backed down after consulting with other Judges, instead joining with them in complaining of the "sensationalism" of the Indian press, which had called Webb "a demon in human shape."[26] One writer appealed to "the good Empress to see how female chastity is outraged in an empire governed in her name."[27] Another paper claimed that "the people of Bengal seem

[n.d.], in a report entitled "Gross Miscarriage of Justice," sharply questioned the rationale of the defense and concluded that this non-trial "adds a fresh instance to the long roll of cases in which Europeans have, with impunity, murdered natives of India."

[25] BL OIOC L/PJ/6/369 Files 459, 464, 467, 468.

[26] *Paridarshak*, 22 June 1884.

[27] *Burdwan Sanjivani*, 19 Aug. 1884.

to see hovering before their eyes, day and night, the apparition of the ravished coolie girl. . . . They seem to hear her saying 'Englishmen, judge impartially!'"[28] The press uproar forced a response by the Viceroy, Lord Ripon, acknowledging the "incomplete and unsatisfactory manner in which the trial was conducted" by the magistrate, and indicating that he "regretted" that the Government of Bengal had failed to provide representation at the High Court hearing.[29] However, having just been forced into a humiliating retreat over the Ilbert Bill, Ripon was in no position to do anything further, and the case remained closed.[30]

In the same months that Webb was exciting attention, a plantation manager named Francis came before a magistrate in the death of a female laborer. He claimed she had died of opium poisoning, but when a police surgeon instead determined that her death was due to violence, native witnesses came forward to swear that he had kicked her to death (at the instigation of another female laborer, his mistress). However, he had never been in trouble with the law before, and the Anglo-Indian Defense Association, fresh from its victory over Lord Ripon on the Ilbert Bill, took up his case. The magistrate found the native witnesses unreliable, since they had waited until the medical finding before coming forward. Although the investigation uncovered evidence of an earlier rape by Francis of a female laborer, this was ruled inadmissible, and on the basis of a further medical examination in which opium was found in her body the magistrate discharged him, recommending that the witnesses for the prosecution be prosecuted for perjury.[31]

The following year yet another tea-planter came before an Assam magistrate in the death of a laborer whose age was given variously as between ten and fourteen. Five Indian witnesses swore that after his absence from work, the youth was summoned to the manager's bungalow, where the manager kicked him fiercely a number of times, in consequence of which he died the next day. Two Europeans testified for the planter, who claimed that the Indian foreman killed the boy without his knowledge. Although the only evidence for the planter's claim was his own words, the magistrate accepted it, and discharged him without trial, deciding, as had the magistrate in the Francis case, that the laborers had

[28] *Bangabasi*, 20 Sept. 1884.
[29] Statement of A. Mackenzie, Secretary to the Government of India, reprinted in *Bengalee*, 8 Nov. 1884, quoted in Sanyal, op. cit., p. 108.
[30] On the Webb case, see Sanyal, pp. 107–116.
[31] *Sanjivani*, 12 July and 9 Aug. 1884; *Ananda Bazar Patrika*, 4 Aug. 1884; *Assam News*, 11 Aug. 1884.

conspired to frame their employer.[32] In the next year, 1886, an Assam planter named Henry was fined Rs. 100 by another magistrate for kicking a laborer to death, but, probably after being queried by his superiors, the magistrate subsequently referred the case to the High Court, which ordered a retrial. All this did was save Henry the money, as his jury acquitted him (the defense had used the common claim that the victim's ruptured spleen had been diseased and would not have ruptured if healthy). Given the required composition of juries, some officials who would have preferred to see such men punished may have justifiably felt that intervening would be futile. Even this outcome did not satisfy Anglo-Indians: *The Englishman* condemned Henry's "persecution" by retrial.[33]

The years immediately after the emasculation of the Ilbert Bill in 1884 may have seen the nadir of equal justice in India. Indian papers claimed to detect a new sense of impunity produced by the guarantee of a European majority on all juries deciding the fate of Europeans, and with it an increase of what one called "the high handedness of oppressive Anglo-Indians."[34] The laxity of justice when Indians were killed by Europeans was in contrast to the excessive vigor when, as happened more rarely, a European was killed. In April 1893 a harsh and grasping manager of an Assam tea estate named Cockburn was murdered, together with his Indian mistress and his watchman. Immediately an intense search was undertaken for culprits – a reward was posted and pardons offered to participants who had not actually committed murder to come forward with information.[35] Nonetheless, the investigation went frustratingly slowly, while the Anglo-Indian press loudly complained of the inefficiency of the police. Finally, on June 27 a suspect who had gone into hiding, a "coolie"

[32] *Paridarshak*, 15 Nov. 1885; *Bengalee*, Dec. 1885 (quoted in Sanyal, pp. 122–125); *Bharat Mihir*, 3 Dec. 1885; *Sanjivani*, 5 Dec. 1885 and 2 Jan. 1886; *Ananda Bazar Patrika*, 18 Jan. 1886.

[33] *Ananda Bazar Patrika*, 11 Jan. and 7 June 1886; *Bharat Mihir*, 14 Jan. 1886; *Samaya*, 7 June 1886; *Sadharani*, 13 June 1886.

[34] *Sadharani*, 12 Apr. 1885.

[35] Violence against Europeans by Indians was always potentially political, and taken most seriously. "Since the legitimation of colonialism," Jenny Sharpe has noted, "was premised on the presumed passivity of the colonized, the killing of even one European took on the exaggerated proportion of a massacre" [*Allegories of Empire: The Figure of Woman in the Colonial Text* (Minneapolis, 1993), p. 63]. In *Burmese Days*, George Orwell described the reaction of Europeans in upcountry Burma to the killing of a minor British official: "they were almost mad with rage. For the unforgiveable had happened – *a white man* had been killed. When that happens, a sort of shudder runs through the English of the East" [London, 1934, p. 238].

named Sajow, was arrested, and after five days in police custody "confessed."[36] As J. F. Stephen had come to see when writing his Code of Criminal Procedure in 1872, "the smallness of the number of the European magistrates makes the police more important and relatively far more powerful in India than they are in England, and . . . no part of the institutions by which India is governed requires more careful watching in order to prevent what is designed for the protection of the people from becoming a means of petty oppression."[37] In practice, however, such "careful watching" was difficult. As a former District Superintendent and then Inspector-General of Police reflected after his retirement, "In all charges against the Native Police the DSP is in a most delicate position. The very object of his existence is to purge the Police and put his foot down on all tyranny and corruption. I certainly never spared a man whom I considered guilty of such misdoings. But in India, where there is always an endless stream of accusation against the Police, whatever they do or whatever they omit to do, and the judiciary, the native press, and the public in general are lamentably prejudiced against them, if the Police, when charges are made against them, cannot look to their own DSP for protection and support, they are between the devil and the deep sea."[38] In such a situation it was not to be wondered that the DSP was more likely to protect than to investigate his men. The District Magistrate, who had the authority to supervise the DSP, had his own interest in not being too scrupulous. As the person accountable to the provincial Government for crime control and conviction rates in his district, his own career prospects (as Lieutenant Governor Elliott's complaints about declining conviction rates suggests) depended on "his" police inspectors not losing too many prosecutions.

In the case of the murdered planter, in consequence of the first dubious confession several other arrests were made, and another confession obtained. On the basis of these, and almost nothing else, the District Magistrate committed seven men for trial. They were tried in September

---

[36] A former Inspector General of Police, who at the time of this case was a District Superintendent of Police, admitted later in his unpublished memoirs that confessions were often obtained by force, blaming it on Indian custom; as he put it, "the traditional idea of detection in the East is to get hold of the man who is suspected of the crime and torture him until he confesses" [Arthur Frederick Cox, *Reminiscences of Seventy Years* (written 1920; privately printed, 1995), p. 134].

[37] Stephen, *History of the Criminal Law in England* (London, 1884), vol. 3, p. 331. He claimed that his Code "is full of provisions intended to guard against this and at the same time to make the police efficient for their purpose."

[38] Cox, op. cit., pp. 135–136.

before a British Sessions Judge and a panel of Indian assessors, with no jury – the prescribed procedure in the mofussil for natives charged with felonies. Although the assessors unanimously recommended acquitting all the men, the Judge, not bound by their recommendation, found four guilty of murder and sentenced them to death, and three guilty of aiding, sentencing them to transportation to the Andaman Islands for life. Here, however, the story took a new turn. In the past this case would probably have ended with this trial, and perhaps, if the convicted men were for-tunate, a commutation of some of the death sentences, but by 1893 there had emerged a critical mass of Indian lawyers, particularly in Bengal, available to intervene. An Indian barrister organized the laborers' appeal without charge, and a sympathetic Anglo-Indian one argued their case strenuously in a weeklong hearing in December (attended by a suspicious Inspector of Police sent by the Assam Government) before a panel of two Judges of the Calcutta High Court.[39] The High Court Judges threw out the convictions, ordering all the men freed. In their ruling, they found a host of "serious irregularities" at "every stage" and called for an inves-tigation into the behavior of police, magistrate, and Sessions Judge. They did not trouble to hide their belief that the Indian police, offered large rewards by the authorities, had coerced confessions, and that the mag-istrate and Judge had not only ignored those abuses but had acted more as prosecutors than as judicial officials.[40]

This ruling created a double sensation – at the overturning of the convictions and at the Judges' indictment of the administration of local justice. It seemed an official acknowledgment of Indian complaints that, as one newspaper put it, "to please the tea planters, the Assam authorities had ordered the police to find out the murderers, but failing to lay their hands on the real culprits . . . took steps to send four innocent men to the gallows and three innocent men to the Andamans for life."[41] Reports reached Britain, questions were asked in Parliament, and the India Office in response prodded the Government of India into an investigation. On the basis of statements from the District Police Commissioner, the Chief Commissioner, the District Magistrate, and the Sessions Judge, the Government formally reprimanded the magistrate and Judge for serious mistakes and "unwise" actions, but in private defended them to the India Office as merely careless and inexperienced, but not ill-intentioned. The

[39] H. T. Prinsep and Ameer Ali, a very conservative and Anglophile Moslem.
[40] BL OIOC L/PJ/6/374, File 963 (High Court hearing); /376, File 1132.
[41] *Dainik-o-Samachar Chandrika*, 14 Dec. 1893.

defendants stayed free, the murders were never solved, the officials all kept their jobs, though with shattered prospects of promotion, and the India Office dropped the matter.[42] Neither Indians nor Anglo-Indians were happy: while the Indian papers called for the dismissal of the officials, the European ones not only objected to the reprimands but pointed out angrily the failure to successfully punish the culprits, whether these or others as yet unapprehended. The leading European paper in Bengal pointed to the vulnerable position of Assam planters:

The conditions obtaining in remote and lonely tea districts, where solitary Englishmen are practically at the mercy of the predatory hordes of the frontier, should make a more imperative demand for protection from Government than any other circumstances under which our fellow countrymen live and work in India. Instead . . . the planter has been left to the protection, visibly growing weaker, of his own prestige as an Englishman.[43]

The Englishman's lament may have been exaggerated, but it would appear that the "Balladhun murder case," as it became known, marked, if not a turning point, at least a sign of a shifting terrain in the treatment of interracial violence.[44] The tensions between the purely judicial High Court and lower judicial officials, enmeshed as they were in executive administration, and between officialdom and the Anglo-Indian community were laid bare for public view, and, most important, the usual and unequal procedures of criminal justice were challenged by the highest judicial officials in India, and then by an official inquiry presented to Parliament. The potential in the British "rule of law" for rectifying injustice – the exposure of official error or misbehavior by a comparatively free press, the appeal to higher courts and to parliamentary inquiry and discussion, and the existence of rules of evidence and procedure that could be insisted upon – was drawn on to halt and undo an act of major injustice.

Such actualization of a dormant potential depended, of course, on changes that were taking place in the political context. On the Indian side, these included the rapid growth of a vigorous press and the number of Indian lawyers, and the rise of organized political activity (most notably the 1885 founding of the Indian National Congress). On the British side, these included the election in 1892 of a Liberal Government more

---

[42] *Papers Relating to the Baladhan Murder Case in Assam*, Parliamentary Papers 1894, House of Commons vol. 58, 321 (C.7456); BL OIOC L/PJ/6/374, Files 963, 1132.

[43] "The Tragedy of Balladhun," *The Englishman*, 13 Dec. 1893.

[44] Kolsky, "Crime and Punishment on the Tea Plantations of Colonial India," gives further information on this case.

responsive to Indian National Congress lobbying,[45] the emergence of a body of Radical M.P.s interested in India, led by several former members of the Indian Civil Service, and the rise of men within the ICS who were more sensitive to the need to conciliate Indian opinion.[46] From this point on, the Indian and Bengal Governments began to make serious efforts to protect Indians against the violence of Europeans. While the Balladhun case was proceeding, the evidence it brought forth of the not exceptional use of flogging on plantations led the Chief Commissioner of Assam to instruct all magistrates "distinctly to recognize the principle that any employer who flogs a coolie woman or causes her to be flogged should be sentenced to a substantial term of imprisonment."[47] Later that year the Assam Labour and Emigration Act was passed, amending the 1882 Act governing labor relations on plantations. The earlier Act had given employers the right to arrest absconding laborers without a warrant; the new Act placed restrictions on the use of this power (planters lobbied fiercely and successfully against an original proposal to abolish this power altogether).

As a consequence of the Balladhun scandal, in 1894 the new Viceroy, Lord Elgin, a friend and political follower of Gladstone, ordered lower officials throughout India to report all cases of interracial homicide to the central Government. Two years later Elgin put through an Act amending the Criminal Procedure Code to make it possible for High Courts to themselves retry cases they considered flawed, and two years after that Stephen's Indian Evidence Act 1872 was amended to prohibit as admissible evidence confessions made only to the police.[48] Elgin appointed

---

[45] A portent for the future was the passage, over the opposition of the Anglo-Indian community, of the first measure providing some degree of political self-government for India, the Indian Councils Act 1892, establishing elections of representatives to the Legislative Councils by municipalities, district boards, and other bodies.

[46] Sir Anthony MacDonnell, who served as Acting Lieutenant Governor of Bengal during Elliott's leave in 1893–1894, was an exemplar of these "new men." From the Irish Catholic landed gentry, he had made his mark by dealing effectively with famine, and pushing through legislation protecting peasants from arbitrary eviction. Through his career he promoted the appointment of Indians to district and provincial councils. He had to decline the lieutenant governorship of Bengal in 1898 owing to the frail health of his wife, and soon thereafter returned home. In later years he helped draft reform legislation for Ireland [L. P. Curtis, Jr., "Sir Anthony MacDonnell," *ODNB*].

[47] Kolsky, "Crime and Punishment on the Tea Plantations of Colonial India," quoting the "Report on Labor Emigration into the Province of Assam for the Year 1893."

[48] This measure partly curbed the widespread imprisonment of innocent Indians, but did not stop it altogether. Even without such confessions, Campion has noted, "investigations and prosecutions unable to assemble a viable case could rely on an army of paid witnesses and clumsily doctored evidence" [Campion, op. cit., p. 159].

Henry Cotton, whom his predecessor had thought too sympathetic to natives, as Chief Commissioner of Assam, and encouraged him to review labor conditions on the plantations. At the same time, Elgin blocked strong calls by Anglo-Indians and some of his own civil servants to meet the rise of nationalist agitation by reimposing the press censorship that had existed between 1878 and 1881.[49] Perhaps another sign of an increasing inclination to protect Indians against Europeans was the quick arrest and prosecution of three soldiers for the death of an Indian town Commissioner. In 1898, these soldiers, stationed at Barrackpore, not far from Calcutta, seized the carriage of Dr. Suresh Chandra Sircar. When he protested they responded by enthusiastically kicking him, from which beating he died. This time the victim was no humble villager. They were quickly convicted of causing grievous hurt and sentenced to seven years' "rigorous imprisonment" – a severe sentence to pass on a European for an offense against a native. In addition, substantial compensation was awarded to the victim's widow. The military authorities made no effort in their favor, other than to see that they were adequately represented.[50]

At the beginning of 1899 a new Viceroy arrived. Although a Conservative, Lord Curzon desired just as much as his Liberal predecessor that justice between Europeans and Indians should be as evenhanded as possible, and added to that desire a far stronger will. As he remarked to the Secretary for India after several years in the post, "since I have been in this country I have never wavered in a strict and inflexible justice between the two races. It is the sole justification and the only stable foundation for our rule." The reality he faced severely tested this aim. "As you know very well," he reminded Lord Hamilton, "our case [in pressing for reform] is one of overwhelming strength, and the only reason why it has never been stated in all its particulars is that it would be so damaging to the character and reputation of the ruling race in this country, that it is almost better to be misrepresented and traduced than to have to give one's countrymen away."[51] Curzon quickly found that

---

[49] Apropos of such demands from members of the ICS, "I think," he wrote the Secretary of State for India, "the Indian Civilian is apt to be somewhat thin-skinned" [BL OIOC Mss. Eur. 125/1–3: Private Correspondence, Hamilton-Elgin Mss. Eur. D 509/1–12, Elgin to Hamilton, 7 Oct. 1896]. After the Liberal electoral victory in December 1905, Elgin was made Secretary of State for the Colonies, where he encouraged greater attention to the treatment of nonwhite races. See Chapter 7.

[50] BL OIOC L/PJ/6/480, file 945. However, after the case had faded from public attention the men received early release.

[51] Curzon to Hamilton, 23 Sept. 1903, BL OIOC Mss Eur. F 111/156 (Curzon Papers).

"the result of the acquittals by European juries is causing a widespread distrust in the Native mind as to the fairness and justice of our judicial system."[52] He could do nothing about the juries themselves, but was determined to do what he could to compensate for their misbehavior. In one case – a mass rape of a Burmese prostitute in 1899 that the military authorities had tried to cover up – Curzon intervened to end the careers of four officers most responsible; in another – the killing of a regimental cook in 1902 – which came to trial but produced a quick acquittal, he famously punished by reassignment the entire unit involved.[53] In others, he pressed provincial Governments to intervene to appeal against acquittals or to seek enhanced punishment for European offenders. In 1900, Bengal authorities intervened in several such cases. In the Dinapur Case, the Government of Bengal appealed the acquittal of nine soldiers on charges of rioting armed with dangerous weapons and causing grievous hurt (two were convicted and sentenced to eighteen months' imprisonment), claiming that the Sessions Judge had misdirected the jury. However, the High Court rejected the Government's appeal.[54] In the Darjeeling Case, the Deputy Commissioner of Darjeeling asked the High Court to enhance the trivial sentence of a Rs. 20 fine imposed on a British soldier by a magistrate for the robbery of an Indian servant. This time the High Court agreed, and altered the sentence to imprisonment for six months.[55] By this time Anglo-Indians had begun to complain of their new Viceroy, and through his period of administration, from 1899 to 1905, a series of criminal cases particularly involving British soldiers kept this pot of discontent with him at the boil. Not only did Curzon find civil justice inadequate, but he was also disappointed with military justice, undermined by "a fierce *esprit de corps*."[56] Despite pressure from Curzon, a 1900 court-martial in Poona of a gunner for culpable homicide ended in acquittal and a complaint by the Lieutenant Colonel in charge about the inordinate delays that such interference had produced.[57]

---

[52] Hamilton to Curzon (summarizing what Curzon had been telling him), 8 Mar. 1900, BL OIOC Mss Eur. C 126/9 (Hamilton Papers).

[53] Descriptions of the "Rangoon outrage case" of 1899 and the "Ninth Lancers case" of 1902 can be found in David Dilks, *Curzon in India* (New York, 1970) vol. 1, pp. 198–200, 211–213.

[54] See K. M. Banerjee, *Reports of Criminal Cases Between Europeans and Indians*, vol. 1 (Calcutta, 1901).

[55] Ibid.

[56] Hamilton to Curzon, 6 June 1900 and 11 Oct. 1900, BL OIOC Mss Eur. C 126/2 (Hamilton Papers).

[57] Curzon to Hamilton, 16 May and 13 June 1900, BL OLOC D 510/5 (Hamilton Papers).

Curzon was frustrated repeatedly as homicide trials of soldiers, pressed by officials, ended in acquittals or derisory sentences. The frequent successful defenses of temporary insanity moved him to sarcasm: of one acquittal in 1903 he privately observed that, like another successful soldier defendant also in Bengal two years earlier, "Private Cassidy seems to possess the peculiar gift of passing with startling swiftness from the full possession to the complete loss of his faculties."[58] The contention Curzon aroused was well captured in an interesting novel, Sara Jeannette Duncan's *Set in Authority* (1906).[59] The author, a Canadian living in India and mixing on close terms with leading Europeans there, built her story around two trials of a British soldier for murdering an Indian. In it she gives all European sides a hearing (Indians, however, are barely present). Her fictional Viceroy, who forces the retrial and conviction of the soldier, is clearly based on Curzon; a Colonel represents the white supremacist attitudes of most, and several Civilian officials (and Duncan's sympathies) fall in between these poles. The Colonel acknowledges that "the state of things between the natives of this country and the army wasn't ideal before [the Viceroy] came" but "at all events we knew where we were. Tommy was a better man than the native, and the native jolly well knew it, and kept his place – got soundly kicked if he didn't, and served him right. And, mind you, in the end it was better for the native." Later, when a retrial is forced, he exclaims, "You can't hang a white man for killing a black one in this country. It isn't in nature. It hasn't been done for two generations out here, and it's not likely to be done for ten." Yet if the Colonel convicts himself by his crude racism, the Viceroy is no hero: he is shown to be a self-righteous prig, filled with contempt for virtually all Europeans in India, and determined that his will should prevail regardless of the cost; ultimately, he is more concerned with his moral image in England than with the maintenance of the complex system of rule he is placed in charge of.

The ubiquity of the backlash against the Viceroy's policy testified, however, to the effectiveness of his efforts. Elgin's 1894 reporting directive was, though still resented, now taken seriously at all levels of administration. "The thing that the soldiers dislike most of all," Curzon

[58] Curzon to Hamilton, 15 July 1903, BL OIOC Mss Eur. F 111/155 (Curzon Papers).
[59] The best account of her work is Thomas E. Tausky, *Sara Jeannette Duncan: Novelist of Empire* (Port Credit, Ont., 1980); in 1900 she had authored an anonymous attack on Curzon in the *Contemporary Review* over his treatment of the Rangoon assault case.

remarked to the Secretary for India, "is that the cases of serious collision between them and the Natives are now reported to the Government of India and taken more notice of than they used to be in former days."[60] It was frequently complained that such a policy was encouraging Indians to be insolent. The Governor of Madras, Baron Ampthill, filling in for Curzon while he was on leave in England in 1904, happily passed on such complaints. "The soldiers say," Ampthill told Permanent Under-secretary Godley, "that they are now 'cheeked' by even the lowest class of Natives in an intolerable way, and as they no longer dare to use or to threaten a good thrashing they are quite helpless. It is said that when a European raises his hand to chastise an insolent Native the latter frequently threatens to 'tell the Lord Sahib'!" He went on to note that "when Sir Michael Hicks-Beach [a former member of the Government front bench] was in India the thing which struck him most was the growing 'cheek' of the Native, and if this is apparent to the casual globe-trotter it is pretty certain that the change of attitude is a considerable one."[61] The complaints were frequent, but the policy worked: the number of recorded assaults on Indians declined sharply between 1901 and 1905, when Curzon left India,[62] and did not rise again afterwards.[63]

A key player in the system of justice was the police, and here Curzon also made a decisive intervention. He soon realized that widespread Indian complaints of police bribery, bullying, and extortion amounting to a "Police Raj" were based on much truth – and not only on the behavior of Indian policemen but too often on that of their British supervisors as well. "The greatest menace to the future of British rule in this country," he told

---

[60] Curzon to Hamilton, 12 Mar. 1903, BL OIOC Mss Eur. F 111/154 (Curzon Papers).

[61] Ampthill to Godley, 27 July 1904, BL OIOC Ampthill Correspondence.

[62] BL OIOC L/P&J/6/781, File 3445: "Return Showing the Number of Assaults Committed by Europeans on Natives, and by Natives on Europeans in the Five Years 1901–1905." Bailkin, op. cit., points out, correctly, that most of the fatal native assaults on Europeans were prosecuted as murder, while none of the more numerous fatal European assaults on natives was so prosecuted. But another equally important characteristic of these statistics was the sharp fall in the number of assaults, both fatal and nonfatal, by Europeans on natives. On this see also N. G. Barrier, *Punjab Politics and the Disturbances of 1907* (Durham N.C., 1966), pp. 153–154. The number of recorded Indian assaults on Europeans, on the other hand, showed no decline.

[63] *Karmayogin*, 15 Jan. 1910 [cited by R. K. Ray, op. cit., p. 177], noted the remarkable virtual cessation of murderous assaults on natives by Europeans, attributing this to the emergence of the Indian volunteer (self-defense) organizations in the course of the Swadeshi movement, although the most marked period of decline preceded the rise of those organizations.

the Secretary for India, "is not, as has sometimes been alleged, the House of Commons, nor the Russian advance, nor the Indian Congress, nor the Indian character, but the attitude and passions of the inferior class of Englishmen who are and will be increasingly attracted to India by the lower grades of employment, or by industrial, mercantile, and professional careers. If this class of man is let loose among the people as a Police Officer, there is no end to the mischief that he may do."[64] To deal with this problem he set up a Commission to investigate the Indian Police. The India Office feared this would undermine respect for British rule, but he pushed on and put together a body of seven that included two Indians, but, he assured Whitehall, highly "reliable" ones – a Maharajah and a high ICS official from Madras. The Commission included no Indian lawyer or magistrate; on the other hand, it included no representative of the Police Service. The result was equally strong complaints from both the IPS and the Indian National Congress, enabling Curzon to argue that it was beholden to neither side. The Commission's 1903 report surprised even Curzon by its strong language: it condemned Indian police officers as corrupt, brutal, and inefficient and if it was easier on their European Commissioners, it was only relatively so, describing them as honest, but often incompetent, and either unable or unwilling to control their men.[65] It was not a report calculated to soothe the Police Service or Anglo-Indians. It was to Curzon's credit that he refused the India Office's urgings to suppress its publication.

The Commission had recommendations for dealing with the problems it found: not only closer supervision of the police by magistrates, but higher pay for both European Superintendents and Indian policemen, and a new policy of appointing educated Indians to positions as Assistant Superintendents and ultimately Superintendents. However, the first and second proved easier to put into practice than the third, which went against both racial prejudices and the career interests of current members of the IPS. Still, after this report, at least a start was made on the "Indianization" of the IPS. Most relevant for the problem of interracial violence was that after the Commission's report, the police were to be, at

---

[64] "Notes by His Excellency the Viceroy on Police Reform," 23 Oct. 1903, sent to Secretary for India, BL OIOC Mss Eur. F 111/281 (Curzon Papers).

[65] Even Arvind Verma, in arguing that the British paid insufficient attention to the corruption or brutality of the police ["Consolidation of the Raj: Notes from a Police Station in British India, 1865–1928," *Criminal Justice History* 17 (2002), 109–132] acknowledged that the early 1900s saw a change in this regard, even if it did not go as far as it should have.

least in cases that might draw public attention, held on a tighter leash. Curzon put new officials in place to carry out these policies, most notably A. H. L. Fraser, who had chaired the Police Commission, as Lieutenant Governor of Bengal, where his progressive outlook contrasted with that of predecessors like Elliott.[66]

This was to be of particular importance in dealing with the group that, after soldiers, was most prone to violence against Indians – planters. In the 1890s, as planters were pressing to improve productivity their laborers were developing a political consciousness. "Coolies," planters complained, were becoming increasingly difficult to manage, as any deleterious changes in pay or conditions of work tended to produce protests, while unusual violence by managers was increasingly leading to counterviolence by coolies.[67] By the turn of the century both sides were thus feeling under siege, and appealing to Government officials for support. The reformist Henry Cotton, in charge of Assam after 1896, welcomed Curzon's arrival as his opportunity to make real changes, and prepared draft legislation regulating indentured labor and working conditions. Curzon encouraged him with frequent words of support, but plantation owners and managers began to organize against him, calling upon the powerful Anglo-Indian community in Calcutta for support. As Cotton told Curzon in 1901,

the unofficial European community in India – and especially the planting interest – has grown altogether intolerant of criticism insisting that good and bad alike in

[66] In his memoirs, Fraser dismissed racial stereotypes, repeatedly noting how much alike Indians and Britons were, differing only in circumstances and culture, and emphasized the importance for effective governance of treating Indians with respect. He was proud that for the most part the members of the ICS did so, although, he conceded, "there are Europeans, sometimes of a class from whom, despite their youth, better things might be expected, but more generally Europeans of low breeding and defective education, who treat their Indian fellow-subjects in a way which leads to bitterness of feeling which it is most difficult to eradicate." This, unfortunately, was sometimes true even of an official. "I have seen an officer assault country carters, and actually beat them severely because they allowed their carts to stray down the middle and on both sides of the road, so as to block his way while he was driving his carriage and pair. That officer, when I reprimanded him for his conduct, told me that he thought we were losing the country owing to such sentiments as mine; but there can be no doubt that a few cases of such violence and injustice do more harm than can be calculated." Such "exceptional" cases were, however, very damaging. "They should be regarded with strong condemnation, and, wherever possible, repressed with rigour" [*Among Indian Rajahs and Ryots* (London, 1911), pp. 86–87].

[67] On the growing "restlessness" in the tea gardens, see Nitin Varma, "Coolie Strikes Back: Collective Protest and Action in the Colonial Tea Plantations of Assam, 1880–1920," *Indian Historical Review* 33 (2006), 259–287.

their ranks shall be treated in the footing of the most favored nation and unless this tendency is checked I fear it will become a most dangerous element in the political situation.[68]

That year Cotton managed to get an Act passed improving labor conditions, though it did not go nearly as far as he wanted. At the same time, he found himself embroiled in an emotional dispute with planters. A manager of an Assam tea garden named Lyall was acquitted by a largely European jury of all charges in the death of a laborer who had been severely beaten at his command; Lyall had claimed that the coolie had afterwards committed suicide. Cotton outraged Anglo-Indians generally, first by officially doubting Lyall's claims and criticizing the pro-planter bias in Assam trials and then, more seriously, by getting the District Magistrate to send the case for review to the High Court of Calcutta, which retried it, convicting the planter of causing hurt and sentencing him to a month's imprisonment and a fine of Rs. 1,000. The European Defense Association, based in Calcutta, sprang into action to demand remission of this sentence, but Curzon curtly refused this demand.[69]

This small achievement, however, cost Cotton dearly, for as an Indian paper observed, "it would be hard to conceive the extent to which the tea-planters have been dissatisfied with Mr. Cotton on account of Mr. Lyall's imprisonment. Any ruler less courageous than Mr. Cotton would have become a puppet in the hands of the planters."[70] After rebuffing it on Lyall, Curzon felt obliged to appease the Defense Association by dissociating himself from Cotton when the latter made further public remarks critical of planters.[71] Felt "thrown to the wolves" by Curzon, Cotton brooded and finally submitted his resignation. He returned to England, where he became a Liberal M.P. and a leader of the "Indian" members there.[72]

Curzon may have sacrificed Cotton, but not his determination to do something to rein in the planters. Several widely publicized cases at this time made the need for reform clear to him. In this same year, 1901, two planters in Madras killed their horsekeeper "by tying him to a tree and

---

[68] Cotton to Curzon, 17 Sept. 1901, BL OIOC Mss Eur. D 1202/2 (Cotton Papers).

[69] On this case, and the efforts of the Defense Association, see K. M. Banerjee, op. cit., pp. 115–122; Renford, op. cit., pp. 294–296.

[70] *Basumati*, 12 Dec. 1901.

[71] Curzon was under pressure from the India Office to avoid conflict. "I was afraid," Hamilton complained, "that Cotton would come into collision with the Assam Planters" as he now had [Hamilton to Curzon, 2 Oct. 1901, BL OIOC Mss Eur. C 126/3 (Hamilton Papers)].

[72] On this episode, see Cotton, *Indian and Home Memories* (London, 1911), chap. 22.

beating him by turns with a rattan" to get him to confess to theft, and then
got him quickly buried and claimed his death was a suicide. It was only
the complaint of his wife a month later that roused the suspicions of the
District Magistrate, who had the body exhumed and examined. They
were charged with culpable homicide, found guilty of the lesser charge of
causing grievous hurt, and sentenced to three and four years' rigorous
imprisonment. Soon the inevitable petition for remission of sentence
arrived. Curzon scornfully forwarded it to Hamilton, who agreed that its
argument was "that it is perfectly right that Europeans should take the
law into their own hands," even when as in this case it meant "flogging a
wretched man to death."[73] This and successive petitions were refused by
the Governor of Madras and then by Curzon, embittering Anglo-Indians.

A strong agitation for Curzon's recall was set off by another rather
similar murder trial. In 1903 an Assam tea garden manager named Bain
ordered a recaptured runaway husband and wife flogged, which led to the
wife's death. He then had the dead woman buried, and sought to hush up
the matter. However, coolies informed the District Superintendent of
Police, who had the body dug up and examined, and instituted criminal
proceedings against him. During his trial he was put up in a hotel instead
of the local jail, which was deemed unsuitable for Europeans. Given such
attitudes, it surprised no one that the jury, made up of fellow planters and
other Europeans in the district, convicted him only of "causing simple
hurt" (the equivalent of common assault), but the District Magistrate
who heard the case gave him the maximum penalty he could, six months'
rigorous imprisonment. Convinced that Bain merited still more severe
punishment, Curzon ordered the magistrate to forward the case to the
Calcutta High Court, asking for enhancement. This action set off a storm
of protest: outraged planters and their friends filled public meetings and
signed petitions of complaint, and Anglo-Indian newspapers sharply
criticized the Bengal Government and the Viceroy. Unfortunately for the
Government, Bain's lawyers managed to get the case heard by the most
sympathetic possible Judge, Justice Sale sitting alone, who decided (in
what Curzon privately called "an astounding judgment") that the original
conviction had been flawed and ordered Bain released. Disgusted, Curzon
sent the entire case file to the India Office. Hamilton agreed that the file
"is ugly reading," and sympathized with him about the demands from
Anglo-Indians in Bengal for his recall, observing that "the function of the

[73] Hamilton to Curzon, 2 Oct. 1901, op. cit.

Viceroy in their judgment is to prevent them from being punished when they whack their niggers."[74]

This commotion, rather than causing Curzon to shy away, convinced him of the need to change the rules governing plantation labor. "The relations between tea-planters and their coolies," he wrote Hamilton, "seem to me to be entering upon a more acute and dangerous phase. The coolies are learning to combine, and very often, upon any provocation, they are apt to gather together and assault the European manager of the plantation. These managers are drawn from a most inferior class of Englishmen and Scotchmen; they do not know the language; they have a profound contempt for the Native, and they are sometimes guilty of serious acts of lust and oppression." The existing labor system on the plantations, even as modified in 1893 and 1901, remained in his view "really a penal contract, and the coolies may almost be described as slaves. They cannot run away except at the cost of being arrested and thrown into prison. As long as these conditions exist, the masters will continue to bully their slaves, and the slaves will resent the tyranny of the masters."[75]

---

[74] Hamilton to Curzon, 30 Sept. 1903, BL OIOC Mss Eur. C 126 (Hamilton Papers), L/PJ/6/628, Files 418, 603, 609. For the extensive coverage of this case in Indian papers, see L/PJ/5/29 [Reports on Native Papers, Bengal 1903], Part 1, pp. 219, 247, 791–792, 816–819, 840, 970–972; Part 2, pp. 337–338, 349–360, 361–362. Later that year another Assam planter was tried in the death of a coolie. A tea garden manager named Reid had slapped around his servant because he believed he had stolen some things from him, and then handed him over to his *chaukidars* to beat the whereabouts of the stolen goods out of him. They applied themselves with enthusiasm, and the servant, bloody and disfigured, died. The chaukidars claimed they were acting under his authorization, and the prosecuting official asked that he be charged with murder or the equivalent of manslaughter; however, the Sessions Judge charged him only with causing simple hurt, and he was fined Rs. 150. The District Commissioner, P.G. Melitus, sought to have the sentence enhanced, arguing that the necessary authority of a plantation manager, which, he noted, Sir Charles Elliott had compared to that of a ship's master, "carries with it its responsibilities as well as its claims to protection. A commander of a ship who handed a culprit over to his sailors with orders to extract information from him, he . . . having first set the sailors the example of beating him, would certainly be held morally responsible for something more than simple assault, if the sailors exceeding their instructions beat him to death." Using his own powers, he ordered statutory inspections of tea gardens to be henceforth more frequent and more thorough. Although Chief Commissioner Fuller passed on the request for review, calling the case "a scandalous one," Curzon was on leave, and neither his temporary replacement, Baron Ampthill, nor Secretary of State Hamilton decided to interfere [L/P&J/6/731, file 2392].

[75] Curzon to Hamilton, 5 Aug. 1903, BL OIOC Mss Eur. F 111/156. He continued: "The planters actually allege in public meeting that they can be certain of no justice, though what they mean by this is that they regard it as the greatest of hardships if a planter is fined Rs. 100 for an assault that terminates in the death of a coolie, while the coolie gets a term of rigorous imprisonment of from three to six years if he so much as lifts his

Consequently, he set Henry Cotton's more conservative successor, J. B. Fuller, to work expanding the regulation of abusive labor recruitment and management practices. Fuller, who was careful to maintain cordial relations with planters, ordered a record put together of serious instances of violence in recent years in the plantations. Then, declaring that "the time has come . . . to cast off some of the bonds in which our labour system is swathed," he skillfully pushed through (without any help from a very cautious India Office still run by Godley) several changes, the most important of which was the abolition of the remaining private power of arrest held by planters, a power which Curzon had declared belonged only in a slave system. Although planters complained that this would destroy labor discipline, they were brought around to accept it by Fuller's diplomatic skill. Even an Indian Marxist historian has acknowledged that Fuller's reforms "substantially transformed the labor system" on Assam plantations.[76] Another change Fuller brought about while Chief Secretary for Assam, perhaps trivial but a sign of the changing times, was to replace in all official usage the term "Native" by "Indian."[77]

Planters were not the only European gentlemen to find the Government unsympathetic when they got into trouble with the criminal law. When in 1903 a colliery manager, Henry Martin, fatally shot with his revolver a native who blocked his right of way on a road and was acquitted by a jury that consisted of four Europeans and one Indian, a friend of one of the defendant's lawyers, the Government of Bengal appealed the acquittal. It cited multiple errors and misdirections by the District Judge, who was notorious among Indians for his bullying of Indian witnesses. Indeed, it would appear that he had practically told the jury to disregard the evidence for the prosecution. An Indian paper noted of the conduct of the trial: "Mr. Martin was permitted to sit on a chair in the Courtroom and his wife sat beside him. He was surrounded by friends; and the whole thing looked as if Mr. Martin was going to be married and Mr. Roe [the Judge] was officiating as priest."[78] The High Court ordered a retrial by

---

hand against a European. In my view this unfortunate state of affairs is likely to continue, and even to develop, so long as the present Labour Law remains in Assam."

[76] Rana P. Behal, op. cit., pp. 167–169. This development reflected more than simply the efforts of a few highly placed individuals; during the same years the Government of nearby Ceylon took the first serious actions to protect tea laborers from exploitation (see R. Wenzlhuemer, op. cit.).

[77] Sir Bampfylde Fuller, *Some Personal Experiences* (London, 1930), p. 127.

[78] *Sri Sri Vishnu Priyta-o-Andnda-Bazar-Patrika*, 8 Apr. 1903. See also *The Englishman*, 28 May 1903.

another District Judge, which convicted Martin. He was sentenced to three years' imprisonment, although his subsequent appeal was heard by Justice Sale, who reduced the sentence.[79]

Planters and other Anglo-Indians were disappointed to find that Curzon's departure at the end of 1905 did not bring back the good old days when the law could be counted on to support their position. When in 1906 another planter named Goss was hacked to death, the upsetting Balladhun scenario of 1893 was replayed. The killing spread alarm through white Assam, and two coolies were soon convicted of murder at a trial in Darjeeling, but this time the Sessions Judge, suspicious of the evidence, referred the case to the High Court. There the coolies' convictions were quashed, as the Judges criticized police misconduct. Of course this led to a strong denunciation of the Court on the part of the Darjeeling Planters Association.[80] They said nothing, however, about the suspicious departure for England just before the trial of a neighbor of Goss's, named by Indian newspapers as a likely suspect. *Hitavadi* remarked that "the natives of Darjeeling believe that some European or Europeans were implicated in the murder and that it was to save their heads that the police spoilt the case." While attacking the behavior of the local Superintendent of Police, it praised "the goodness and impartiality of the Sessions Judge of Darjeeling" for preventing judicial murders.[81]

The next year an indigo planter named Bloomfield, who was also tax collector in his district, refused to register the land claims of some peasants, and was in consequence mobbed and beaten, later dying from his injuries. After his death, *The Englishman* urged that "no efforts and no expense should be spared" to find the culprits.[82] As one might expect, the police "terrorized" the locality (in the words of an Indian paper) and arrested many men, and the Sessions Judge sentenced four to death and one to transportation.[83] These sentences provoked not only Indian

---

[79] See L/PJ/6/636, File 1060; *Bengalee*, 19 July 1903; and *Indian Empire*, 21 July 1903. On the efforts of the European Defense Association, see Renford, op. cit., p. 297. Curzon commented to Hamilton: "The miscarriage of justice [in this case] was so flagrant that the Local Government had to order the case to be retried. . . . Here the evidence was so overwhelming that the Jury found him unanimously guilty of culpable homicide. However, the Judge . . . once again came to the rescue, and let him off with the minimum sentence of three years' imprisonment. That he should have got even this has made everybody positively gasp with surprise" [29 July 1903].

[80] See L/R/5/32, Part. 1, p. 741; Part. 2, p. 347; R. K. Ray, op. cit., p. 140.

[81] *Hitavadi*, 12 Aug. 1906.

[82] *The Englishman*, 21 July 1907.

[83] Renford, op. cit., p. 304; L/R/5/33, Part 2, pp. 809–811.

protests but also questions in the House of Commons. On appeal, the Calcutta High Court, in an opinion written by an Indian Judge, set aside the murder convictions and drastically reduced the sentences to three years each for two defendants (for rioting with dangerous weapons) and seven years each for three (for causing grievous hurt). This in turn led to planter outrage: the Behar Planters Association met and passed a resolution of protest to the Viceroy, which the European press, as well as *The Times* back in England, publicized. The High Court had, they claimed, gravely endangered British prestige in Assam, and Bengal generally.[84] Anglo-Indian feelings were raised to a fever pitch, leading even the Planters Association to state that it "deprecate[d] the hysterical tone of many letters that have appeared in the public Press" and to urge everyone to "retain a cool, level and clear-headed judgment on the matter."[85] However, the Government made no concession to the planters or to the Anglo-Indian public.

The new Liberal Secretary for India, John Morley, carried on this part of Curzon's policies, pressing his successor as Viceroy, Lord Minto, to bear down on those beneath him. "One great mischief," he told Minto during his first year in office, "is the overbearing manners etc. of the European, not quite excepting officials."[86] In the face of the rise of revolutionary agitation, Morley pushed Liberal appointments such as that of Sir Lawrence Jenkins – "a regular Congress man," Morley called him – first to the Council of India in 1908 to help draft what became the "Morley-Minto reforms" in local Government, and the following year to the Chief Justiceship of the Calcutta High Court.[87] On the bench Jenkins was a frequent critic of the police and even of magistrates, infuriating many Anglo-Indians.[88]

---

[84] "Prestige" was generally thought by planters to be essential to managing Indians. As one missionary in Fiji remarked of the Indian workers, "it is really only by prestige that the people can be kept in check; and when that goes, there goes all along with it all control. The Indian can scarcely be frightened. When his temper is fully roused, no power on earth can hold him back" [John Wear Burton, *The Fiji of Today* (London, 1910), pp. 293–294].

[85] L/PJ/6/825, File 2982 (2 Sept. 1907); *The Times*, 27 Aug. 1907, p. 3 (*The Times's* correspondent, a partisan of the planters, remarked that henceforth the planters would not trust in the law but arm themselves – "this is a point of grave significance"); *The Englishman*, 27 Feb. 1908.

[86] Morley to Minto, 23 Nov. 1906, Minto Papers, National Library of Scotland.

[87] Morley to Minto, 4 Dec. 1908, Minto Papers.

[88] Jenkins wrote Morley how a colleague he admired, Justice Fletcher, "after deciding a case in favor of an Indian and against a European got hate mail," and was now "anathema to the white man" in Bengal [18 July 1909, IO, Mss Eur. D 573(Morley

High officials now found themselves caught between increasingly fearful Europeans, seeing the arm of British authority slacken, and increasingly demanding Indians.[89] When a man named Sterling, the assistant editor of the leading European paper in the Punjab, who had been a leading champion of the rights of Anglo-Indians, was himself charged in the fall of 1907 with having shot his Indian bearer to death, the case inevitably was followed throughout India. Sterling's arrest took place just as mass political agitation was building in the Punjab, and, indeed, with Punjabis already awaiting trial for a political "riot." The police at first charged Sterling only with committing a "rash and dangerous act," but the District Judge added the more serious charge of culpable homicide and sent the case to the Punjab Chief Court for trial. Further, very unusually in the case of a European defendant (particularly one who was not a soldier), he refused bail. As an Indian paper in the Punjab observed, "such a course would not have been taken ... but for the fact that the authorities are anxious to avoid giving an opportunity for hostile criticism in these days of unrest."[90] At his trial, native witnesses told of a quarrel and of his first kicking the servant and then angrily getting his gun and brandishing it at the man. Sterling acknowledged the quarrel and the kicks, but claimed that it went no further, and that he had then turned to cleaning his pistol when it accidentally fired. Out of great regret he had immediately and voluntarily paid Rs. 300 compensation to the widow. Sterling's counsel emphasized the hardships of the five weeks he had already spent in prison, and complained that the Government had attempted, unsuccessfully, to influence the selection of the jury. He then reminded the jury of the well-known unreliability of native testimony, and of his client's previous excellent character.

Papers)/46]. Morley consequently intended to appoint Fletcher Chief Justice of the North West Provinces High Court, but left office before he could get it done. This was the Judge the next Viceroy, Lord Hardinge, complained of as an obstruction to the executive. Morley, however, thought the executive often needed some obstructing. "One thing," he had written Lord Minto, "I do beseech you to avoid – *a single case* of investigation in the absence of the accused. . . . [I]t has an ugly continental, Austrian, Russian look about it, which will stir a good deal of doubt or wrath here" [Morley's underlining, 24 Dec. 1908; IO, Mss. Eur. D 573(Morley Papers)/46].

[89] As has been recently observed, although the liberalism which the Raj was unable to disavow was "selective, intermittent and invariably hedged around more or less explicitly by the threat of repression or entrapment," it "nonetheless provided a crucial opportunity to exert influence. It was by seizing on these liberal pretensions, or departures from them, that the tables could, albeit briefly, be turned" [Nicholas Owen, *The British Left and India: Metropolitan Anti-Imperialism, 1885–1947* (Oxford, 2007), p. 27].

[90] *Aftab*, 29 Oct. 1907 [L/R/5/189: Reports on Indian Papers, Punjab, 1907–1908].

The Judge of the Punjab Chief Court who was trying the case had just been flayed in the Indian press for his conduct of the trial of a European stationmaster charged with the rape of a young Indian woman, a trial which had ended in an acquittal.[91] Perhaps in reaction, he made a point of instructing Sterling's jury that their "duty is to weigh the facts and return a verdict without any feeling of pity or compassion towards the prisoner. Any regret the prisoner may feel does not affect your verdict. . . . Extenuating circumstances do not affect the question of conviction."[92] The jury at first returned to find him not guilty of culpable homicide, although guilty of a "rash and negligent act," but recommended mercy "as we are not unanimous." They were five to four for this verdict, which the Judge refused to accept as too narrow. After retiring again, they returned with a majority of six to three on the second charge, repeating their recommendation to mercy. Sterling was sentenced to six months' rigorous imprisonment, together with payment of a Rs. 200 fine.[93] Most Indian papers complained of the leniency; *Mahratta* argued that the rape acquittal two weeks before and Sterling's trial "both go unmistakably to prove that the only business of European juries in India is to acquit the European accused brought before them, when the latter do not confess to having done the incriminating act, and to unwillingly give a verdict of guilty and that too on the lowest count when the accused has made such a confession." It expected to see Sterling eventually none the worse for the experience, "installed [back] in the editorial chair of the *Civil and Military Gazette*."[94] A Bengal paper concluded that "while the Government fears to see the offenders acquitted, it does not at the same time possess sufficient moral courage to have them adequately punished."[95]

Greater sensitivity in the Government of India was paralleled by growing assertion by Indians. Following the example of the Anglo-Indian press, the rapidly developing Indian-owned newspaper press began to turn British legal rhetoric against the everyday realities of British rule. Repeatedly, this press urged England, as Madan Mohan, a newspaper

---

[91] It became known as the "Rawalpindi Outrage Case." See BL OIOC L/P&J/6/848 File 453.

[92] *Hindu*, 27 Nov. 1907.

[93] *The Englishman*, 23 Nov. 1907, p. 6: "The Lahore Shooting Case"; *Hindu*, 27 Nov. 1907; *Panjabee*, 27 Nov. 1907. He could have been given up to two years for this offense (as another European was in Bengal a few months later in the killing of a European: *The Englishman*, 26 Feb. 1908, p. 5: "The Sitarampur Tragedy").

[94] 1 Dec. 1907 [BL OIOC L/R/5/189. p. 553].

[95] *Marwari Bandhu*, 5 Dec. 1907.

editor, had already put it at the 1887 meeting of the Indian National Congress, to "be true to her traditions, her instincts and herself and grant us our rights as free born British citizens."[96] In 1903 Denzil Ibbetson, a Conservative member of the Viceroy's Council, warned that "the schoolmaster (and what is more the pleader) is abroad. The respect for authority as such, which is on the whole traditional with the Indian people, is yearly diminishing; the English ideas of liberty and independence are yearly spreading more widely among a people whom we do not propose to allow to be free or independent; the habit of obedience which alone enables a handful of Englishmen to control the millions of Indians is weakening; the disposition to question orders instead of obeying them is strengthening, even in the rural areas."[97] A few years later Lord Minto responded to Morley's criticism of European behavior towards Indians by cautioning him that there was "just now a dangerous condition of affairs, which is likely to be fanned for political purposes, viz., the extremely insulting behaviour of the Babu class to British residents, whether soldier or civilian. . . . I am in constant anxiety lest some case of assault [against an Indian] should be brought about for political purposes in hopes of producing a great scandal here. . . . We are a manly race ready enough to resent an insult, and we have already only managed with difficulty to prevent publicity being given to some very disagreeable incidents."[98] Such incidents were now more likely to become public, as in the new century the criminal courts saw an increasing number of charges brought by Indians against Europeans.

Railways, which despite having cars divided by class inevitably brought the races together, were a fertile site of clashes, and these now began to reach the courts. In 1901 a servant of an Assistant District Superintendent of Police (no doubt with the implicit support of his employer, who however did not testify at the trial) brought a charge of assault against an Army officer, Major A. G. Cartwright. The servant had entered his master's first-class carriage upon his arrival in Benares to take out his luggage and the Major without a word threw him out, then stepped outside and shook his fists at the man. While several Indians gave evidence for the prosecution, Major Cartwright claimed that the servant had

---

[96] Quoted in Harish Kaushik, *The Indian National Congress in England 1885–1920* (Delhi, 1973), p. 11. See D. Naoroji, *Poverty and Un-British Rule in India* (London, 1901).

[97] Minute, 1 Aug. 1903, quoted in Barrier, op. cit., p. 222.

[98] Minto to Morley, 26 Dec. 1906, Minto Papers. He went on to complain that it was not always appreciated at home that "natives are very irritating to deal with in many ways."

tried to push him aside upon entering the carriage, and he had simply pushed back. However, the magistrate, while regretting that the matter "should ever have come into Court," found Cartwright guilty of common assault, and ordered a fine of Rs. 10, to be paid to the complainant. The outraged Major appealed to the Allahabad High Court. At the subsequent hearing, the Government Advocate hardly bothered to present an argument, calling it merely a "technical" assault. Justice Knox, who heard the case, quashed the conviction, calling the charge "frivolous and vexatious," and complained that servants were not behaving as respectfully as they had "twenty years ago," when a servant "would stand by while a master, whoever that master might be, made his way past."[99] Still, the bringing of the charge, and the initial conviction of the English officer, were remarkable enough.

Nor was it isolated; in the same year an Indian clerk in the Calcutta office of *The Englishman* charged the English manager with assault. The case was heard by a Bench composed of one Indian and two European magistrates. By the time of the trial, the prosecuting clerk's witnesses failed to appear; he claimed, probably correctly, that they feared losing their jobs, and the case was dismissed.[100] In 1903, however, a Captain was fined Rs. 50 in Bombay police court for a gross insult to an Indian barrister and his wife in a first-class rail carriage (he had objected to riding with a "dirty little black man"), after the barrister brought charges. Even though the officer had, when the proceedings opened, offered a public apology, the case continued; the fine was necessary, the magistrate declared, to "deter" others.[101] One can see why Anglo-Indians were concerned about natives increasingly stepping out of their place. As time went on, such once-unheard-of cases became more common, even against officials. In 1908, a Deputy Inspector-General of Police for the United Provinces was convicted of assault and fined after a Jain priest brought charges.[102] An Assistant Superintendent of Police was forced in 1912, by an Indian Judge, to apologize in open court for slapping an Indian boy who had gotten in the way of his bicycle.[103]

---

[99] *New India*, 4 Nov. 1901. R. K. Ray has observed that "racialism was to be encountered in a more personally humiliating form in railway carriages where men and women often had the bitter experience of being unceremoniously thrown out" [op. cit, p. 22].
[100] K. M. Banerjee, op. cit., pp. 78–79.
[101] L/P&J/6/630, File 557 (a question about this was raised in the House of Commons).
[102] Report on Native Papers, Bengal, 1908, p. 961.
[103] *Amrita Bazar Patrika*, 6 Dec. 1912: "Rangpur slapping case"; *Bangavasi*, 4 Jan. 1913.

assault

Feeling some inhibition now against directly responding to native "insolence" as they had been accustomed to, some Europeans themselves began to make use of the courts to further criminal complaints against Indians. The "Chandighat tea garden case" of 1913 revealed a changed situation in Assam. Here a European manager named Stuart had apparently insulted an Indian gentleman, who had responded by striking him with his walking-stick. Instead of retaliating physically, the European went to court with assault charges. The magistrate sentenced the Indian to a year's imprisonment, but the District Judge cut the sentence in half; upon further appeal to the High Court the sentence was reduced to a fine only.[104] "We know," one Indian paper observed, "that one can get justice done if one appeals to the High Court [something unlikely to have been conceded a decade or more earlier], but not everybody can go up to the High Court for reasons of expense."[105]

Such change had its limits, and in the great mass of cases, inequality of treatment, if diminished, certainly continued. Similar offenses drew much more severe punishment when committed by an Indian than when the perpetrator was European, and in cases crossing the racial line, harms to Indians were still regarded less seriously than harms to Europeans. In particular, the guarantee of European-majority juries to Europeans made conviction and serious punishment of European offenders against Indians extremely difficult, even when Judges and executive officials sought them. This "right of freeborn Englishmen" ensured in India, as elsewhere in the Empire, the continuation of racial inequality in criminal justice. Thus, cases in which Europeans were acquitted of causing death (on grounds either of accident or of temporary insanity) continued, as did, more numerously, cases in which they were convicted but merely fined, yet they occurred much less often than in the later nineteenth century. The great fall in such fatal incidents, together with more frequent convictions and more severe punishments of Europeans when they did take place, and the decline in convictions and the less severe penalties given to Indians when charged with personal violence against Europeans, all testified to long-term change, which ensured that the ideal of equality under the law survived, along with widespread respect for the rule of law. When the nationalist B. G. Tilak's appeal of his sedition conviction to the Privy Council succeeded in 1915, one Indian paper observed (if perhaps

---

[104] *Basumati*, 8 Mar. 1913; *Bangavasi*, 5 July 1913.
[105] *Hitavadi*, 4 July 1913.

overenthusiastically), "The English Government is loved by the Indian public on account of its justice. Though it costs a good deal to reach the highest courts of appeal, yet in the end everything is properly sifted and measured."[106]

The postwar repression that culminated in the Amritsar massacre of course changed feelings, but one should resist the temptation to read back the alienation and radicalism of the post-Amritsar era into earlier times. Moreover, the postwar crisis itself produced further reform – not only of the structure of Government but also in criminal justice. A Committee on Racial Differences in the Administration of Criminal Justice was appointed in 1920. Its recommendations to abolish nearly all racial distinctions went further than could be adopted, but specific changes in this direction were instituted, for example, ending the European exemption from being judged by Indians in the mofussil. Its report also served to give official legitimacy to the views of its Hindu and Moslem members on the workings of the criminal law. The year after the Committee reported saw the first murder conviction of a European in the death of an Indian since 1880. A gunner in the Royal Field Artillery, Lucknow, named Eaton was charged with murdering a watchman employed by the battery's tailor. After heavy drinking, without provocation he had attacked the man with a knife. The Chief Justice of the Allahabad High Court told the jury that intoxication was no excuse in murder. They returned a verdict of guilty but recommended mercy on the grounds of his youth (he was twenty-three) and the want of premeditation. The Judge then pronounced the sentence of death, although Eaton was later to be spared the gallows as the jury had requested; still, the Indian papers took note of this most unusual verdict.[107]

The postwar years saw fundamental changes in British rule in India, as Indians gained political power and administrative positions, and as the Independence movement built up its strength among the populace. From outside India, the Government was increasingly constrained by a more liberal British public opinion and by international scrutiny, through the League of Nations, to more carefully uphold its proclaimed principles of non-racism and equality under the law. In this new situation, with British

---

[106] *Dainik Bharat Mitra*, 1 Apr. 1915.
[107] *The Englishman*, 27 July 1922, p. 8; L/R/5/203: Punjab Press Abstract, 1922, pp. 365, 390. Another murder conviction, this time of three English soldiers, described in Bailkin, op. cit., took place in 1931.

rulers permanently on the defensive, criminal cases of serious personal violence by Europeans to Indians became still less frequent and their outcomes less scandalous. George Orwell's fictional Police Superintendent in *Burmese Days* complained in the 1920s, "'It's all this law and order that's done for us,' said Westfield gloomily. The ruin of the Indian Empire through too much legality was a recurrent theme with Westfield. . . . 'All this paper-chewing and chit-passing. Office babus are the real rulers of this country now.'"[108] The freedom of official and non-official Europeans in India was in the postwar years hemmed in as never before. Down to Independence, enough reality existed in the "English gospel" of law to help shape the India of today. As an Indian legal historian observed in 1984, "the Rule of Law is among the most precious legacies of England to India."[109]

Perhaps just as important in the British Government of India as the racial distinctions emphasized by recent historians was the maintenance and gradual strengthening of a framework of legality, however often distorted in practice. Rather than being "indefinitely deferred," as postcolonial critics have claimed, equal treatment under law (like self-government) would appear to have been advancing, even if slowly and unevenly, from the 1890s onward. What sometimes had served as an "alibi of empire" also served to prevent a British slide toward real despotism of the kind of which the twentieth century has sadly given all too many examples – a despotism which would have also made likely a despotic independent India. The extent to which the British sometimes lived up to the promise of equal justice under law – even the existence of mavericks like Cotton who insisted against their fellow Britons, sometimes against their superiors, on applying the law to all – helped shape a nationalist movement committed to a constitutional order. The visiting English radical journalist H. W. Nevinson was surprised and indeed

---

[108] P. 32.

[109] A. C. Banerjee, *English Law in India* (Delhi, 1984). Even when the Executive interfered to curb basic rights, he noted, "the *form* of law was maintained, i.e., the Executive exercised arbitrary power in terms of laws or ordinances which were passed in accordance with the established legal procedure, even though the *spirit* of the law was violated. The expression 'lawless law', used by the nationalists, is a meaningful description of the two contradictory aspects of this system which was a product of political necessity" [p. 274]. Indeed, Banerjee concluded his study by asserting, in contradiction to many nationalist writers, that "the democratic values which we hold so dear cannot be traced even remotely to Hindu Law or Moslem Law," but stem from the English legal infusion [p. 288].

irritated by the attachment of leading members of the Indian National Congress even in 1907 to British rule. Nevinson was especially taken aback when G. K. Gokhale defended Curzon's notion that "inscrutable providence" had brought Britain to govern India, since "England was supplying what most was lacking in the race – love of freedom and self-assertion against authority."[110] If many of contemporary Africa's political problems have been traced back to the era of British colonialism,[111] surely some of the credit for modern India's comparative political success should be allotted to this attachment of so many of its nationalist leaders to British liberal traditions.

The ideals of the rule of law and the rights of the subject could be found in the most surprising places among the British in India, even among the most committed imperialists. In this connection, it might be enlightening to conclude this chapter with one of Kipling's less-remembered poems, written just months after the endlessly cited poem "The White Man's Burden" – "The Old Issue":

> ...All we have of freedom, all we use or know –
> This our fathers bought for us long and long ago.
>
> Ancient Right unnoticed as the breath we draw –
> Leave to live by no man's leave, underneath the Law.
>
> Lance and torch and tumult, steel and grey-goose wing
> Wrenched it, inch and ell and all, slowly from the King.
>
> Till our fathers 'stablished, after bloody years,
> How our King is one with us, first among his peers.
>
> So they bought us freedom – not at little cost
> Wherefore must we watch the King, lest our gain be lost. . . .
>
> He shall break his Judges if they cross his word;
> He shall rule above the Law calling on the Lord. . . .
>
> Over all things certain, this is sure indeed,
> Suffer not the old King: for we know the breed. . . .

---

[110] Quoted in Nicholas Owen, "British Progressives and Civil Society in India, 1905–1914," *Civil Society in British History: Ideas, Identities, Institutions*, ed. Jose Harris (Oxford, 2003), p. 161. Ironically, soon after this meeting Gokhale was called by the Indian Government's Criminal Investigation Department "the most dangerous man in India" [Kaminsky, op. cit., p. 168].

[111] Mahmoud Mamdani, *Citizen and Subject: Contemporary Africa and the Legacy of Late Colonialism* (Princeton, 1996).

Long-forgotten bondage, dwarfing heart and brain –
All our fathers died to loose he shall bind again. . . .

Step by step and word by word: who is ruled may read.
Suffer not the old King: for we know the breed –

All the right they promise – all the wrong they bring.
Stewards of the Judgment, suffer not this King!

7

Kenya, 1905–1934

It will be an ill day for these native races when their fortunes are removed from the impartial and august administration of the Crown and abandoned to the fierce self-interest of a small white population.

Winston Churchill, *My African Journey* (1908)[1]

On a June day in 1923, a substantial Kenya farmer, Jasper Abraham, son of the Bishop of Norwich, ordered an African employee named Kitosh to deliver to the farm a horse that had been left at a railway station. When Abraham was told that the employee had been seen riding the horse, rather than walking it as he had been told to do, he flew into a tirade, demanding over and over again to know why the "boy" had defied his instructions and ridden it. The African finally replied that he was not a thief. Taken aback by this "insolent" answer, Abraham flogged him with an ox rein for fifteen minutes, then, tiring, ordered other African employees to continue the flogging, finishing off after a few more minutes by personally delivering a kick to the head. He then had him tied to a post in the storeroom for the night. By morning the man was dead. He died, as Dane Kennedy has astutely observed, "because he had ridden the European's horse." The "right to mount" the horse was "an emblem of social rank and authority reserved for Europeans. By riding the horse, the African employee unwittingly challenged a symbolic boundary that distinguished and separated the two races, thereby sparking the explosive response of the European farmer."[2] On being informed of the man's death, Abraham called the local police chief and told him that, injured

[1] P. 38.
[2] Dane Kennedy, *Islands of White: Settler Society and Culture in Kenya and Southern Rhodesia, 1890–1939* (Durham, N.C., 1987), p. 181.

and humiliated, the African had wished himself to death – a phenomenon settlers claimed to be familiar with. This may appear a peculiar belief, but it was widely held. "Men who appeared to be quite healthy would sometimes die because they wanted to," the writer Elspeth Huxley recalled in her memoir of growing up on an East African farm.[3] Isak Dinesen, in her famous work *Out of Africa*, gave a fictionalized version of this case, from which she drew the "beautiful lesson" that the African, like all the "wild things" of Africa, was in touch with a power beyond the reach of Europeans: "It seems...a strange, a humiliating fact that the Europeans should not, in Africa, have power to throw the African out of existence. The country is his Native land, and whatever you do to him, when he goes he goes by his own free will, and because he does not want to stay."[4] Whatever may have been believed about African suicidal powers, Abraham was charged with murder. A Bishop's son in this position naturally drew the attention of the British press, and his subsequent trial in August before a jury of nine Europeans was, unlike previous such trials, widely reported in Britain, opening up a window for the home public into life in the colony.

Kenya came under British control in 1895 and was placed under the Colonial Office in 1905. It was thus one of the newest imperial acquisitions, and unlike the old possessions in the West Indies, had a growing European population, who hoped to fill it with farms and make it a "white man's country." Yet, as in India, Europeans remained vastly outnumbered by the natives (and outnumbered even by the Indians immigrating there at the same time). Unlike in India, however, they did not recognize the mostly pastoral African population as at all civilized, and thus having a legitimate claim on the land. In contrast to Australia, on the other hand, this population was not dying out from European diseases, but was instead increasing under European rule, and thus could not simply be pushed aside. Like each of these colonial possessions, then, Kenya's situation was unique.[5] Yet, like them, it became a stage on which were played out a similar set of struggles – between Europeans and

---

[3] *The Flame Trees of Thika*, p. 55.

[4] [1937] (New York, 1972), pp. 278–283.

[5] It differed also from the other white settler colonies of Africa, Rhodesia, and South Africa: "Kenya held an ambiguous position among the white settler domains of Africa. While it was often referred to as a white man's country, the European community never achieved the numerical strength of its counterparts to the south" [Christopher P. Youé, *Robert Thorne Coryndon: Proconsular Imperialism in Southern and Eastern Africa, 1897–1925* (Waterloo, Ont., 1986), p. 160].

subordinate races and, in consequence of this basic conflict, secondary struggles between British officials and European settlers, and among British officials (and even at times among settlers) themselves. African land and African labor formed the basic currencies of conflict, to which eventually were added political rights – of Indian immigrants as well as of native Africans.

As twentieth-century settlers, white Kenyans found themselves in a new relationship to the imperial Government. The great improvement in communication produced by the undersea telegraph cable and then the wireless and the airplane enabled British politicians and bureaucrats to become much more involved than their predecessors with the details of colonial administration. At the same time, the rise of a mass-circulation press in Britain was giving greater home publicity to violent or scandalous events in the colonies, while the arrival of democracy was making that public's reactions more important and British Government more socially and racially liberal and less acquiescent in settler ambitions to exercise unchecked power in their new land. Not that the new conditions of the new century were all bad for the settlers: the same technological improvements enabled settlers to remain in closer touch with the homeland, and more able than their nineteenth-century counterparts to maintain a strong base of political support with their "kith and kin" there. Although officials at the Colonial Office agreed from the start that Kenya was "not a white man's country in the best sense of the word," and doubted that its economic future lay in white farming, they were unable to find a Governor who would not "go over" to the settlers.[6]

Along with land, labor was essential to European development of Kenya. All of the trials we will be viewing, except the very first, involved European farmers and African farm employees, and originated in the struggle to control African labor. As in some other parts of the Empire, white farmers policed their own farms, and labor "discipline" was often violent, sometimes getting out of control. In general, the homicides discussed here were unintended – the consequences of times when "discipline" – or anger – went too far. These unfortunate events seemed to settlers only technically crimes, and they expected British officials to see this. Yet the latter, as elsewhere in the Empire, had their own perspective. In the colony's first years, it resembled Fiji in that white settlers were few, and officials could virtually dictate to them. As settler numbers grew, so did their power, and officials soon were bending over to

[6] W. D. Ellis, cited in Ronald Hyam, "The Colonial Office Mind, 1900–1914," op. cit., p. 47.

accommodate them. However, this happy situation for settlers did not last long; soon they faced new challenges – from the demands of an imperial Government enlarged and strengthened by the World War; from increasingly active humanitarians and anti-imperialists in Britain; from the supervision of new international institutions like the League of Nations and the International Labor Organization; from Indian immigrants, now encouraged by political reform in India to claim the rights of imperial citizens; and, initially least but ultimately perhaps most important, from the emergence of African political agitation.[7] Counterbalancing these challenges was the strong pressure that immediately developed toward white solidarity and the greater proportion of members from the upper classes among them than was typical of other settler colonies; besides inflecting the East African settler community with their own self-confidence, such members could draw on influential family and business connections in Britain.[8] Often, indeed, settlers were their own worst enemies in winning support from Government and the British public.[9] Winston Churchill had already noted after a 1907 visit that "the white population here, though small in numbers, is loud and vehement in its opinions. English people dislike being governed so intensely, that they shut their eyes to all the advantages they derive, and I must say many of their complaints have appeared to me to be most ungrateful."[10]

Complaints about the criminal justice system were loud and prolonged after the first two convictions of white men in the deaths of Africans. The

---

[7] See John Cell, ed., *By Kenya Possessed: The Correspondence of Norman Leys and J. H. Oldham 1918–1926* (Chicago, 1976); E. S. Atieno Odhiambo, *Siasa: Politics and Nationalism in East Africa 1905–1939* (Nairobi, 1981); Charles Chenevix Trench, *Men Who Ruled Kenya* (London, 1989); Bruce Berman, *Control and Crisis in Colonial Kenya* (London, 1990).

[8] "Because the *East African Chronicle* was considered 'openly hostile to Europeans in this country,' its editor was commanded in 1921 to resign his membership in the Lumbwa Farmers' Association. Some years later the same association protested the opinions expressed by one of its members in a letter to the *East African Standard*. The controversy resulted in the unanimous passage of a resolution stating that, 'before individual members ventilate their political views in the public press, they should first bring them before their Association for full discussion in order that they may be dealt with through proper channels'" [Kennedy, *Islands of White*, p. 181].

[9] A businessman and Conservative M.P., Sidney Henn, privately observed to his friend Governor Coryndon at the peak of Kenyan political tensions in 1924 that white settlers unfortunately tended to notice only their British critics and "forget that they have plenty of friends at this end who are steadily working away to help them." The settlers, he complained, "do not realize that many of their troubles are created by themselves" [25 Aug. 1924, Bodleian Library, RHL Mss. Afr. s 633 (Coryndon Papers), Box 9, file 6, f. 43].

[10] Quoted in Hyam, *Elgin and Churchill at the Colonial Office*, p. 347.

first Kenyan High Court jury trial, in early 1905, was that of a newcomer, Max Wehner, charged with the murder of a native guide. Wehner and a friend had been doing some hunting, and had stopped in a hotel in Nakuru for dinner. Leaving the hotel in a drunken state, they headed for their camp some miles outside the small town, engaging several natives as guides. Halfway there an argument arose as to the correct direction; Wehner angrily concluded that they were being misled, struck several of their guides with a heavy stick, and shot one. His body was found the next day, with both bullet wounds and head battered in. Wehner had only recently arrived from South Africa, and when the police checked with that country they discovered that he had been jailed for murder in a South American country, and had then served time in South Africa for serious crimes, only recently having been released from prison in Durban.[11] Wehner and his white companion were then held and charged with murder. Wehner immediately claimed the right to a jury trial which, since he had been charged with a capital offense, he was readily granted. He was tried in Nairobi at the High Court, established less than three years earlier. The other Africans hired that fatal night were called as witnesses. The Court's inexperience was apparent: only after the first African had been giving evidence for a short while did the Crown Advocate prose- cuting the case realize that he had not been sworn; the trial was halted, the witness sworn, and the evidence resumed. At the conclusion of the exami- nation of the second native witness, Judge R. W. Hamilton remembered that the jury had not been sworn. This was done immediately, but the two native witnesses were not recalled to repeat their evidence. These tech- nical errors were to prove fateful. Although Wehner's counsel offered a weak and inconsistent defense, the jury of five white men (at least two of whom were Government employees) returned a verdict that he had indeed caused the death of the native, but was not responsible for his actions due to drink. Chief Justice Hamilton, however, interpreted this as a guilty verdict with a recommendation to mercy, since it was well- established English law that drunkenness, unless it was so dominating as to prevent the formation of an intent to seriously harm, could not excuse murder. He accordingly sentenced Wehner to death (the only sentence for murder), and his companion to a term of penal servitude, and retired

[11] See W. Robert Foran, *A Cuckoo in Kenya: The Reminiscences of a Pioneer Police Officer in British East Africa* (London, 1936), pp. 313–316. However, Foran's account is inaccurate in some details; see the contemporaneous trial report in the *African Standard*, 4 Feb. 1905, on which I have relied on points of difference.

to prepare his report for the expected plea for commutation of the capital sentence.

That was not what was to follow, however. A storm of protest at the sentence itself immediately ensued. Lost in the furor was Wehner's criminal past; he now became in public discourse a gentleman victimized by an ignorant and willful Judge, who, the *African Standard* was to complain, "is apparently determined to hang somebody before he is relieved from his responsibilities in this unhappy country."[12] On the evening of the trial's conclusion a mass meeting of sixty or seventy "indignant settlers" was held in Nairobi. It was told that "the accused was convicted on purely circumstantial evidence," while "white evidence" had shown that the gun from which the cartridge was fired was in the possession of another at the time. Moreover, the failure to swear in the African witnesses and the jury was noted, as was the (perfectly legal) use of officials on the jury. A barrister volunteered to head a committee to seek appeal of the decision.[13]

The Court of Appeal in Zanzibar recommended commuting the death sentence, but only to penal servitude for life, and Commissioner Sir Donald Stewart, acting as head of the East Africa Protectorate, did so, but told the Colonial Office that it was only to respond to the jury's plea. "I consider that the prisoner was guilty of a brutal and cold-blooded murder."[14] Mere commutation did little to soothe the settlers, and a defense fund was set up to carry the appeal to the Privy Council. Wehner was now described in the local press as "grandson of General Wehner, last Commander-in-Chief of the Hanoverian Army under King George." The appeal focused on procedure: the failure to properly swear in witnesses and jury, the Judge's supposed misdirection of the jury, and his misinterpretation of its intent. "The jury have, we understand," announced the *African Standard* in urging its readers to contribute to the defense fund, "stated that their intention was to bring in a verdict of manslaughter, or causing death by a negligent act while in a state of intoxication, while Judge Hamilton recorded their finding as a verdict

[12] *African Standard*, 18 Mar. 1905, p. 3.
[13] *African Standard*, 11 Feb. 1905, p. 11.
[14] CO 533/1/17600 (26 Apr. 1905). Two days later Stewart requested that "arrangements be made for [Wehner's] reception in an English prison. . . . I have reason to believe that the prisoner is a desperate character. He has already made one ineffectual attempt to escape from prison here, and it is stated that he was sentenced to death on a former occasion in Mexico" [CO 533/1/17606]; see also CO 533/6/194905, CO 533/2/26675, CO 533/10/29693, CO 533/3/27643, and CO 533/3/28859.

of murder."[15] A King's Counsel was hired, and an appeal duly went forth to the Privy Council. A Colonial Office official, sizing up the situation, correctly predicted Wehner's escape: "He is probably going to get out of prison on a technicality," noted H. B. Lucas, "though there is little doubt that he was guilty of a cowardly and brutal murder. These people treat him as a persecuted innocent. This sort of thing will not do."[16] Indeed, in early 1906 the Judicial Committee of the Privy Council did overturn both convictions, citing serious procedural errors – the failures in swearing in and the Judge's misreading of the jury's verdict. The counsel appearing for the Government did not seem to put much effort into his brief, and the Committee's tone was sharply critical: Lord Halsbury observed in the ruling that "the whole proceedings were from the first irregular."[17] Wehner and his associate, having been held in Mombasa prison for almost a year, and now seen even in Britain as victims of official excess,[18] were released and put aboard a steamer for Bombay.

While Wehner's case wound its way to London, two further trials kept settler indignation stoked. In March 1905 Justice Hamilton tried two white men named McLeish and McCormick for a number of offenses, from shooting elephants to shooting at natives to kidnapping native girls. Their counsel asked for a nine-man jury, but, as he had with Wehner, Hamilton ruled that only five were necessary, and in the event two of them, as in Wehner's case and over the objections of defense counsel, were officials. The men were acquitted on most charges but found guilty of compelling the girls to labor against their will, and sentenced by Hamilton to six months' imprisonment and Rs. 500 fines. The *African Standard* called it a "flagrant perversion of justice" by a Judge who, as with Wehner, seemed determined to convict of something. These "trumped up charge[s]," it warned, "are rapidly bringing the law into ridicule in British East Africa."[19] Finally, in July a farmer was tried for seriously wounding a native by shooting. A group had "created a

[15] *African Standard*, 18 Feb. 1905, p.3: "Sad Case of Mr. Wehner." Contributors, it promised, would have their names recorded in the paper. The jury's memorial to the Privy Council stated that "we are of opinion that the condemned man was only guilty of culpable homicide not amounting to murder as these terms are used in English law and that the native's death though due to the hand of the condemned was not a premeditated crime."

[16] CO 533/10/37484: minute, 24 Oct. 1905.

[17] *The Times*, 9 Feb. 1906, p. 9.

[18] *The Times* observed in a leader on 10 Feb. 1906 that Wehner did not receive the "fair play" English law prided itself on, and concluded that "the whole matter is not reassuring to Europeans living in or visiting these parts."

[19] *African Standard*, 11 Mar 1905, p. 7.

disturbance" near his house while his wife was in the last stages of pregnancy, and when they ignored his call to disperse, he angrily fired a shotgun at them "in order to frighten them," injuring one man, who was taken to the hospital. The District Commissioner had him arrested and taken to Nairobi for trial before a Sessions Judge alone, who found him guilty of causing hurt and sentenced him to six months' imprisonment. As upsetting to settlers as his trial was his public degradation before the African population, for when arrested, he was handcuffed to a native policeman and taken this way sixty miles to Nairobi, for passers-by to see. A protest meeting was held after the arrest at which outrage was vented and a resolution passed. One writer to the *African Standard* declared, "no community of white men should ever allow it to happen again." A settler leader, Lord Hindlip, complained to the Colonial Office: "I do not now intend to discuss the legality or equity of either the sentence or the absence of a jury. But with all respect I do wish to convey to the Right Honourable The Secretary of State that I regard the handling of white men by black as extremely dangerous. There is a very strong feeling in East Africa on the subject, and I earnestly hope that steps will be taken to prevent a similar occurrence before any reprisal happens and a murder is committed."[20]

These cases produced a settler campaign against the criminal justice system in Kenya and against the judiciary. From its beginning the colony had been governed by the Indian Penal and Criminal Procedure Codes in their 1882 form, which, settlers complained, put too much power in the hands of officials and gave accused persons too few rights. The fact that under this system non-Europeans had even fewer rights was not of course of concern. What the settlers demanded were the full rights of freeborn Englishmen for themselves; as one of their leaders, a lawyer, declared at a public meeting, "wherever Englishmen settled in any new country they were entitled to the English common law."[21] In East Africa in 1905, as in India before 1884, only for the most serious offenses did Europeans have a right to a jury trial, and such a jury did not need to be unanimous to

---

[20] CO 533/10/31595, Lord Hindlip to Secretary of State, 2 Sept. 1905; *African Standard*, 29 July 1905, p. 4, and 5 Aug. 1905, p. 5. Another letter to the *African Standard* from a visitor sympathetically repeated what a settler had told him about this incident: "We take it Sir, as a deliberate and studied insult from the authorities to the white inhabitants of this country. . . . There is hardly a man among us who at some time or other has not had to put up with the overbearing insolence and impertinence of these black police . . . which the authorities must know from the number of complaints sent to them." The colonial authorities, he concluded were using "German methods" [12 Aug. 1905, p. 9].

[21] *African Standard*, 29 July 1905, p. 4.

convict. Moreover, a Judge could send a case whose verdict he thought wrong to the High Court for retrial. All of this was both practically and symbolically intolerable to settlers, placing their fates in the hands of judicial officials and branding them as second-class Englishmen. Feeding their legal grievances was the social condescension that imperial officials seemed unable to avoid in dealing with ordinary Europeans in the Empire.[22]

Immediately upon Wehner's conviction, the *African Standard* had run a leader attacking the Indian Penal Code, followed the next week by a leader criticizing the appointment of Judges unfamiliar with life in the colony.[23] By July of that year, a petition to the Colonial Secretary had been drawn up and widely signed calling for the abolition of the Indian Penal Code in East Africa. It was absurd, the petition noted, for the East African Protectorate to be "governed as if it were a province of India." Colonists, it declared, "object altogether to be made subject to any criminal law which is different from, or in excess of the English statute and common law." It particularly objected to "the very large powers which [the Code] entrusts to magistrates, frequently young and inexperienced . . . and the inadequate provision it makes for trial by jury of many important offences." Most galling of all was that East African settlers did not even have the protection given since the Ilbert Bill controversy to Europeans in India, of claiming a jury trial for any offense in which a defendant faced the possibility of more than a few days' imprisonment. The petition went even further than these specific grievances, however, to declare trial by jury in all criminal or civil cases the colonists' "inalienable right."[24] The *African Standard* in particular scrutinized the courts, and did not let many weeks go by that year without a story of judicial practical ignorance or overreaching.[25] These efforts got results: a 1906 ordinance provided that all Europeans and Americans committed to a Court of Session (which in East Africa could be just a single magistrate) would be entitled in most instances to claim a jury, *all* of whose members were to be European or American. This actually made them better off than

---

[22] Robert Foran, op. cit., recalled various examples of official snobbery toward settlers – and toward himself, a mere policeman.

[23] *African Standard*, 11 Mar. 1905, p. 6, and 18 Mar. 1905, p. 3. It repeated the latter complaint twice, on 29 Apr. 1905, p. 6, and 13 May 1905.

[24] *African Standard*, 8 July 1905, p. 3: "The Grievances of East African Colonists."

[25] See for example, 13 May 1905, p. 4: "Our Judiciary and Their Ways"; 5 Aug. 1905, p. 3: "The Indian Law," "Another Peculiarity"; 12 Aug. 1905, p. 9: "Black and White," "Autocrat Officialism."

Europeans in India, whose juries only had to have a majority of their race; and it said nothing about Indians, Arabs, or Africans, who continued without any right to jury trial.[26]

The guarantee of jury trial in almost all criminal trials was a crucial victory for settlers. Henceforth, it would be a most unusual case of European violence to Africans that would produce any criminal sanctions. Such an unusual case appeared the very next year, but despite producing a conviction it nonetheless illustrated the rise of settler assertiveness and confidence. In the spring of 1907, Captain Ewart Grogan, a leader of the growing settler community, together with four other men publicly flogged three African rickshaw drivers in front of the Nairobi courthouse, as several hundred whites gathered to watch. Their provocation was the men's supposed verbal insulting of ladies of his family, but the Acting Commissioner of the East African Protectorate, F. J. Jackson, regarded "the whole incident as deliberately engineered and planned... with a view to bringing the Administration, and more particularly the Judicial and Police Departments, into contempt." Jackson had the group arrested and charged with "taking part in an unlawful assembly," a charge minor enough not to require jury trial. Grogan was given one month's imprisonment and the others shorter periods in jail. The convictions were denounced as "political" and, because they did not involve a jury, an illegitimate procedure taken from "an alien code." A delegation of settlers immediately got the Acting Commissioner to agree to place them not in the common jail where African offenders were kept, which would "degrade them in the eyes of the surrounding native population," but in a separate location under guard. Their brief sojourn even in this special and not uncomfortable facility still became a grievance frequently cited thereafter, and at the same time a mark of honor among their fellows. If the law was in part vindicated by their conviction, the inability of the Government to punish more severely their very public act of defiance underlined the fragility of the law's hold over the settler community (under questioning, one of the defendants at the trial had declared that "as it has always been the first principle with me to flog a nigger on sight who insults a white woman, I felt it my bounden duty to take the step I did, and that in a public place as a warning to the natives").[27]

---

[26] CO 533/13/17685.

[27] *The Times*, 20 May 1907, p. 10; 6 July 1907, p. 14. This generated a parliamentary report: "Correspondence Relating to the Flogging of Natives," Cd. 3562, 1907. In African colonies, as in the West Indies, black hopes correspondingly came to be vested

More characteristic of the emerging legal balance of power was a solicitor's request recalled by W. R. Foran in his 1936 memoirs: "defending a European on a charge of the manslaughter of a native [he] actually asked the Magistrate to discharge the accused as the Court was perfectly well aware that no white jury in East Africa would convict any European on a charge of causing the death of a native. I actually heard that statement made, openly and without correction, in the Town Magistrate's Court at Nairobi during 1909."[28] This was borne out in the intensely followed 1911 trial of Galbraith Cole, brother-in-law of Lord Delamere, the settler community's unofficial leader. Plagued by thefts of sheep, Cole fatally shot one of a group of unknown natives whom he found on his property. "There was a lot of feeling about stock thefts, at this time," recalled Elspeth Huxley many years later, "between Government and farmers. The tiny, scattered police force could not possibly protect the farmers' property, yet when they protected it themselves, they were had up and condemned."[29] The death was only reported some days later by one of the natives who escaped, to a magistrate over a hundred miles away. At trial Cole admitted to having shot the man, and Justice Hamilton summed up firmly against him, but the jury of eight white men still acquitted him of all charges. The Colonial Office was most unhappy – "in spite of [Governor] Girouard's apologetics, it seems to me," the young official Herbert Read minuted, "that murder is murder, and that it is out of the question to let the matter slide in the easy manner which he appears to contemplate." He and another clerk, F. W. Fiddes, pointed out that it was the duty of the Kenya Government to appeal the verdict, as the Indian Penal Code allowed, and Secretary of State Lewis Harcourt agreed with them.[30] Told that an appeal would be useless and only inflame the settler community, the Colonial Office ordered Governor Girouard to deport Cole, which he did, but only after dragging his feet for months.[31] As Cole

---

in Judges. The South African activist Sol Plaatje, who had long supported the Cape jury tradition, revised his views once Afrikaners came to power. In 1924 he unsuccessfully called for the South African Criminal Procedure Act to be amended so that "all indicted cases of violence between white and black should be tried by a court of judges, or by judges and assessors" [quoted in Robert Turrell, *White Mercy: A Study of the Death Penalty in South Africa* (London, 2005), p. 159].

[28] Foran, op. cit., p. 312.

[29] *Flame Trees of Thika*, p. 199.

[30] Minute, CO 533/88/18665

[31] When Harcourt decided to deport Cole, a pleased Read noted that "this will show the settlers," and then urged the Secretary to consider restricting the jury system in the

passed through Nairobi under escort on his way to the Coast he was cheered by settlers. His deportation became another frequently cited grievance in the settler community – a newspaper condemned "those arbitrary powers with which the deportation ordinance endows [officials]" – and seven years later he was readmitted.[32]

When a few months later another farmer, named Langridge, was tried and acquitted of causing grievous hurt to an African employee, settlers objected bitterly that he should ever even have had to go through a trial. It was charged that the local magistrate should have heard the case himself and dismissed it, but because he and Langridge had been feuding, he had sent it on for full trial in Nairobi. The *Leader of British East Africa* denounced the "blind class prejudice" of officials, and the *East African Standard* editorialized that any charges by Africans against whites should be carefully investigated before being submitted for trial:

No policy [it continued] is so dangerous to a young colony in Africa as that which encourages or gives an opening to natives, by which they may carelessly lay serious charges against Europeans. It is equally as bad for the native people as for their white rulers. It encourages the native, particularly the revengeful native, to lie and plot and concoct evidence, and it is very apt to cause the British whiteman to forget his deeply rooted love of law and order, and take the law into his own hands.[33]

For the insecure settlers, many of them farmers, conscious of how vastly outnumbered by Africans they were, white prestige, or "respect for

colony, before "fresh cases of a similar nature" occurred. This was a step too far for his superiors, however, and nothing was done [CO 533/88/18665].

[32] The *Leader of British East Africa,* 7 Oct. 1911, p. 8 (this paper eulogized Cole as "a man who has been a pattern of industry; who has led a blameless life, and one who is of the few who have turned this wilderness into a fruitful domain"). For fuller contemporary accounts from differing points of view, see W. McGregor Ross, *Kenya from Within: A Short Political History* (London, 1927), and Elspeth Huxley, *White Man's Country: Lord Delamere and the Making of Kenya* (London, 1935), pp. 281–286; for a recent scholar's account, see Robert M. Maxon, *The Struggle for Kenya: The Loss and Reassertion of Imperial Initiative, 1912–1923* (Rutherford, N.J., 1993), pp. 38–40, 78. Girouard, a military engineer who had succeeded Lord Lugard in governing Northern Nigeria, had been appointed Governor in 1909 both for his experience in managing railways and for his supposed care for native interests. On the latter score, he proved a great disappointment to the Colonial Office, for from the start he threw his lot in with the settler community; he was removed in 1912, over the protests of the settlers [John Flint, "Sir Percy Cranwell Girouard," *ODNB*].

[33] The *Leader of British East Africa,* 7 Oct. 1911, p. 8; *East African Standard,* 6 Oct. 1911; for the official view of the case, see CO 533/91/36359.

Europeans," as they usually called it, was critical, as Elspeth Huxley later explained:

[R]espect was the only protection available to Europeans who lived singly, or in scattered families, among thousands of Africans accustomed to constant warfare and armed with spears and poisoned arrows, but had themselves no barricades, and went about unarmed. This respect preserved them like an invisible coat of mail, or a form of magic, and seldom failed; but it had to be very carefully guarded. The least rent or puncture might, if not immediately checked and repaired, split the whole garment asunder and expose its wearer in all his human vulnerability. Kept intact, it was a thousand times stronger than all the guns and locks and metal in the world; challenged, it could be brushed aside like a spider's web.[34]

To make their growing numbers more politically effective, in 1910 settlers merged the two organizations that had been founded – the Colonists' Association, led by Grogan, made up of farmers, and the Pastoralists' Association, sheep-raisers who had originally come together to protest the grants of huge holdings to a favored few colonists. The new merged organization, the Convention of Associations, sank its class differences and indeed was led by the largest landholder in the colony, Lord Delamere. It quickly became the political voice of white settlers.[35] One of its first accomplishments was to win further revision in the Criminal Procedure Code. In 1914 an ordinance established that only Europeans were qualified to serve as jurors (blocking the bid of increasingly prosperous Indians to serve on them), and that they need meet no property or literacy requirements.[36] Moreover, their verdicts henceforth had to be unanimous, which further protected Europeans from criminal prosecution. These procedural safeguards underpinned European farmers' control of their African laborers.

The World War stimulated changes in Kenya, some of which strengthened settlers' power, but others of which posed new challenges for them. In the short run, the former predominated. The immediate aftermath of the war found the Government funding the resettlement of ex-soldiers on farms in Kenya, doubling the settler population within a

---

[34] *Flame Trees of Thika*, p. 16.
[35] See G. Bennet, "Development of Political Organization in Kenya," *Political Studies* 5 (1957), 113–130.
[36] John Ainsworth, a Native Commissioner, disapprovingly observed at this time that "Kenya must be one of the very few countries where there are no property or literacy requirements in the jurors' qualifications" [Robert M. Maxon, *John Ainsworth and the Making of Kenya* (London, 1980), p. 42].

few years.[37] Growing numbers and loyal military service during the war were recognized in political reorganization: in 1920 Kenya ceased to be a Protectorate and became a Crown colony; more unofficial members were added to its Legislative Council, and they were now to be elected, rather than nominated by the Governor. While Whitehall continued to rule, settlers could justifiably feel that they were well on their way to self-government.[38] The Governor from early 1919, Major General Sir Edward Northey, had led the invasion of German East Africa and strongly supported white immigration. He himself bought a coffee plantation, and moved comfortably in the society of fellow planters. He initiated the practice, which continued until 1927, of the Governor opening the annual sessions of the settler Convention of Associations.

During the war a series of "emergency measures" tightened control on the African population, and remained in force after it ended. Africans now had to register and obtain identity cards, and their movements were subject to official permission. Together with the Master and Servant ordinances passed in 1906 and 1910, this made it difficult for Africans to change jobs; prosecution of workers under these ordinances steadily increased in the aftermath of the war, as the growing European population created an ever-rising labor "shortage."[39] In the aftermath of the war, white settlers attained a position of unprecedented strength. Yet, rather than rejoicing in their gains, settlers soon found new grievances. In their view Government should have been actively assisting their development of the country by moving Africans off more land, and by "recruiting" African workers for European farms. Even a sympathetic Governor like Northey could not go as far in accommodating settlers' "needs" as settlers thought appropriate. He had to deal with often-recalcitrant civil servants beneath him whose task was to supervise the African areas, and who often stood up for the interests of their charges. Even more, the Colonial Office was clearly opposed to both settler demands. The postwar years saw intense disagreements between the Colonial Office and settler spokesmen over the moving of Africans off land and over African "forced labor,"

---

[37] 1914: 5,438; 1921: 9,651 (by 1926, 12,529).

[38] See Nicholas Best, *Happy Valley: The Story of the English in Kenya* (London, 1979).

[39] David Anderson, "Policing the Settler State: Colonial Hegemony in Kenya, 1900–1952," in *Contesting Colonial Hegemony: State and Society in Africa and India*, ed. Dagmar Engels and Shula Marks (London, 1994), 248–264; Anderson, "Master and Servant in Colonial Kenya, 1894–1939," *Journal of African History* 41 (2000), 349–485; Anderson, "Kenya: Registration and Rough Justice," in *Masters, Servants, and Magistrates in Britain and the Empire, 1562–1955,* ed. Douglas Hay and Paul Craven (Chapel Hill, N.C., 2004), 498–528.

whether directly, through the orders of chiefs, or indirectly, through hut taxes that required Africans to take employment for wages. Although Churchill, as Colonial Secretary in 1921, had banned the practice that had emerged during the war of officials "assisting" private employers to find workers, compulsory labor continued for state projects. This practice supported the efforts of private employers much as the workhouse had supported nineteenth-century employers at home, since if Africans did not work "freely" for private farmers they were legally liable to work under usually harder conditions compulsorily for the colonial state.[40]

Even this arrangement failed to satisfy most settlers. In a similar fashion, the security that a jury trial provided to shield them from criminal conviction for "excesses" in disciplining their workers was not enough; there were still complaints of "vexatious" even if unsuccessful prosecutions against them and complaints that although the number of prosecutions of employees under the Master and Servant laws kept increasing, these were so time-consuming as to be a waste of their time. Workers would desert, and the law was in practice not very effective in either punishing them or getting them back to work. As many Queensland or Fiji sugar plantation or Assam tea garden managers had lamented, magistrates' courts in Kenya also were not providing farmers the assistance they felt their due. Some called for these courts to be held right on their farms; others demanded "plenary powers" to judge their employees themselves. None of these desires were granted, and so even as their power solidified, settlers remained an unsatisfied group, continually pressing their demands upon Government.

Yet the war also set in motion forces that worked against settlers' newly improved position. The imperative to mobilize resources stimulated the growth of central Government in Britain and the centralization of Empire. At the same time, the war hastened completion of telegraph lines connecting Britain with Kenya, bringing the colony much closer to Whitehall, to Parliament, and to the British and worldwide press. George Orwell, who served in the imperial police in Burma after the war, later remarked that the autonomy of the local official in the Empire (to which, despite his anti-imperialism. he remained nostalgically attached) was "killed" by the telegraph and related innovations:

In a narrowing world, more and more governed from Whitehall, there was every year less room for individual initiative. . . . By 1920 nearly every inch of the

---

[40] Opolot Okia, "In the Interests of Community: Archdeacon Walter Owen and the Issue of Communal Labour in Colonial Kenya, 1921–1930," *Journal of Imperial and Commonwealth History* 32 (2004), 19–40.

colonial empire was in the grip of Whitehall. Well-meaning, over-civilised men, in dark suits and black felt hats, with neatly rolled umbrellas crooked over the left forearm, were imposing their constipated view of life in Malaya and Nigeria, Mombasa and Mandalay.[41]

If local officials found their autonomy increasingly hemmed in, the intrusion of Whitehall and Westminister – and Fleet Street – was to eventually press even more on the non-officials who had often been able to co-opt local Governors. For Whitehall itself was, partly as a result of the war, coming under new pressures to counteract settler interests, pressures arising from within the colony, within Britain, and internationally. In Kenya, promises made to ensure African and Indian support during the war were being submitted for redemption, first by Indians but then by Africans as well.[42] At the same time, new international bodies – the League of Nations and the International Labor Organization – provided new forums for widely publicized criticism of the treatment of African workers and farmers, and new demands placed on the British Government, which had now to think of its international image.[43] Even more important perhaps were the new domestic pressures. The 1918 Franchise Act (and its 1928 supplement) made Britain for the first time a democracy with universal suffrage, and opened the way for the rise of the Labour Party and its more critical attitude to Empire, and especially to settlers. In turn, Labour's rise fostered the emergence of a humanitarian lobby stronger than anything in Britain since the 1830s. Two former Kenyan civil servants, Norman Leys and W. McGregor Ross, forged

[41] *England, Your England* [orig. 1940] (London, 1953), pp. 216–217.

[42] As the voice of hard-line settlers, *The Leader*, observed in 1921, "those who play with the principles of political equality when no racial equality exists are playing with fire with risk of grave disaster" [7 July 1921]. In 1923, *The Leader* failed economically, and was absorbed by the largest white newspaper, *The East African Standard*. New divisions within the hitherto solid ranks of settlers were suggested by the appearance in 1922 of a paper, the *Kenya Critic*, which took the part of the "small men" among the Europeans against the wealthy businessmen and farmers of large estates who had long dominated settler politics.

[43] See Susan Pedersen, "The Meaning of the Mandates System: An Argument," *Geschichte und Gesellschaft* 32 (2006), 560–582. As Youé has noted, if self-government for Africans was still not contemplated, still "there was a striking new feature about the postwar world: imperialists should at least be seen to uphold standards of decency within their realms. . . . While talk of African paramountcy and Indian political equality [in Kenya] did not lead to any substantial encroachments on white power, it did not lead to any enhancement either. Trusteeship may well have been rhetoric but it did act as a clamp on settler ambitions for self-government" [op. cit., pp. 160–161].

connections with the surviving Victorian humanitarian bodies and kept up a drumbeat of publicity about the ongoing sacrifice of African interests to those of a comparatively few settlers. As time went on they were joined by other former colonial officials, like Robert Hamilton, the colony's first Chief Justice, who during more than a decade in that position became thoroughly exasperated not only by white juries but by the biases in favor of white employers held by most magistrates.[44] After retiring from judicial service in 1918 he entered Parliament as a Liberal M.P. in 1922, remaining until 1935. Such men nurtured the growth of a British (and even international) public opinion unfavorable to East African settlers, a new domestic pressure upon the Colonial Office that counterbalanced that of settlers' traditional friends at home.[45] Meanwhile, politics in Britain was shifting leftward as far as Empire was concerned; as Labour became the second party and a home for critics of Empire, the Conservatives moved toward a middle position, from Milner's to Baldwin's. New Conservatives like Edward Wood, to become Lord Halifax, and William Ormsby-Gore, as Parliamentary Undersecretaries at the Colonial Office, were more skeptical of settlers' claims and more sympathetic to Africans than their Conservative predecessors.[46] Similarly the new generation in Whitehall reflected these shifts, becoming ever more impatient with the excesses of settlers.[47]

The postwar years also witnessed new developments inside Kenya that, as much as those in Britain and at Geneva, were to turn the power balance against the settler community. One was Indian political activism; another, less effective at the time but of great long-run significance, was the beginnings of African political consciousness. The desperate need during the war for Indian troops had hastened political concessions to Indian

---

[44] M. K. Banton, "The Colonial Office, 1820–1955: Constantly the Subject of Small Struggles," in Hay and Craven, op. cit., pp. 274–275, quotes extensively from memoranda issued by Chief Justice Hamilton to encourage magistrates to be receptive to grievances of African workers, and quotes his rebuke of a magistrate in a 1910 case for an ill-considered conviction of an African.

[45] See Diana Wylie, "Confrontation over Kenya: The Colonial Office and Its Critics 1918–1940," *Journal of African History* 18 (1977), 427–447.

[46] Youé observed that not long before his appointment by Baldwin in 1922 Ormsby-Gore had suggested in the House of Commons that "Kenya would be best developed on West African lines since the policy of white settlement had failed miserably. Not unnaturally the settlers protested against the appointment. Delamere's vitriolic attack on the young MP at a Nakuru meeting did not go unnoticed by [Secretary of State] Lord Devonshire, who regarded the outburst as 'grossly improper'" [op. cit., pp. 160–161].

[47] Permanent Undersecretary Sir John Masterton was another comparative liberal, having been picked from the Ministry of Labour by Churchill, who was vexed with the settlers.

nationalism, and this sea change in the Raj in turn awakened the large Indian community in Kenya, which was twice the size of the white. The winning by white settlers in 1920 of the right to elect unofficial representatives to the Legislative Council led Indians to demand the same, as well as other rights held by whites, such as freedom of entry into the colony and the right to purchase land in the "White Highlands." The next few years saw a bitter conflict over these claims, with the whites by 1923 successfully preventing Indians from winning any of their chief demands.[48] At the same time, witnessing the political effectiveness of settlers and the efforts to copy them of Indians, some urban Africans began to create their own organizations. In March 1922, Harry Thuku, a Nairobi telephone operator and organizer of the urban-based East African Association, was arrested in Nairobi for his agitation against the introduction of an identification card for Africans. His arrest led to an angry demonstration numbering in the thousands, which police fired upon, killing about twenty persons. Thuku was exiled, the East African Association banned, and the Government given a lasting fear of African revolt. This meant tightening controls on Africans, as settlers had been calling for; but in the long run it was to sensitize British officials and politicians to the risk that concessions to settlers would carry a heavy price in African discontent.

For the moment, however, the position of settlers seemed stronger than ever.[49] With magistrates freely ordering corporal punishment for Africans convicted of petty offenses, farmers felt little hesitation about doing the same on their own farms, without going through the bother of legal process.[50] When faced with what appeared to them an infraction by a worker, rather than invoking the Master and Servant laws, they were more likely to withhold pay, confiscate passbooks, or simply have the

---

[48] See Maxon, *Struggle*; Berman, *Control*.

[49] As local officials were well aware. "I honestly feel," Chief Native Commissioner Maxwell, who had been administering compulsory state labor for the past few years, wrote Governor Coryndon in 1924, "that the Government must admit to itself that the natives of the Colony have not had fair treatment, that they have been exploited, that their economic development has been definitely repressed instead of advanced, that they have been overtaxed, that they have not received anything like a fair proportion of the Colony's expenditure on medicine, education and other beneficial services" [Maxwell to Coryndon, quoted by Odhiambo, op. cit., p. 25].

[50] In 1919, Chief Justice Hamilton felt impelled to write a pamphlet, "Hints to Magistrates," pointing out that corporal punishment was "not for every day but is a power in reserve for exceptional cases which call for sharp and stern punishment." It is not clear if it had the desired effect.

offending worker flogged, without much fear of legal retribution, even though all these procedures were formally illegal and had by this time more or less disappeared from most other parts of the Empire. As one farmer had told the commission investigating "native punishments" in 1921, the "raw native" required a punishment that was immediate and stern.[51] There was no furtiveness about this; one farmer had written home to his mother in 1919 that "my Africans wanted a 10 instead of 11 hour day, so I flogged the nearest, and a few more, and then got them to flog the others."[52] As David Anderson has put it, " 'rough justice' was the norm on the European-owned farms."[53]

Occasionally this "justice" was rougher than intended, and the worker died. Such cases would usually end in court. Prosecutors, however, faced the great hurdles not only of all-white juries but also of the lack of witnesses other than Africans. "White witnesses do not come forward readily to implicate fellow Colonists," one Kenyan official complained.[54] Two such cases during the war produced convictions of causing hurt only, and fines.[55] By 1918, however, more complex feelings among the white community began to be evident, as this lenience began to be greeted with some unease. When two Europeans beat a thief to death and the subordinate was acquitted and the employer only fined Rs. 1,000, the *East Africa Standard* editorialized in disapproval, calling the verdict of causing simple hurt "extraordinary." Since the deceased had clearly been treated with "great brutality," the lenient verdict, the paper concluded, was a "grave miscarriage of justice."[56] In 1920, a farmer named Hawkins, already known to be something of a brutal man, flogged several workers, including a pregnant woman, to extract a confession of theft and one died. He was convicted of causing grievous hurt and sentenced to two years' imprisonment – the first imprisonment for violence against an

---

[51] Anderson, "Policing the Settler State," op. cit., p. 260. The evidence of the Native Labour Commission 1912–1913 and the Native Punishments Commission 1921–1923 shows clearly how common it was for employers to resort to coercive methods to recruit and keep workers, to flogging their workers, to withholding their pay, although all these practices were formally illegal.

[52] Noel Smith, 31 July 1919, quoted by C. S. Nicholls, *Red Strangers: The White Tribe of Kenya* (London, 2005), p. 56.

[53] Anderson, "Master and Servant," op. cit., p. 472.

[54] Quoted in Kennedy, *Islands of White*, op. cit., p. 181.

[55] *R v Van Rooyen* 1915; *R v Watts* 1918. It is clear that these were regarded as compromises, in which the conviction on the minor charge allowed the State Prosecutor and the Judge to save appearances; a fine – unlike imprisonment, however brief – was a civil-like penalty that did not impugn the "prestige" of the accused.

[56] 10 Sept. 1918, p. 11.

African since the Grogan scandal of 1907. The appeal against this sentence as "savage" was rejected without raising the kind of press outrage evident before the war. Later that same year another farmer named Harries, who found one of his workers beating a valuable pig, flogged the man badly enough to put him in the hospital for three months and was convicted of inflicting simple hurt, but this time the Judge instead of fining him gave him three months' imprisonment; again, appeal was denied.[57]

The Colonial Office was also taking a closer look at such cases, urging the Governor to remind settlers that it was quite against the law for private employers to flog employees, and after another acquittal in a case of serious injury, in 1921 forced against heated local opposition the passage of an ordinance giving the Crown the right of appeal against acquittals that it had acquired in India.[58] Whitehall officials became exasperated with Northey, who was removed in 1922. His successor as Governor, R. T. Coryndon, who served from 1922 to 1925, was appointed because of his reputation as a man sensitive to African interests, but again, the appointment disappointed Whitehall. By 1924, the men in the East Africa Department had concluded that Coryndon had been co-opted by the settlers. At the same time, the settlers themselves had become ever more disaffected and militant, as they saw the British Government trying to accommodate, rather than repel, the double threats posed by Indian demands for suffrage and African political mobilization.[59]

It was in the midst of this spiral of mutual alienation between Whitehall and white farmers, and of mutual suspicion between Whitehall and Government House, that the Bishop's son, Jasper Abraham, found himself in the dock in a Nairobi courtroom. The case was heard by Acting Chief Justice Sheridan, who had been a puisne Judge in Kenya for some years. Several medical men testified for the defense that the injuries from the flogging were not enough to have caused death. If this were India, one might expect at this point evidence of a dangerously inflamed spleen, but African spleens were known to be in better shape; in fact, unlike the fragile Indians, Africans, again, as part of being "closer to nature," were thought to recover rather more readily from serious injury than

---

[57] C. S. Nicholls, op. cit.

[58] Ordinance No. 48 of 1921 [for the text, see W. M. Ross, op. cit.] was deeply resented by settlers, who won its repeal in 1924 (Ordinance No. 12 of 1924).

[59] C. J. D. Duder, "The Settler Response to the Indian Crisis of 1923 in Kenya: Brigadier General Philip Wheatley and 'Direct Action,'" *Journal of Imperial and Commonwealth History* 17 (1989), 349–373.

Europeans. Instead, his death was explained in part by his having eaten little the preceding few days, and in part by the ability of Africans to "will to die." This latter explanation was supported by the evidence of another African farm employee that he had heard the victim cry out during the night that he wanted to die. The defense pled "grave and sudden provocation" to a man known to be excitable. However, the Judge questioned this provocation plea in summing up (telling the jury they could not take Abraham's supposed excitability into account, but must ask whether a man of ordinary temperament would have been provoked). The European jury found Abraham guilty of causing grievous hurt, and Sheridan sentenced him to two years' imprisonment.

The psychological distance between East Africa and Britain was evident in the sharp reaction to the verdict and sentence not only of the Colonial Office but of both the Liberal and Labour press. The Colonial Office immediately requested a report. Neither Justice Sheridan nor Governor Coryndon saw any problem; the Judge pronounced himself fully satisfied with the jury's verdict, and without second thoughts on the sentence he had awarded. In the Kenyan context, neither the verdict nor the sentence were especially lenient; Sheridan tried to point that out to the Colonial Office, citing previous cases where those charged with similar killings had been simply fined. He noted that Hawkins, to whom in 1920 he had given the same sentence, was a worse character than the well-respected Abraham. As for Abraham, Sheridan concluded, "I do not think he is criminal by nature, but he is a powerful man with a naturally hot temper."[60] The Governor transmitted Sheridan's report without comment. However, the report produced outrage at the Colonial Office. Sheridan's descriptions of the even more lenient earlier trials only convinced the Office of the inability of the Kenyan courts to deal justly with settler assaults on natives. One official, William Bushe, laid out the full circumstances of the Abraham case and concluded that "if all this had happened in this country I have no doubt that the accused would have been charged with murder and I am inclined to think that in law the offence would have amounted to murder. . . . I should regard any verdict less than manslaughter to be unthinkable. . . . [L]ooking at this story as

---

[60] Sheridan pointed out that (white) "feeling was inclined to run high" at that time on the Indian Question. "I particularly directed the Jury not to allow themselves to be influenced by any question of political expediency – to put out of their heads anything to do with a political atmosphere. That they obeyed my direction seems clear" [CO 533/298, Judge's Report, 3 Oct. 1923].

calmly and as coldly as you like, it seems to me to be a horrible and revolting proceeding."[61] Herbert Read, now Assistant Undersecretary, fully agreed that the case was "revolting," and asked his superiors: "If the positions had been reversed and the native had been on trial for a similar offence against the white, who can doubt what would have been his fate?" Read also pointed out the Colonial Office's political exposure, warning that the case, already criticized in the press, was sure to be raised in Parliament and pressed by a number of reformist organizations like the Anti-Slavery and Aborigines Protection Society and the African Progress Union.

Read's superiors, up to the Conservative Secretary of State, the Duke of Devonshire, agreed (if with a lesser intensity of outrage), and in consequence Devonshire sent an open letter to the governor (drafted by Read) expressing his "abhorrence of a crime which appears to me to offer no extenuating circumstances." The letter went on to state that his "legal advisers...are of opinion that a verdict of anything less than manslaughter is quite irreconcilable with the facts," and also to generally deplore the outcomes of unnamed other recent similar cases. It concluded that "so long as this condition of affairs remains, the jury system [in Kenya] can only be regarded, so far as cases of this nature are concerned, as on its trial." Henceforth, shorthand reports of all trials involving serious interracial violence were required to be furnished to the Colonial Office. Moreover, the case exposed the persistence of practices by farmers that had been clearly declared illegal, from docking pay to confiscating ID cards to flogging; Devonshire observed not only that such practices were indeed illegal but that their persistence marked "a wide distinction between Kenya and any other tropical colony in which natives work under the employment of white men."

The Colonial Secretary, however, knew the limits of his power over colonial justice. Although his political Undersecretary, William Ormsby-Gore (soon to be Colonial Secretary himself), suggested that "we may have to remove Justice Sheridan," Devonshire dismissed that suggestion. Further, he had the words of Read's draft letter that had called the punishment given Abraham "totally inadequate" struck out from his dispatch, noting that "we could hardly leave in [these] words unless we were prepared to secure the removal of the judge." Nor could he do anything beyond vague threats about the jury system in Kenya, too deeply

---

[61] Bushe was to head a Commission on Criminal Justice in East Africa in 1934 that recommended sweeping changes.

rooted, as he noted, in "British traditions of justice" as well as in settler values and interests.[62]

The strong response in Whitehall, even more than the sharp questions in Parliament, showed that a new generation of officials no longer thought of the Empire as a place quite different from Britain and requiring its own set of rules. The outlook of this generation had been shaped in the post-Victorian climate of new progressive thinking. While of course aware of the complex and unequal multiracial situation in East Africa, they responded to the case with the more liberal values of home. Moreover, as Permanent Undersecretary Masterton-Smith noted, this case "has come at a bad moment for [settlers]. The decisions [just] taken by His Majesty's Government upon the Indian controversy are based upon the principle of British trusteeship for the African native; and even the most extreme advocate of responsible Government among the white settlers in Kenya must appreciate that the kind of thing that has happened in the Abraham case proves clearly that they are quite unfitted at the present time to be entrusted with the guardianship of the interests of non-European communities."[63]

The Colonial Office decided to take several steps: it ordered a change in the law to require interracial criminal cases to be heard elsewhere than in the district where the offense had taken place, and, in a related controversy, a change in the Master and Servant laws removing desertion from the list of offenses cognizable to the police (forcing employers to go to the magistrate to request a summons); it required a Judge's reports and other information to be immediately forwarded to it in all cases of interracial violence; and it requested a report on the nature and extent of the administration of corporal punishment to their employees by employers, and proposals from the Governor on how this practice was to be eliminated, along with other illegal practices by employers.[64] It also decided to try to speed up the long-planned change of Kenyan criminal law from the Indian Penal Code to a code more closely modeled on England, which would make it easier to indict for murder in homicide cases.[65] In addition, the Office also began to prod the inspectors of

---

[62] CO 533/298.

[63] CO 533/298, minute, 5 Dec. 1923. By "the decisions just taken" he was referring to the "Devonshire Declaration" of that year indicating that in Kenya "African interests" had to be "paramount" (as against both Indian and European interests).

[64] CO 533/298 and CO 533/371/4.

[65] H. F. Morris and J. S. Read, *Indirect Rule and the Search for Justice: Essays in East African Legal History* (Oxford, 1972), pp. 120–121.

labor, created only in 1919, into more effective activity. Although implementation of some of these decisions was slowed down by the arrival in November 1924 of a more settler-friendly Secretary of State, L. S. Amery, they had set a new direction that was never reversed. The tide was turning for Kenyan settlers, and with Amery's departure in 1929, their last friend in Whitehall was gone. Settlers no longer ruled the roost in East Africa, and the possibility of self-government for them henceforth steadily receded. Even on their own farms, their control was no longer unchallenged, as African employees began to make increasing use of provisions of the law to protect their own interests.[66]

The feelings of insecurity that settlers had voiced in the years before the war in consequence revived. In 1927, Amery's sympathy had enabled them to win, over the resistance of permanent officials in the Colonial Office, the creation of an exclusively white military force, service in which was to be compulsory for all white men in the colony. However, it was never to be employed, and Amery's Labour successor, Sidney Webb, cut its funding and removed its compulsory character; thereafter, its numbers shrank and in 1936 it was abolished.[67] The feelings that lay behind its creation can be seen in extreme settler reactions to violence – or the possibility of violence – against whites. When a white farmer was murdered in 1929, it was not enough that two natives were sentenced to death; farmers passed a resolution asking the Government for public hangings, to be witnessed by representatives of their village, plus a large fine on that village and confiscation of all property held by the culprits. All these requests were immediately refused.[68] When a settler was found dead in the wilderness in 1931 in what was almost surely an accident, many settlers insisted that he had been murdered by Africans and forced a lengthy and futile investigation.[69]

The replacement that year of Governor Edward Grigg by the "tough and suspicious" former police official Joseph Byrne deprived white employers, who had already lost any sympathy from the Colonial Office,

---

[66] Anderson, "Kenya: Registration and Rough Justice," p. 515.

[67] On its history, see C. J. D. Duder, "An Army of One's Own: The Politics of the Kenya Defence Force," *Canadian Journal of African Studies*, 25, 2 (1991), 207–225.

[68] CO 533/390/10.

[69] C. J. Duder and G. L. Simpson, "Land and Murder in Colonial Kenya: The Leroghi Land Dispute and the Powys 'Murder' Case," *Journal of Imperial and Commonwealth History* 25 (1997), 440–465.

of an advocate on the ground in Government House. During his years there, Byrne forced through almost a miniature "New Deal," a series of measures bringing Kenya into line with International Labor Organization conventions legalizing trade unions, protecting the right to strike, and setting minimum wages for various categories of worker. In 1938, when Byrnes's departure revived their hopes, settlers sent a spokesman to visit the Colonial Office to complain of "undue subservience to Geneva ideals." However, he was told that rather than being relaxed, the recent legislation might have to be "tightened" further.[70] Underneath these political changes was an economic one: the Great Depression had struck harder at white farming, directed as it was at a world market, than at African peasant farming, tilting the economic power balance against settlers. Government revenue was increasingly dependent upon African rather than white farming, which inevitably made local officials pay greater attention to African grievances. At the same time as employees were receiving greater statutory attention, hut and poll taxes, which had forced Africans to take employment with Europeans in the first place, were reduced (the lost revenue was replaced by restoring the income tax, which had been abolished in the heyday of settler dominance).[71] At the same time, white farmers' fresh calls to Whitehall for financial assistance got nowhere; it was now sink or swim for them.[72]

This shift was reflected also in the courts. In 1930 the Indian Penal Code was finally scrapped, and from then on the number of African complaints lodged with magistrates and the number of prosecutions of employers who breached the Master and Servant laws rose, with magistrates imposing more severe sentences on them. As David Anderson has shown, convictions of Europeans rose markedly in the 1930s, and bindings-over were mostly replaced by fines. From 1931 to 1938, 80 percent of Europeans prosecuted under the Master and Servant laws were convicted, the highest rate ever. Although they were in general liable only to fines, fines got larger and nonpayment of fines (in part due to the

---

[70] Anthony Clayton and Donald C. Savage, *Government and Labour in Kenya, 1895–1963* (London, 1975), pp. 184–195.

[71] In addition, the 1918 law requiring (African) squatters to pay in labor was repealed.

[72] This was the case throughout East Africa; the Chief Secretary of Nyasaland complained as early as 1931 that the Governor and the Colonial Office were "relentless" in determining to end a temporary aid program for tobacco farmers despite their desperate straits. Minute quoted in Robin Palmer, "White Farmers in Malawi: Before and After the Depression," *African Affairs* 84 (1985), 226.

Depression) led to many employers being jailed. in 1934, the worst year of the Depression, no fewer than 598 European employers were jailed for such failure.[73] At the same time, legal disciplining of Africans moved in the opposite direction. The replacement of the Indian Penal Code greatly narrowed magisterial discretion, and in consequence perhaps magistrates ordered far less flogging (and the same was happening with police and military authorities' disciplining of their men).[74] This change was accelerated by the 1934 report of the Bushe Commission on criminal justice, which complained that flogging was still being used as a punishment, and insisted that it should be done away with.[75] Any suggestion of flogging had become an embarrassment; the East Africa Marketing Board produced a poster in 1931, "East African Transport – New Style," showing a road bridge being built, in which a white supervisor was holding a pipe as he directed his African workers. In the original form of the poster he was holding a horsewhip; the Governor objected, the whip was removed, and a pipe inserted instead.[76]

It was in this altered climate that on July 13, 1934, Major Geoffrey Selwyn and his wife, Helen, were jointly charged with the murder of an African employee. The major died of blackwater fever before the case came to trial, and his wife stood alone in the dock. She herself was not well (though the precise nature of her illness, beyond "nerves," was never specified), and much solicitude in the press was expressed for her situation (a Government motion to move the trial to Nairobi was successfully resisted on grounds of her health).[77] Although their farm employed eleven African men, it was apparently under severe economic pressure, for it was the nadir of the world depression. When some cowbells were stolen, she lost her temper and ordered six men whom she suspected whipped until they confessed and returned them. They did not confess, and one had to

[73] Anderson, "Master and Servant," op. cit., p. 482.
[74] Anderson, "Master and Servant"; David Killingray, "The 'Rod of Empire': The Debate over Corporal Punishment in the British African Colonial Forces, 1888–1946," *Journal of African History* 35 (1994), 201–216.
[75] The thrust of the Commission's recommendations (strongly supported in Parliament and press by the former Chief Justice, Sir Robert Hamilton) was to move away from aspects of "indirect rule" toward a more direct, uniform, and equal rule based on English legal procedures and principles.
[76] CO 956/215 [Adrian Allinson illustrator]; Ramamurthy, op. cit., p. 150.
[77] At the preliminary hearing, Mrs. Selwyn "was too ill to stand when she appeared in Court and was provided with an easy chair and footstool" [*East African Standard*, 4 Aug. 1934, p. 32].

be taken to the hospital, where a few days later he died. As with Abraham, their high family connections back in England – the Dean of Winchester was Major Selwyn's brother – could not prevent a trial.[78] It was held in the nearest rural district to the Selwyns, with a jury of white farmers, though none personal acquaintances, and the colony's Attorney General prosecuting. When she gave her evidence, Mrs. Selwyn frequently broke into tears, and before her cross-examination began the Court adjourned for ten minutes, "in order that she might refresh herself with tea." After five days, the Attorney General concluded by warning that taking the law into one's hands would lead to anarchy, and the Judge summed up strongly for a verdict of manslaughter; the jury gave it, with the expected recommendation to mercy. The Judge responded that as "a newcomer to Kenya," on hearing the evidence of Mrs. Selwyn,

I must say I was amazed. If the boys who were beaten had actually stolen and been found in possession of the cow-bells there would have been perhaps some excuse for what happened though it would have been an unlawful thing to do. But in fact it appears that Mrs. Selwyn admits that what she was doing was beating them in the hope of obtaining evidence and she treated her act as a thing that hardly called for comment at all. . . . I will give full weight to your recommendation to mercy and also to the state of Mrs. Selwyn's health. I may say that had this offense been committed by a man I should have felt myself bound to impose an extremely severe sentence. As things go, Mrs. Selwyn is going to hospital where she will remain until her condition permits removal. I must pass sentence upon her of twelve months' imprisonment.

The Africans who did the whipping under her orders were given one month in prison. Patrick Collinson has observed that "in only one other case in the history of the colony was a white woman sentenced for causing death or injury to an African."[79]

The British press gave prominence to the case and to the trial, with headlines like "Native Flogged to Death." In Parliament, too, questions were asked about the persistence of private corporal punishment on Kenyan farms. Governor Byrne insisted that "illegalities of this nature

---

[78] The distinguished historian Patrick Collinson, who married the Selwyns' daughter, has written of this case, drawing on both written records and family memory; see "The Cow Bells of Kitale," *London Review of Books* 25, no. 11 (5 June 2003), pp. 15–18. When Major Selwyn died in custody (he had already been quite ill), the Dean sought damages from the Colonial Office, but it rejected his claims.

[79] For reports on the hearing and trial, see *East African Standard*, 28 July 1934, p. 43; 4 Aug., p. 32; 25 Aug., p. 17; 8 Sept., p. 17; 29 Sept., pp. 6–8, 41; 6 Oct., pp. 14–15. A petition was gathered asking for remission of her sentence; she was released after six and a half months.

are unreservedly condemned by this Government," while conceding
that they continued to occur without being reported by either party
(Africans would often prefer being whipped to losing their job). He
pledged to renew his efforts to stamp out the practice. As Collinson has
pointed out, many settlers felt, with disgust, that the authorities were
determined to see Mrs. Selwyn imprisoned in order to show Africans that
British justice applied to whites as well as blacks.[80] Just the week before
her trial, the same Judge had presided over the trial of eight Africans for
the murder of a settler, Alex Semini, and the rape of his wife. Six of the
eight were condemned to death. It is certainly true that to immediately
follow that with an acquittal or a mere fining of a white woman would
have deeply embarrassed the British Government. Moreover, the Bushe
Commission on criminal justice in East Africa, though focused on the
administration of native areas, had just released its report containing a
sharp criticism of the continuation of illegal private corporal punishment
on white farms. In such a setting, Mrs. Selwyn had to be condemned and
punished. In a sense, with the Abraham case Kenya had reached the stage
of India under Lord Curzon, when whites could no longer expect virtual
legal immunity in their use of violence against native employees, particularly when such violence had fatal consequences, and with Selwyn
had reached the situation of India after the World War. And not just
of India: across the postwar Empire, lethal violence by private white
individuals was being more seriously addressed in the courts. Peter
Fitzpatrick has described this change in postwar New Guinea, where in
1931 the death of a native by flogging resulted in the unexpected manslaughter conviction of an European and his sentencing to ten years'
imprisonment.[81]

In the postwar Empire, a variety of forces – pressures from international organizations, increasingly influential humanitarian bodies, and
growing numbers of interested Members of Parliament, combined with
emerging native nationalist movements and with growing economic
pressures on an overstretched imperial Government – all worked to

---

[80] Collinson quoted his mother-in-law as remarking about government officials, "They are
all shopkeepers, and all for the native at all costs."

[81] Fitzpatrick, "Tears of the Law," op. cit., pp. 140–141. He noted the increasingly
important "purposive promotion of legality by colonial officials as a powerful mode of
rule. This, in terms of its own rationalities, obliged officials to require white people to
behave in the same basic ways as they required black people to do. There was a calculated aspect of reciprocity, or hoped-for reciprocity, in this."

reduce the freedom of action that settlers had earlier enjoyed. One result was to diminish the drastic imbalance in the courts when private violence against natives was the issue. What Collinson remarked about Kenya in 1934 – that it was becoming apparent that "settler aspirations were never going to be fulfilled" – was becoming similarly evident across the Empire, and one of the venues in which this was becoming evident was in the courts.

8

British Honduras, 1934

In the Colony men of every race are on an equal footing politically and before the law, and . . . the poorest black man has his rights as sedulously protected as the richest white man.

Report of the British Honduras Commission of Enquiry following the "Ex-Servicemen's Riot" of 1919[1]

A few months before Helen Selwyn had her workers whipped, another fatal encounter took place on the other side of the world in the colony of British Honduras. A lumber mill owner from Alabama, Thurman Eugene Gantt, also seeking recovery of stolen goods, searched the house of a black employee and found nothing. When the man taunted him, he shot him to death.[2]

A small territory in Central America, British Honduras – today the state of Belize, like the Bahamas a major tourist destination – was in 1934 extremely poor, heavily dependent upon the mahogany lumber industry. Like the Bahamas, it was one of the first British colonies. British settlement began in the 1650s, and although Spain continued to dispute ownership down to the end of its Empire in the Americas, the colony was under continuous British control from that time forward, remaining, however, perhaps even more than the Bahamas, a backwater of Empire. In 1934 its economy was almost in shambles, suffering not only from the

[1] Quoted in Peter David Ashdown, "Race, Class and the Unofficial Majority in British Honduras 1890–1949," Ph.D. thesis, University of Southampton, 1979, p. 158. After this riot thirty-one nonwhite men were convicted and sentenced to terms of imprisonment from six years to six months.

[2] Information on this case and quotations that follow are drawn from CO 123/348/2 and *Belize Independent*, 17 Jan. 1934, pp. 1, 9–10.

world depression but also from the aftereffects of a devastating hurricane in September 1931, which practically razed Belize City. After his trip through Central America in 1933, Aldous Huxley reflected that "if the world had any ends British Honduras would certainly be one of them. It is not on the way from anywhere to anywhere else. It has no strategic value. It is all but uninhabited."[3] Its population of about sixty thousand was unusually mixed, from a few thousand whites, chiefly of British origin but including a growing number of Americans, to black descendants of slaves, to "Latins" who had come from Mexico and Guatemala, to Maya and Carib peasants.[4] Alan Burns, Governor from 1934 to 1939, who tried to encourage farming to diversify the economy, later described the black majority as "good workers on work they understand and like, such as forestry, but they have not the gift of perseverance and are inclined to blame others, and not their own shortcomings, for any lack of success. They have a great sense of humour and are very musical . . . [but] they are easily misled by irresponsible agitators."[5] Such agitators had first appeared in the aftermath of the World War and, more seriously, began to gain a following in 1934, just as Gantt's case was being tried. The economy's labor laws had not changed since the nineteenth century, with unions still illegal and Master and Servant Acts still in force.

After the Jamaica rebellion of 1865, British Honduras shared in the general renovation and tightening of imperial control throughout the Caribbean colonies. However, this effort was undone by a political counterrevolution in 1890–1892 (more formal, but in outcome not unlike what took place at the same time in Trinidad and the Bahamas). Gubernatorial incompetence and favoritism had provoked a movement for "representation for taxpayers," during which much was said about the rights and liberties of British subjects. This movement of "leading men," unlike the contemporaneous ones in the Bahamas and Trinidad, was supported by the colony's Chief Justice and directed against its Governor. It gained the concession, unique for Crown colonies, of an unofficial majority on the Legislative Council. Although these unofficial members had to be nominated by the Governor, they thereafter formed a cohesive block that virtually controlled the Government of the colony. The result was to restore the oligarchic situation that had existed before the Colonial Office's earlier strengthening of executive power. Although

---

[3] Aldous Huxley, *Beyond the Mexique Bay* (London, 1934), p. 30.
[4] Sir Alan Burns, *Colonial Civil Servant* (London, 1949), pp. 136–137.
[5] Ibid., p. 137.

it remained constitutionally a Crown colony without elected representatives, in effect British Honduras's political system after 1892 differed
little from that of the Bahamas, and the characterization of its oligarchy
by one Whitehall official in 1932 as "a gang of superior bootleggers"
could as well have applied to the latter colony's ruling group in the age of
American Prohibition.[6] British Honduras's merchant-landowner oligarchy, in which the largest firm, the Belize Estate and Produce Company,
known as B.E.C., came to play a leading role, discouraged peasant pro-
prietorship or other economic diversification as a threat to its labor
supply. Though oligarchs prospered after 1892, the colony as a whole did
not; average income seems to have risen little, and public health and
housing conditions continued to be abysmal.[7]

Crown rule returned in practice after the devastating hurricane of
1931, which led to urgent requests for aid to the British Government. In
return for a long-term loan to the local Government, the Treasury and
Colonial Office demanded and got an alteration to the colony's constitution giving imperial authorities closer control of legislation. The loan
was applied, apart from restoring infrastructure, to assisting politically
powerful businesses (most of all B.E.C., controlled by the influential
Hoare family, whose head by this time was in the British Cabinet) in
recovering and fending off the growing incursion of American interests.
The Government's subsequent rearrangement of taxes favored large
businesses at the expense of the unorganized poor and working classes,
and discontent continued to mount over the next few years, leading to the
outbreak of political protest in 1934. In contrast to Kenya, British
Honduras's nonwhites, like others in the Caribbean, who had been under
British rule for a long time, were more politically organized, and the
Depression, accentuated in British Honduras by the hurricane, provided
the spur to activate those organizations. In return, the Colonial Office
viewed the black and brown laborers of the colony as decidedly more
"advanced" than East Africans. When the colony's Attorney General
remarked in 1936, to justify keeping the Master and Servant laws that had
been abolished in some other parts of the Empire, that "it is extremely
doubtful whether the majority of workers of this Colony can be said to be
sufficiently evolved to understand the binding nature of contracts," he

[6] CO 123/337, Stephen Luke minute, 29 Apr. 1932, on Pilling (O.A.G.) to Secretary of
State Cunliffe-Lister, 7 Mar. 1932.
[7] Of all deaths in Belize in 1931–1933, 36% were attributed to malaria and 29% to
dysentery [P. D. Ashdown, op. cit., p. 212].

produced only irritation in Whitehall. One official doubted whether "the Attorney-General is 'sufficiently evolved' to appreciate the difference between civil contract and criminal law."[8] At the same time similar statements from the Government of Kenya were accepted without complaint. The laws of British Honduras, like those of the rest of the British West Indies but unlike those of Kenya in the 1930s, made no distinction between the races.

British Honduras's economy in the 1930s had one novel aspect: like some other West Indian possessions by this time but perhaps even more so, it was the site of significant and growing American business penetration. This penetration was dividing the elite, as some smaller businessmen took employment with American interests, and others sided with American firms in resentment of the special favors B.E.C. received. Such discord strengthened the hand of the Governor and the Colonial Office, while also perhaps reinforcing their existing dislike of "ruthless" American businessmen.[9] A good proportion of the new American arrivals were from the nearby U.S. South, and brought with them a fiercer form of racism, which also repelled British officials. All of this was to influence how Gantt's case was to play out.

At his murder trial, Thurman Gantt claimed that the shooting had been accidental: he had taken his shotgun with him to confront the presumed thief, but only for protection, and had no idea that the safety catch had come off; he explained the firing as the result of tripping. Several black witnesses, however, described his pointing the gun straight at the victim, and the firing taking place right after a heated exchange of insults. "Be careful how you speak to me, Amos," he was quoted by witnesses. When the victim told him he was not afraid of him, he was cited as replying, "then perhaps you'll fear this," and pointed the gun straight at him. The next event was its firing. As a Deep Southerner, Gantt no doubt felt his blood easily reach the boiling point when faced with an insolent black. He had come to British Honduras a few years earlier to build and run a lumber mill, and was part of a growing community of Americans, disproportionately from the nearby U.S. South, which integrated easily with resident British settlers and businessmen, who were gaining an increasing part of their income from lumber exports to, and related trade with, America. Thus it was not surprising that his deliberating jury, whose

[8] Cited by Banton, op. cit., pp. 292–293.
[9] C. H. Grant, *The Making of Modern Belize: Politics, Society and British Colonialism in Central America* (New York and London, 1976).

foreman was one of the business leaders in the colony, sent a message to the Judge's clerk to get assurance that if they returned a verdict of manslaughter, as the Judge had almost urged in his summation, the Judge in turn would heed their accompanying mercy recommendation and be lenient in sentencing. The clerk gave them the impression that the Judge read and accepted their request. However, in fact he failed to pass the message to the Judge. In the event, the Judge, Chief Justice C. W. Greenidge, sentenced Gantt to life imprisonment, shocking the jury, most of the white population, and certainly Gantt himself (who had had evidence of his good character given in court by a family friend, a U.S. Federal Judge from Alabama).

Gantt's wife and friends immediately began to seek to overturn the verdict. The U.S. Consul in Belize visited Gantt and urged that he, the only white prisoner, be removed to better conditions than existed in the local jail, claiming his health was being adversely affected. Indeed, he suggested that Gantt could be removed to an American prison, thus saving the British Government the cost of incarcerating him. His lawyer argued that the jury had been misled, and would not have convicted him if it knew that the Judge would sentence him as he did. Gantt wrote to Cordell Hull, the U.S. Secretary of State, and his wife wrote President Franklin D. Roosevelt an emotional plea. More effectively, the Federal Judge spoke to a Senator from Alabama, who prodded the State Department to have its embassy in London intervene with the Foreign Office, which in turn communicated to the Colonial Office.[10] The U.S. officials asked if the case could be reviewed for improprieties, and perhaps overturned. This was too much; after consulting the Judge, the Colonial Office told the Foreign Office to tell the Americans that "the Secretary of State has no power to order a retrial or to interfere with the verdict in this case."[11] It continued, "and on the information before him he would not be disposed to do so even if he had the power" – this part the Foreign Office tactfully dropped from their reply to the United States. The United States accepted this, but not willing to drop the matter altogether, asked if the sentence could then be reduced by the Governor's prerogative of mercy. The Foreign Office was naturally concerned not to ruffle Anglo-American relations over this minor issue, and recognized that, as one official noted, "US states' views about killing negroes are rather different

---

[10] NA, FO 371/17596 [orig. #1872].
[11] The Chief Justice told the Colonial Office that "this was a case of murder and nothing less."

from ours." While sharing the annoyance evident in the Colonial Office at American interference with the workings of British justice, the Foreign Office wanted to be able to "assure [the Americans] truthfully that we are still doing something." Despite their annoyance, officials at the Colonial Office seemed ready to find some accommodation: if the conviction could not be overturned, then surely the sentence could be reduced; if Gantt could hardly be moved to an American prison (that suggestion was quickly rejected as a fundamental insult to British sovereignty, especially in view of the ever-increasing American economic penetration of Central America), there was no reason he could not be moved to "more tolerable quarters" in Britain.[12] It so urged the Government in Belize.

At this point, however, Honduran politics entered the story and further complicated it. While these communications were going on, a militant labor movement had emerged in Belize, throwing politics into turmoil. The month following Gantt's trial, a large number of unemployed people formed themselves into the "Unemployed Brigade" and marched around town carrying placards and chanting slogans. They petitioned the Governor for economic relief. The next month, Antonio Soberanis Gomez, a barber by trade, seized control of the movement and turned it in a more militant direction, holding large public meetings twice a week to denounce the Governor, the wealthy merchants, and the B.E.C. Before the end of 1934, he had organized a strike and been arrested in connection with a major riot. This was not a situation in which the Government wanted to take any step to help Gantt, a mill owner convicted of murdering a worker. The harassed Acting Governor (waiting anxiously for the newly appointed Governor to arrive) refused to reduce his sentence, and urged the Colonial Office not to remove him to a British prison (the colony would be required to pay the costs of his incarceration wherever it was, and so such removal would not even save it money), which, he said "would cause a storm of justifiable protest from all sections of the community," and indeed even a riot with possible loss of life and property. Do not, he telegraphed London, "add to the difficulties of the Colonial Government by this apparently unwarrantable action." The Colonial Office heeded this plea, and sent an official to call in person on the Foreign Office, since "neither the moment nor the subject matter of what he had to say was particularly suitable for an official letter." First, a point of principle was made: concern was expressed – "Mr. and Mrs. Gantt are evidently an elderly couple and their case must certainly command

---

[12] There was statuory provision for this in the Colonial Prisoners Removal Act of 1884.

sympathy" – but, it was stressed, "justice must take its course." All the more since "there was no distinction between white and black in British Honduras, so that anything savouring of favoured treatment for a white man would be exceedingly unpopular with the inhabitants and might lead to serious riots in the colony." Then, a practical solution: the incoming Governor, it was suggested "off the record," would be asked to review the sentence "with a view to granting him a pardon or reducing his sentence." So it was likely that Gantt could be released after a few years. This message was transmitted to the U.S. Embassy, which passed it on to Gantt's partisans as the best that could be arranged.

Gantt stayed in the Belize jail. After two years, the U.S. Embassy in London requested consideration of early release, which was forwarded to Governor Burns. Burns considered it premature and put it aside. The next time he was prodded, Burns agreed, and Gantt was released after serving two and a half years as the only white prisoner in Belize; he left immediately for home. While Gantt had been sitting in jail, the colony's politics had undergone large changes; by his release, it had a new constitution, providing for the return of elected officials and representatives, though with a restricted franchise, and by 1939, the "popular" party controlled the Belize Town Council. In 1941, trade unions were legalized, and two years later the old Master and Servant law was repealed.

Gantt's case, and its post-trial handling, reflected a number of things about the Empire. One was the somewhat special situation of an American on trial for murder. In the U.K. in the later nineteenth century, Carolyn Conley has found, courts "were hardest on Americans (a quarter of those tried [for murder] were executed). There was a consensus that Americans were more savage and placed less value on human life than any of their British or Irish cousins. As *The Times* lamented [in 1867], "one is sometimes tempted to think that the life of a man is thought little more of in America than the life of a rat.'"[13] Another was the special situation of British Honduras at the time, its officials under pressure both from the Depression and from American economic penetration – there is a thread running through officials' discussions of disdain for this unattractive American racist, and one wonders if Justice Greenidge would have come down quite so hard on a defendant who had not arrived only a few years before from a state known for its lynchings. At the same time that colonial justice was being shaped by the old order in relations between the races, and between employers and workers, it was also being shaped by the

[13] Conley, op. cit., p. 59.

beginnings of that order's disintegration. Everywhere in the Empire in the 1930s, old racial distinctions were losing the underpinning that the criminal justice system had once provided, and were increasingly challenged and sometimes even overthrown. Equal justice under law was beginning to become a practical principle, perhaps the only principle that had a hope of preserving British authority.

Conclusion

"The great genius of the English-speaking peoples was in holding two sets of ideas in their minds at the same time: both 'racial pride'. . . and 'the inviolable freedom of the individual conscience [and] the equality of all human persons.'"

John Derbyshire [quoting George Orwell], "In Memory of Private Moyse," *New English Review*, April 2007

Viewed through the lens of interracial homicide trials, several aspects of the British Empire have, I hope, been brought into sharper focus. One is its diversity – most obviously the fundamental difference between colonies of white settlement, moving to self-government and local control of relations with their indigenous and other nonwhite inhabitants, and predominantly nonwhite colonies, governed directly by imperial officials. In this sharp distinction, the uncertain position of East Africa stands out, part of the second group but with a growing body of white settlers eager to join the first. Yet this distinction was not the only element of diversity in the Empire; every colony, it should have become clear, presented its own unique set of circumstances.

Within this diverse array of territories and peoples, one common element was the permanent tension between the forces pressing toward centralization and those pressing towards localization. These trials were all conditioned by the tug between Judges, Governors, and other officials on the spot (backed up in varying degrees by the Colonial Office) attempting for the most part to enforce Empire-wide laws and principles, and local white populations pushing to expand their own autonomy. Depending on the relative power of each side, these trials might produce differing outcomes. Colonial courtrooms were arenas for struggles in which both sides often appealed to the British inheritance of "the rule of law," but interpreted this heritage in different ways. Was its heart "the same law for all British subjects" or was it "the Englishman's birthright" of rights against Government, including trial by a jury of his peers? And if it was the former, what place did it leave for an appreciation of subject peoples' own laws and traditions, and of their specifically disadvantaged social and economic situation? If it was the latter, why did it not apply also to nonwhite subjects of the Crown? And if "the rule of law" was indeed "the gospel of the English," at the heart of British Government everywhere, how was it to be reconciled with a virtually absolute political domination in the colonial territories over nonwhite majorities?

These trials show not only ongoing tensions but also change over time, as in the second half of the nineteenth century, settlers increased their power almost everywhere, in India and the Caribbean as well as in Australia, and then, just as colonies like Australia became essentially independent, imperial officials (ironically aided by the rise of nonwhite political consciousness) regained the initiative against settlers in the remaining parts of the Empire. These trials also highlight the inadequacies of the two most common narratives of the British Empire's history. Neither the narrative of celebration nor that of indictment prepares us for the complex struggles that these trials stimulated and focused. These struggles suggest the fallacy of thinking of the Empire in terms of an "imperial project," whether one of good or evil. Rather, the Empire was a site of many simultaneous "projects," worthy of both celebration and indictment, often at the same time. Throughout its history, interests and ideologies among the British themselves were in competition. The racism of most settlers was not shared by most officials, who usually held some variant of what has been called a "civilizational" perspective on the differences between the British and less "advanced" peoples.[1] Throughout the nineteenth and twentieth centuries most officials saw most of the peoples they ruled over as simply less advanced in the universal march of civilization, a march led by themselves. Full "civilization" was, in the view of most of them, attainable by virtually all their subjects, in the fullness of time. How long that might be, of course, was a topic on which they differed – the more conservative saw British rule as necessary for an indefinite time far into the future, while the more liberal envisaged a speedier development, beginning in their own day. At the same time, if few officials shared settler racism, neither did they share settler exaltation

[1] Peter Mandler, " 'Race' and 'Nation' in Mid-Victorian Thought," in *History, Religion, and Culture: British Intellectual History 1750–1950*, ed. Stefan Collini, Richard Whatmore, and Brian William Young (Cambridge: Cambridge University Press, 2000), 224–244.

of the rights of individuals against Government. Officials sought, in administering the law, to treat all subjects similarly as far as they could without risking social disorder, but they did not shy away from their duty to rule, even against the wishes of those they ruled, white or colored.

Thus both officials and settlers could sincerely express their reverence for the rule of law, while giving that ideal quite different practical meanings. The crucial ambiguities in the ideal nurtured conflicts, between the official and unofficial parts of the "ruling race" and, increasingly, between its representatives and nonwhite peoples, both indigenous and imported. The vigorous strains of egalitarianism and liberalism contained within a system of political authoritarianism and racial domination provided all actors in the complex drama of Empire – Governors, white settlers, and nonwhite peoples – with ideological leverage to push for their concerns against others. Indeed, in an historical irony, both the official ideology of egalitarian paternalism and the settlers' unofficial one of "the Englishman's birthright of liberty" proved in the long run self-extinguishing. Nonwhite subjects increasingly claimed the equal treatment of the former against white settlers, and similarly came to ask why they should not be included in the settlers' political "birthright" of liberty. First Indian and then other nonwhite politicians came to charge British rule with being "un-British" in its failure to live up to its egalitarian ideology, while also (in an ever-shrinking world) laying claim to the rights of British citizenship. It proved a significant moment when George Yule, a Scottish businessman in Calcutta who became the first non-Indian President of the Indian National Congress, pointed out at the fourth Congress in 1888 that many Indians already met English standards for full citizenship:

There are many thousands of Hindus, Mohammedan, Eurasian, Parsee and other gentlemen in the country who, if they were to transfer their persons to England (which they had a full right to do) for twelve months or more and pay certain rates, would be qualified to enjoy all the rights and privileges of British subjects [i.e., voting, jury service, etc]. If you and I go to England we are qualified. If we return to India our character changes, and we are not qualified. In England we should be trusted citizens. In India well, the charitably-minded among our opponents say that we are incipient traitors! (Loud and prolonged cheers and laughter).[2]

---

[2] Presidential address, in W. C. Bonnerjee (Introduction), *Indian Politics* (Madras, 1898), Part II, pp. 25–26.

"English freedom" was contagious, and could not be forever restricted by racial bounds; nor could imperial rulers forever justify the practical absence of equal treatment between the races, nor their own resort, in maintaining their rule, to breaching the principle of the rule of law. When nationalists in the twentieth century began to condemn the "lawless law" of British rule, they turned the most sacred British values against the Empire, and signaled that the game was up.

Bibliography

Unpublished Manuscripts and Collections

The National Archives, Kew:
   Colonial Office Papers
   Foreign Office Papers
   Home Office Papers
Bodleian Library (Oxford), Mss. Eng.:
   Coryndon Papers
   Wodehouse Papers
British Library Oriental and India Office Collection:
   Ampthill Correspondence
   Cotton Papers
   Cross Papers
   Curzon Papers
   Government of India Official Papers
   Hamilton Papers
   Lansdowne Papers
   Morley Papers
National Library of Scotland:
   Minto Papers
Queensland State Archives, Brisbane

Unpublished Secondary Sources

Ashdown, Peter David. "Race, Class and the Unofficial Majority in British Honduras 1890–1949." Ph.D. thesis, University of Southampton, 1979.

Beattie, Allen, and Patrick Dunleavy. "New Perspectives on the British Imperial State." Unpublished paper, 2004.

Cain, Robert J. "The Administrative Career of Sir Anthony Musgrave." M.A. thesis, Duke University, 1965.

Campion, David. "Watchmen of the Raj: The United Provinces Police, 1870–1931 and the Dilemmas of Colonial Policing in British India." Ph.D. diss., University of Virginia, 2002.

Compton, John Michael. "British Government and Society in the Presidency of Bengal, c. 1858–1880," D.Phil. thesis, Oxford, 1968.

Conley, Mary. "From Jack Tar to Union Jack: Images and Identities of British Naval Men, 1870–1918." Ph.D. diss., Boston College, 2000.

Datta, Damayanti. "The Europeans of Calcutta, 1858–1883." Ph.D. thesis, Cambridge, 1995.

Kercher, Bruce. "Sovereigns at Sea." Unpublished paper, 2005.

McLaren, John. "The Perils of Judicial Tenure in Britain's Caribbean Colonies in the Post-Emancipation Era, 1830–1870." Paper presented at The British World Conference, Bristol, July 14, 2007.

Subrahmanyam, Gita. "Schizophrenic Governance and Fostering Global Inequalities in the British Empire: The UK Domestic State vs. the Indian and African Colonies, 1890–1960." Paper presented at the annual meeting of the American Political Science Association, Chicago, 2004. <.PDF> Retrieved 2006-10-05 from http://www.allacademic.com/meta/p61046_index.html.

Newspapers

African Chronicle (Nairobi)
African Standard (Nairobi)
Belize Independent
Brisbane Courier
Cooktown Courier
East African Standard (Nairobi)
Englishman, The (Calcutta)
European Mail (Port of Spain, Trinidad)
Fiji Argus
Fiji Times
Freeman, The (Nassau)
Glasgow Herald
Leader of British East Africa, The (Nairobi)
Liverpool Courier
Liverpool Evening Express
Liverpool Mercury
Morning Post (London)
Nassau Guardian
Pall Mall Gazette (London)
Port of Spain Gazette
Sydney Daily Telegraph
Sydney Morning Herald
Times, The (London)
Townsville Herald
Truth (London)

Published Secondary Sources

Abbott, Charles, and William Shee. *A Treatise of the Law Relative to Merchant Ships and Seamen* (London, 1854).

Anderson, David. "Kenya: Registration and Rough Justice." In *Masters, Servants, and Magistrates in Britain and the Empire, 1562–1955*, ed. Douglas Hay and Paul Craven, 498–528 (Chapel Hill, N.C., 2004).

"Master and Servant in Colonial Kenya, 1894–1939." *Journal of African History* 41 (2000): 349–485.

"Policing the Settler State: Colonial Hegemony in Kenya, 1900–1952." In *Contesting Colonial Hegemony: State and Society in Africa and India*, ed. Dagmar Engels and Shula Marks, 248–264 (London, 1994).

Arnold, David. *The Problem of Nature: Environment, Culture and European Expansion* (Oxford, 1996).

Arthur, T. C. *Reminiscences of an Indian Police Official* (London, 1894).

Atkinson, Alan. *The Europeans in Australia. A History.* Vol. 2: *Democracy* (Sydney, 2006).

Bailkin, Jordanna. "The Boot and the Spleen: When Was Murder Possible in British India?" *Comparative Studies in Society and History* 48 (2006): 462–493.

Balachandran, G. "Recruitment and Control of Indian Seamen: Calcutta 1880–1935." *International Journal of Maritime History* 9 (1997): 1–18.

Ballhatchet, Kenneth. *Race, Sex and Class Under the Raj: Imperial Attitudes and Policies and Their Critics, 1793–1905* (New York, 1980).

Banerjee, A. C. *English Law in India* (Delhi, 1984).

Banerjee, K. M. *Reports of Criminal Cases Between Europeans and Indians*, vol. 1 (Calcutta, 1901).

Banivanua-Mar, Tracey. *Violence and Colonial Dialogue: The Australia-Pacific Labor Trade* (Honolulu, 2007).

Banton, M. K. "The Colonial Office, 1820–1955: Constantly the Subject of Small Struggles." In *Masters, Servants, and Magistrates in Britain and the Empire, 1562–1955*, ed. Douglas Hay and Paul Craven, 251–301 (Chapel Hill, N.C., 2004).

Barker, George. *A Tea Planter's Life in Assam* (Calcutta, 1887).

Barns, Margarita. *The Indian Press: A History of the Growth of Public Opinion in India* (London, 1930).

Barrier, N. G. *Punjab Politics and the Disturbances of 1907* (Durham N.C., 1966).

Beames, John. *Memoirs of a Bengal Civilian* (written 1896; published London, 1961).

Behal, Rana P. "Power Structure, Discipline, and Labour in Assam Tea Plantations Under Colonial Rule." *International Review of Social History* 51 (2006), Supplement: 143–172.

Bellot, Hugh H. L. "A Judicial Scandal: Are Judges Above the Law?" *Westminster Review* 145 (Jan.–June 1896): 237–246, 388–406.

Bennet, George. "Development of Political Organization in Kenya." *Political Studies* 5 (1957): 113–130.

Berman, Bruce. *Control and Crisis in Colonial Kenya* (London, 1990).

Best, Nicholas. *Happy Valley: The Story of the English in Kenya* (London, 1979).

Bishop, Gilbert. *The Beachcombers, or Slave-Trading Under the Union Jack* (London, 1889).

Black Experience and the Empire, ed. Philip D. Morgan and Sean Hawkins (Oxford, 2004).

Blakeley, Brian. *The Colonial Office, 1868–1892* (Durham, N.C., 1972).

Bloch, Michael. *The Duke of Windsor's War* (London, 1982).

Bonnerjee, W. C. *Indian Politics* (Madras, 1898).

Bose, P. N., and H. W. B. Moreno. *A Hundred Years of the Bengali Press* (Calcutta, 1920).

Brantlinger, Patrick. "Missionaries and Cannibals in Nineteenth Century Fiji." *History and Anthropology* 17 (2006): 21–38.

Brereton, Bridget. *Law, Justice and Empire: The Colonial Career of John Gorrie, 1829–1892* (Barbados, 1997).

 Race Relations in Colonial Trinidad 1870–1900 (Cambridge, 1979).

Brown, George. *George Brown, D.D., Pioneer-Missionary and Explorer: An Autobiography* (London, 1908).

Brown, Lawrence. "Inter-colonial Migration and the Refashioning of Indentured Labor: Arthur Gordon in Trinidad, Mauritius and Fiji." In *Colonial Lives Across the British Empire: Imperial Careering in the Long Nineteenth Century*, ed. David Lambert and Alan Lester, 204–227 (Cambridge, 2006).

Burns, Sir Alan. *Colonial Civil Servant* (London, 1949).

Burton, John Wear. *The Fiji of Today* (London, 1910).

Capper, John [Anon.]. "Law in the East." *Household Words* 5 (1852): 347–352.

Cell, John, ed. *By Kenya Possessed: The Correspondence of Norman Leys and J. H. Oldham 1918–1926* (Chicago, 1976).

Chadwick, Roger. *Bureaucratic Mercy: The Home Office and the Treatment of Capital Cases in Victorian Britain* (New York, 1992).

Chanock, Martin. "The Law Market: The Legal Encounter in British East and Central Africa." In *European Expansion and Law*, ed. W. J. Mommsen and J. A. De Moor, 279–305 (New York, 1992).

Chapman, J. K. *The Career of Arthur Hamilton Gordon, First Lord Stanmore 1829–1912* (Toronto, 1964).

Chatterjee, Priya. *A Time for Tea: Women, Labor and Post-Colonial Politics on an Indian Plantation* (Durham, N.C., 2001).

Chaturvedi, Umesh. "The Image of British Administration of Justice as Reflected in the Hindi Press in the Last Quarter of the Nineteenth Century." *Quarterly Review of Historical Studies* (Calcutta) 10 (1970): 202–208.

Chippendall, Rev. John. *A Plea for Inquiry into the Conduct of Sir A Gordon . . . in the Case of Lt. E. C. Chippendall* (Manchester, 1880).

Clayton, Anthony, and Donald C. Savage. *Government and Labour in Kenya, 1895–1963* (London, 1975).

Cobley, Alan. "Black West Indian Seamen in the British Merchant Marine in the Mid-Nineteenth Century." *History Workshop Journal*, issue 58 (Autumn 2004): 259–274.

Cocks, Raymond. "Social Roles and Legal Rights: Three Women in Early Nineteenth-Century India." *Journal of Legal History* 22 (2002): 77–106.

Collingham, Elizabeth M. *Imperial Bodies: The Physical Experience of the Raj, c. 1800–1947* (Oxford, 2001).

Collinson, Patrick. "The Cow Bells of Kitale." *London Review of Books* 25, no. 11 (5 June 2003): 15–18.

Comaroff, John. "Colonialism, Culture and the Law: A Foreword," *Law and Social Inquiry* 26 (2001): 305–314.

Conley, Carolyn. *Certain Other Countries: Homicide, Gender, and National Identity in Late Nineteenth-Century England, Ireland, Scotland, and Wales* (Columbus, Ohio, 2007).

Cooper, Frederick. *Colonialism in Question: Theory, Knowledge, History* (Berkeley and Los Angeles, 2005).

Cotton, Henry. *Indian and Home Memories* (London, 1911).

Course, Captain A. G. *The Merchant Navy: A Social History* (London, 1963).

Cox, Arthur Frederick. *Reminiscences of Seventy Years* (written 1920; privately printed, 1995).

Cromar, John. *Jock of the Islands* (London, 1935).

Curry, J. C. *The Indian Police* (London, 1931).

Dasgupta, Uma. *The Rise of an Indian Public* (Calcutta, 1977).

Davidson, J. W., and Deryck Scarr. *Pacific Island Portraits* (Canberra, 1970).

Denman, Terence. "'Ethnic Soldiers Pure and Simple'? The Irish in the Late Victorian Army." *War in History* 3 (1996): 253–273.

den Otter, Sandra M. "The Political Economy of Empire: Freedom of Contract, Commercial Civilization and Colonial Law in British India." In *Worlds of Political Economy*, ed. Martin Daunton and Frank Trentman, 69–94 (London, 2004).

Des Voeux, G. W. *My Colonial Service* (London, 1903), 2 volumes.

Dicey, A. V. "Digby on the History of English Law," *Nation* 21 (9 Dec. 1875): 373–374.

Lectures Introductory to the Study of the Law of the Constitution (London, 1885).

Dilks, David. *Curzon in India* (New York, 1970), 2 volumes.

Neville Chamberlain. Vol. 1: *1869–1929* (Cambridge, 1984).

Dinesen, Isak. *Out of Africa* [orig. 1937] (New York, 1972).

Dinwiddy, J. R. "The Early Nineteenth Century Campaign Against Flogging in the Army." *English Historical Review* 97 (1982): 308–331.

Docker, E. W. *The Blackbirders: The Recruiting of South Seas Labour for Queensland, 1863–1907* (Sydney, 1971).

Duder, C. J. D. "An Army of One's Own: The Politics of the Kenya Defence Force." *Canadian Journal of African Studies* 25, no. 2 (1991): 207–225.

"The Settler Response to the Indian Crisis of 1923 in Kenya: Brigadier General Philip Wheatley and 'Direct Action.'" *Journal of Imperial and Commonwealth History* 17 (1989): 349–373.

Duder, C. J. D., and G. L. Simpson. "Land and Murder in Colonial Kenya: The Leroghi Land Dispute and the Powys 'Murder' Case." *Journal of Imperial and Commonwealth History* 25 (1997): 440–465.

Duff, Sir M. E. Grant. *Sir Henry Maine: A Brief Memoir of His Life* (London, 1892).

Dunlop, J. K. *The Development of the British Army 1899–1914* (London, 1938).

Dyos, H. J., and D. H. Aldcroft. *British Transport: An Economic Survey from the Seventeenth Century to the Twentieth* (Harmondsworth, 1974).

Eves, Richard. "Unsettling Settler Colonialism: Debates over Climate and Colonization in New Guinea, 1875–1914." *Ethnic and Racial Studies* 28 (2005): 304–330.

"Ex-Civilian" [G. Graham]. *Life in the Mofussil* (London, 1878).

Farewell, Bryan. *Armies of the Raj: From Mutiny to Independence* (London, 1989).

Faught, C. Brad. "An Imperial Prime Minister? W. E. Gladstone and India, 1880–1885." *Journal of the Historical Society* 6 (2006): 555–578.

Finnane, Mark, and Clive Moore. "Kanaka Slaves or Willing Workers? Melanesian Workers and the Queensland Criminal Justice System in the 1890s." *Criminal Justice History* 13 (1992): 141–160.

Finnane, Mark, and Jonathan Richards. "'You'll Get Nothing Out of It': The Inquest, Police and Aboriginal Deaths in Colonial Queensland." *Australian Historical Studies* 35 (2004): 84–105.

Fitzgerald, Rear-Admiral C. C. Penrose. *Life of Vice-Admiral Sir George Tryon, K.C.B.* (London, 1897).

Fitzpatrick, Peter. "Tears of the Law: Colonial Resistance and Legal Determination." In *Human Rights and Legal Theory*, ed. Katherine O'Donovan and G. R. Rubin, 126–148 (Oxford and New York, 2000).

Foran, W. Robert. *A Cuckoo in Kenya: The Reminiscences of a Pioneer Police Officer in British East Africa* (London, 1936).

Francis, Mark. "Colonial Political Culture and the Mentality of British Governors, 1825–1860." *Political Science* [Wellington, N.Z.] 38 (1986): 133–146.

Fraser, A. H. L. *Among Indian Rajahs and Ryots* (London, 1911).

Froude, J. A. *The English in the West Indies* (London, 1888).

Fuller, Sir Bampfylde. *Some Personal Experiences* (London, 1930).

Gatheru, R. Mugo. *Kenya: From Colonization to Independence, 1888–1970* (London, 2005).

Gatrell, V. A. C. "Crime, Authority, and the Policeman-State, 1750–1950." In *The Cambridge Social History of Britain, 1750–1950*, ed. F. M. L. Thompson, vol. 3, 243–310 (Cambridge, 1990).

Geertz, Clifford. "From the Native's Point of View: On the Nature of Anthropological Understanding." In *Interpretive Social Science: A Reader*, ed. Paul Rabinow and William M. Sullivan, 225–241 (Berkeley, 1979).

Genocide and Settler Society: Frontier Violence and Stolen Indigenous Children in Australian History, ed. A. Dirk Moses (Sydney, 2004).

Ghosh, Amitav, and Dipesh Chakrabarty. "A Correspondence on Provincializing Europe." *Radical History Review*, issue 83 (Spring 2002): 146–172.

Ghosh, Anindita. *Power in Print: Popular Publishing and the Politics of Language and Culture in a Colonial Society, 1778–1905* (Oxford, 2006).

Gilmour, David. *The Ruling Caste: Imperial Lives in the Victorian Raj* (London, 2006).

Gorrie, John. "Fiji As It Is." *Proceedings of the Royal Colonial Institute* 14 (1882–1883), 159–199.

Grant, C. H. *The Making of Modern Belize: Politics, Society and British Colonialism in Central America* (New York and London, 1976).

Gray, Rev. William. *The Kanaka* (Adelaide, 1895).

Gregg, Robert. *Inside Out, Outside In: Essays in Comparative History* (London, 2000).

Griggs, Peter. "Sugar Plantations in Queensland, 1864–1912: Origins, Characteristics, Distribution and Decline." *Agricultural History* 74 (2000): 609–647.

Guha, Ranajit. "Chandra's Death." *Subaltern Studies* 5 (1986): 135–165.

Dominance Without Hegemony: History and Power in Colonial India (Cambridge, Mass., 1997).

Guillemard, Sir Lawrence. *Trivial Fond Records* (London, 1937).

Hall, Benjamin T. *Socialism and Sailors*, Fabian Society Tract 46 (London, 1893).

Hall, Catherine. *Civilizing Subjects: Metropole and Colony in the English Imagination, 1830–67* (Chicago, 2002).

Hall, Henry L. *The Colonial Office* (London, 1937).

Harrison, Jennifer. "The People of Queensland, 1859–1900: Where Did the Immigrants Come From?" *Journal of the Royal Historical Society of Queensland* 13 (1988): 189–200.

Harrison, Mark. *Public Health in British India: Anglo-Indian Preventive Medicine, 1859–1914* (Cambridge, 1994).

Haynes, Douglas M. "Victorian Imperialism in the Making of the British Medical Profession: An Argument." In *Decentering Empire: Britain, India, and the Transcolonial World*, ed. Dane Kennedy and Durba Ghosh (London, 2006).

Henty, G. H. *A Final Reckoning: A Tale of Bush Life in Australia* (London, 1887).

Highland, Gary. "Aborigines, Europeans and the Criminal Law: Two Trials at the Northern Supreme Court, Townsville, April 1888." *Aboriginal History* 24 (1990): 182–196.

"A Tangle of Paradoxes: Race, Justice and Criminal Law in North Queensland, 1882–1894." In *A Nation of Rogues? Crime, Law and Punishment in Colonial Australia*, ed. David Philips and Susanne Davies, 123–140 (Melbourne, 1994).

Hindley, Charles. *Curiosities of Street Literature* (London, 1871).

Hirschmann, Edwin. *"White Mutiny": The Ilbert Bill Crisis in India and the Genesis of the Indian National Congress* (New Delhi, 1980).

Holthouse, Hector. *Cannibal Cargoes* (Sydney, 1969).

Hood, W. H. *The Blight of Insubordination: The Lascar Question and the Rights and Wrongs of British Shipmasters* (London, 1903).

Hunter, W. W. "The Character of British Rule in India." *Westminster Review* 34 (July 1868): 1–36.

Hutchins, Francis. *The Illusion of Permanence: British Imperialism in India* (Princeton, 1967).

Huttenback, Robert A. *Racism and Empire: White Settlers and Colored Immigrants in the British Self-Governing Colonies 1830–1910* (Ithaca, N.Y., 1972).

Huxley, Aldous. *Beyond the Mexique Bay* (London, 1934).

Huxley, Elspeth. *The Flame Trees of Thika: Memories of an African Childhood* (Harmondsworth, 1959).

White Man's Country: Lord Delamere and the Making of Kenya (London, 1935).

Hyam, Ronald. "Bureaucracy and 'Trusteeship' in the Colonial Empire." In *The Oxford History of the British Empire*. Vol. 4: *The Twentieth Century*, ed. Judith M. Brown and William Roger Louis, 255–279 (Oxford, 1999).

"The Colonial Office Mind, 1900–1914." In *The First British Commonwealth: Essays in Honour of Nicholas Mansergh*, ed. Norman Hillmer and Philip Wigley, 30–55 (Cambridge, 1979).

Elgin and Churchill at the Colonial Office (London, 1968).

In the Matter of the Release by the Governor of the Bahamas of Alfred E. Moseley. Notes by the Chief Justice of the Colony (London, 1892).

Jeffries, Sir Charles. *The Colonial Office* (London, 1956).

Joyce, R. B. *Samuel Walker Griffith* (St. Lucia, Queensland, 1984).

Kaminsky, Arnold P. *The India Office, 1880–1910* (New York, 1986).

Karsten, Peter. *Between Law and Custom: "High" and "Low" Legal Cultures in the Lands of the British Diaspora* (Cambridge, 2002).

Kaul, Chandrika. *Reporting the Raj: The British Press and India c. 1880–1922* (Manchester, 2003).

Kaushik, Harish. *The Indian National Congress in England 1885–1920* (Delhi, 1973).

Kelly, John D. "Gaze and Grasp: Plantations, Desires and Colonial Law in Fiji." In *Sites of Desire/Economies of Pleasure: Sexualities in Asia and the Pacific*, ed. Lenore Manderson and Margaret Jolly, 72–98 (Chicago, 1997).

Kemp, Peter. *The British Sailor: A Social History of the Lower Deck* (London, 1970).

Kennedy, Dane. *Islands of White: Settler Society and Culture in Kenya and Southern Rhodesia, 1890–1939* (Durham, N.C., 1987).

The Magic Mountains: Hill Stations and the British Raj (Berkeley, 1996).

Kilbracken, Lord [Sir Arthur Godley]. *Reminiscences* (London, 1931).

Killingray, David. "The 'Rod of Empire': The Debate over Corporal Punishment in the British African Colonial Forces, 1888–1946." *Journal of African History* 35 (1994): 201–216.

Kirk-Greene, Anthony. *Britain's Imperial Administrators, 1858–1966* (Oxford, 2000).

Knaplund, Paul, ed. "The Gladstone-Gordon Correspondence." *Transactions of the American Philosophical Society* 51 (1961): 1–116.

Kolsky, Elizabeth. "Codification and the Rule of Colonial Difference: Criminal Procedure in British India." *Law and History Review* 23 (2005): 631–684.

"Crime and Punishment on the Tea Plantations of Colonial India." In *Modern Histories of Crime and Punishment*, ed. Markus Dirk Dubber and Lindsay Farmer, 272–298 (Stanford, 2007).

Koss, Stephen E. *John Morley at the India Office, 1905–1910* (New Haven, Conn., 1969).

Kostal, Rande. *A Jurisprudence of Power: Victorian Empire and the Rule of Law* (Oxford, 2005).

Kubicek, Robert V. *The Administration of Imperialism: Joseph Chamberlain at the Colonial Office* (Durham, N.C., 1969).

Lahiri, Shompa. "Patterns of Resistance: Indian Seamen in Imperial Britain." In *Language, Labour and Migration*, ed. Anne J. Kershen, 155–178 (Aldershot, 2000).

Lai, Walton Look. *Indentured Labor, Caribbean Sugar: Chinese and Indian Migrants to the British West Indies, 1838–1918* (Baltimore, 1993).

Lal, Brij V. "Labouring Men and Nothing More: Some Problems of Indian Indenture in Fiji." In *Indentured Labour in the British Empire 1834–1920*, ed. Kay Saunders, 126–157 (London, 1984).

Lal, Brij V., Doug Munro, and Edward D. Beechert, eds. *Plantation Workers: Resistance and Accommodation* (Honolulu, 1993).

Lambert, David, and Alan Lester, eds. *Colonial Lives Across the British Empire: Imperial Careering in the Long Nineteenth Century* (Cambridge, 2006).

Land, Isaac. "Customs of the Sea: Flogging, Empire, and the 'True British Seaman' 1770 to 1870." *Interventions* 3 (2001): 169–185.

Lane, Tony. "The Political Imperatives of Bureaucracy and Empire: The Case of the Coloured Alien Seaman Order 1925." In *Ethnic Labour and British Imperial Trade: A History of Ethnic Seafarers in the U.K.*, ed. Diane Frost, 104–129 (London, 1995).

Lester, Alan. "British Settler Discourse and the Circuits of Empire." *History Workshop Journal*, issue 54 (Autumn 2002): 25–48.

Imperial Networks: Creating Identities in Nineteenth Century South Africa and Britain (London and New York, 2001).

Levine, Philippa. *Prostitution, Race and Politics: Policing Venereal Disease in the British Empire* (London, 2003).

Liberal by Principle: The Politics of John Wodehouse, 1st Earl of Kimberley, ed. John Powell (London, 1996).

Lonsdale, John. "Kenyatta's Trials: Breaking and Making an African Nationalist." In *The Moral World of the Law*, ed. Peter Coss, 196–239 (Oxford, 2000).

Loos, Noel. *Invasion and Resistance: Aboriginal-European Relations on the North Queensland Frontier 1861–1897* (Canberra, 1982).

Macgregor, William. "British New Guinea." *Journal of the Royal Colonial Institute* 26, no. 4 (1895): 295–300.

Mamdani, Mahmoud. *Citizen and Subject: Contemporary Africa and the Legacy of Late Colonialism* (Princeton, 1996).

Mandler, Peter. "'Race' and 'Nation' in Mid-Victorian Thought." In *History, Religion, and Culture: British Intellectual History 1750–1950*, ed. Stefan Collini, Richard Whatmore, and Brian William Young, 224–244 (Cambridge, 2000).

Marsden, Ben, and Crosbie Smith. *Engineering Empires: A Cultural History of Technology in Nineteenth-Century Britain* (Basingstoke, 2005).

Marsh, Peter. *Joseph Chamberlain: Entrepreneur in Politics* (New Haven, Conn., 1994).

Mason, Philip. *The Men Who Ruled India*. Vol. 2: *The Guardians* (London, 1954).

Maxon, Robert M. *John Ainsworth and the Making of Kenya* (London, 1980). *The Struggle for Kenya: The Loss and Reassertion of Imperial Initiative, 1912–1923* (Rutherford, N.J., 1993).

Mayhew. Henry. *The Morning Chronicle Survey of Labour and the Poor: The Metropolitan Districts*, vol. 3 (Horsham, 1981).

Mayne, John D. *The Criminal Law of India* (Madras, 1896).

McCulloch, Jock. "Empire and Violence, 1900–1939." In *Gender and Empire*, ed. Philippa Levine, 220–239 (Oxford, 2004).

McHugh, P. G. *Aboriginal Societies and the Common Law* (Oxford, 2004).

McLaren, John. " 'The Judicial Office... Bowing to No Power but the Supremacy of the Law': Judges and the Rule of Law in Colonial Australia and Canada, 1788–1840." *Australian Journal of Legal History* 7 (2003): 177–192.

McLean, Janet. "From Empire to Globalization: The New Zealand Experience." *Indiana Journal of Global Legal Studies* 11, no. 1 (Winter 2004): 161–181.

Mehta, Uday. *Liberalism and Empire: A Study in Nineteenth-Century British Liberal Thought* (Chicago, 1999).

Merry, Sally Engel. "Law and Colonialism." *Law and Society Review* 25 (1991): 889–922.

Metcalf, Thomas. *Forging the Raj: Essays on British India in the Heyday of Empire* (New York, 2005).
Ideologies of the Raj (Cambridge, 1995).

Misra, Maria. *Business, Race and Politics in British India c. 1850–1960* (Oxford, 1999).

Mohapatra, Prabhu P. "Assam and the West Indies, 1860–1920: Immobilizing Plantation Labor." In *Masters, Servants, and Magistrates in Britain and the Empire*, ed. Douglas Hay and Paul Craven, 455–480 (Chapel Hill and London, 2004).

Morgan, Philip. "Encounters Between British and 'Indigenous' Peoples, c. 1500–c. 1800. In *Empire and Others*, ed. Martin Daunton and Rick Halpern, 42–78 (Philadelphia, 2000).

Morris, H. F., and J. S. Read. *Indirect Rule and the Search for Justice: Essays in East African Legal History* (Oxford, 1972).

Moses, A. Dirk, ed. *Genocide and Settler Society* (New York, 2004).

Munro, Doug. "Patterns of Resistance and Accommodation." In *Plantation Workers: Resistance and Accommodation*, ed. Brij V. Lal et al., 1–44 (Honolulu, 1993).

Naipaul, V. S. *A Way in the World* (New York, 1994).

Naoroji, D. *Poverty and Un-British Rule in India* (London, 1901).

Newland, Simpson. *Paving the Way: A Romance of the Australian Bush* (London, 1893).

Nicholls, C. S. *Red Strangers: The White Tribe of Kenya* (London, 2005).

Nourse, Victoria F. "Reconceptualizing Criminal Law Defenses." *University of Pennsylvania Law Review* 151 (2003): 1691–1746.

Odhiambo, E. S. Atieno. *Siasa: Politics and Nationalism in East Africa 1905–1939* (Nairobi, 1981).

O'Dwyer, Michael. *India As I Knew It, 1885–1925* (London, 1926).

Okia, Opolot. "In the Interests of Community: Archdeacon Walter Owen and the Issue of Communal Labour in Colonial Kenya, 1921–1930." *Journal of Imperial and Commonwealth History* 32 (2004): 19–40.

Orwell, George. *Burmese Days* (London, 1934).

    England, Your England [orig. 1940] (London, 1953).

    Unsigned Review of Maurice Collis, *Trials in Burma. The Listener*, 9 Mar. 1938.

Owen, Nicholas. *The British Left and India: Metropolitan Anti-Imperialism, 1885–1947* (Oxford, 2007).

    "British Progressives and Civil Society in India, 1905–1914." In *Civil Society in British History: Ideas, Identities, Institutions*, ed. Jose Harris, 149–176 (Oxford, 2003).

Oxford Dictionary of National Biography.

Palmer, Edward. *Early Days in North Queensland* (Sydney, 1903).

Palmer, Capt. George. *Kidnapping in the South Seas* (London, 1871; reprinted 1971).

Palmer, Robin. "White Farmers in Malawi: Before and After the Depression." *African Affairs* 84 (1985): 211–245.

Parnaby, O. W. *Britain and the Labor Trade in the Southwest Pacific* (Durham, N.C., 1954).

Peck, John. *Maritime Fiction: Sailors and the Sea in British and American Novels, 1719–1917* (London, 2001).

Pedersen, Susan. "The Meaning of the Mandates System: An Argument," *Geschichte und Gesellschaft* 32 (2006), 560–582.

Peers, Douglas M. "Britain and Empire." In *A Companion to Nineteenth-Century Britain*, ed. Chris Williams, 53–78 (London, 2004).

Pitts, Jennifer. *A Turn to Empire: The Rise of Imperial Liberalism in Britain and France* (Princeton, 2005).

Polden, Patrick. "Doctor in Trouble: *Anderson v Gorrie* and the Extension of Judicial Immunity from Suit in the 1890s." *Legal History* 22, no. 3 (Dec. 2001): 37–68.

Porter, Andrew. *Atlas of British Overseas Expansion* (London, 1994).

Powell, John, ed. *Liberal by Principle: The Politics of John Wodehouse, First Earl of Kimberley* (London, 1996).

Powles, Louis D. *The Land of the Pink Pearl, or, Recollections of Life in the Bahamas* (London, 1888).

Queensland Law Journal Reports.

Race Relations in Colonial Queensland: A History of Exclusion, Exploitation and Extermination, ed. Raymond Evans et al. (St. Lucia, Queensland, 1975; rev. ed. 1988).

Radical Brisbane, ed. Raymond Evans and Carole Ferrier (Melbourne, 2004).

Ramamurthy, Ananda. *Imperial Persuaders: Images of Africa and Asia in British Advertising* (Manchester, 2003).

Rankin, George Claus. *Background to Indian Law* (Cambridge, 1946).

Rasor, Eugene. *Reform in the Royal Navy: A Social History of the Lower Deck 1850 to 1880* (London, 1976).

Ray, Rajah Kanta. *Social Conflict and Political Unrest in Bengal 1875–1927* (Delhi, 1984).

Raychaudhuri, Tapa. *Perceptions, Emotions, Sensibilities: Essays on India's Colonial and Post-Colonial Experiences* (Delhi, 1999).

Renford, Raymond K. *The Non-Official British in India to 1920* (Delhi, 1987).

Reports of Cases Argued and Determined in the Supreme Court of Queensland, vol. 2 (Brisbane, 1900).

Richards, Frank. *Old Soldier Sahib* (London, 1936).

Roberts-Wray, Sir Kenneth. "The Adaptation of Imported Law in Africa." *Journal of African Law* 4, no. 2 (Summer 1960): 66–78.

Rodger, N. A. M. *The Wooden World: An Anatomy of the Georgian Navy* (London, 1996).

Romilly, Hugh Hastings. *From My Veranda in New Guinea: Sketches and Traditions* (London, 1889).

Ross, W. McGregor. *Kenya from Within: A Short Political History* (London, 1927).

Roy, Kaushik. "Spare the Rod, Spoil the Soldier? Crime and Punishment in the Army of India, 1860–1913." *Journal of the Society for Army Historical Research* 84 (2006): 9–33.

Sanyal, Ram Gopal. *The Record of Criminal Cases, as Between Europeans and Natives, for the Last Hundred Years* (Calcutta, 1896).

Sarkar, Mahua. *Justice in a Gothic Edifice: The Calcutta High Court and Colonial Rule in Bengal* (Calcutta, 1997).

Sarkar, Sumit. *Modern India, 1885–1927* (London, 1983).

Scarr, Deryck. *Fragments of Empire: A History of the Western Pacific High Commission* (Canberra, 1967).

The Majesty of Colour: A Life of Sir John Bates Thurston. Vol. 1: *The Very Bayonet* (Canberra, 1973). Vol. 2: *Viceroy of the Pacific* (Canberra, 1980).

Seal, Anil. *The Emergence of Indian Nationalism* (Cambridge, 1968).

"Imperialism and Nationalism in India." In *Locality, Province and Nation: Essays on Indian Politics 1870 to 1940*, ed. John Gallagher, Gordon Johnson, and Anil Seal, 1–27 (Cambridge, 1973).

Sharpe, Jenny. *Allegories of Empire: The Figure of Woman in the Colonial Text* (Minneapolis, 1993).

Shrine, Francis H. *Life of Sir William Wilson Hunter* (London, 1901).

Shutt, Allison K. " 'The Natives Are Getting Out of Hand': Legislating Manners, Insolence and Contemptuous Behaviour in Southern Rhodesia, c. 1910–1963." *Journal of Southern African Studies* 33 (2007): 653–672.

Singha, Radhika. *A Despotism of Law: Crime and Justice in Early Colonial India* (Delhi, 1998).

Sinha, Mrinalini. *Colonial Masculinity: The "Manly Englishman" and the "Effeminate Bengali" in the Late Nineteenth Century* (Manchester, 1995).

Snelling, R. C., and T. J. Barron. "The Colonial Office and Its Permanent Officials 1801–1914." In *Studies in the Growth of Nineteenth Century Government 1801–1914*, ed. Gillian Sutherland, 139–166 (Cambridge, 1972).

Solomos, John. *Race and Racism in Britain* (London, 2003).

Spangenberg, Bradford. *British Bureaucracy in India: Status, Policy and the I.C.S. in the Late Nineteenth Century* (Delhi, 1976).

Spiers, Edward M. *The Late Victorian Army, 1868–1902* (Manchester, 1992).

Stanmore, Lord [Arthur Hamilton Gordon]. *Fiji, Records of Private and Public Life, 1875–1880* (London, 1897–1912), 4 volumes.

Stenhouse, John. "Imperialism, Atheism and Race: Charles Southwell, Old Corruption, and the Maori." *Journal of British Studies* 44 (2005): 754–774.

Stephen, James Fitzjames. *History of the Criminal Law in England* (London, 1884), 3 volumes.

Stirling, A. W. *The Never-Never Land* (London, 1884).

Stobie, W. "An Incident of Real Life in Bengal." *Fortnightly Review* 42 N.S. (1887): 329–341.

Tausky, Thomas E. *Sara Jeannette Duncan: Novelist of Empire* (Port Credit, Ont., 1980).

Taylor, Miles. "Colonial Representation at Westminster, c. 1800–1865." In *Parliaments, Nations and Identities in Britain and Ireland, 1660–1850*, ed. Julian Hoppit, 206–219. (Manchester, 2003).

The Times special correspondent. *Letters from Queensland* (London, 1893).

Thomas, J. J. *Froudacity: West Indian Fables by J. A. Froude Explained* (London, 1889).

Tracy, Louis. *Meeting the Sun: Some Anglo-Indian Snapshots* (Allahabad, 1898).

Trainor, Luke. *British Imperialism and Australian Nationalism: Manipulation, Conflict and Compromise in the Late Nineteenth Century* (Cambridge, 1994).

Travers, Robert. *Ideology and Empire in Eighteenth-Century India: The British in Bengal* (Cambridge, 2007).

Trench, Charles Chenevix. *Men Who Ruled Kenya* (London, 1989).

Trodd, Anthea. "Collaborating in Open Boats: Dickens, Collins, Franklin, and Bligh." *Victorian Studies* 42 (1999): 201–225.

Trotman, David Vincent. *Crime in Trinidad: Conflict and Control in a Plantation Society* (Knoxville, Tenn., 1986).

Turrell, Robert. *White Mercy: A Study of the Death Penalty in South Africa* (London, 2005).

Varma, Nitin. "Coolie Strikes Back: Collective Protest and Action in the Colonial Tea Plantations of Assam, 1880–1920." *Indian Historical Review* 33 (2006): 259–287.

Verma, Arvind. "Consolidation of the Raj: Notes from a Police Station in British India, 1865–1928." *Criminal Justice History* 17 (2002): 109–132.

Vickers, Daniel. *Young Men and the Sea: Yankee Seafarers in the Age of Sail* (New Haven, Conn., 2005).

Visram, Rozina. *Ayahs, Lascars and Princes: Indians in Britain 1700–1947* (London, 1986).

The Way We Civilise (Brisbane, 1880).

Wenzlhuemer, Roland. "Indian Labour Immigration and British Labour Policy in Nineteenth-Century Ceylon." *Modern Asian Studies* 41 (2007): 575–602.

Wiener, Martin J. *Men of Blood: Violence, Manliness and Criminal Justice in Victorian England* (Cambridge, 2004).

"Murder and the Modern British Historian." *Albion* 36, no. 1 (Spring, 2004): 1–12.

Williams, David. "Mid-Victorian Attitudes to Seamen and Maritime Reform: The Society for Improving the Condition of Merchant Seamen, 1867." In *Merchants and Mariners: Selected Writings of David M. Williams*, ed. Lars U. Scholl, 229–252 (London, 2000).

Wilson, Kathleen. *The Island Race: Englishness, Empire and Gender in the Eighteenth Century* (London, 2003).

Wodehouse, John. *Journal of John Wodehouse, First Earl of Kimberley*, ed. A. Hawkins and J. Powell (London, 1997).

Wylie, Diana. "Confrontation over Kenya: The Colonial Office and Its Critics 1918–1940." *Journal of African History* 18 (1977): 427–447.

Wyndham, Horace. *The Queen's Service; or the Real 'Tommy Atkins'* (London, 1899).

Youé, Christopher P. *Robert Thorne Coryndon: Proconsular Imperialism in Southern and Eastern Africa, 1897–1925* (Waterloo, Ont., 1986).

Index